G.I.GURDJIEFF: A LIFE

G. I. Gurdjieff: A Life

Paul Beekman Taylor

EUREKA EDITIONS 2020

By the same Author:

Shadows of Heaven: Gurdjieff and Toomer (1998)
Gurdjieff and Orage (2001)
Gurdjieff's America (2004)
The Philosophy of G.I.Gurdjieff (2007)
Gurdjieff's Invention of America (2007)
G.I.Gurdjieff: A New Life (2008)
Real Worlds of G.I.Gurdjieff (2012)
Gurdjieff's Worlds of Words (2014)

© Eureka Editions 2019
ISBN: 978 94 92590 046

Acknowledgments

This book is a revised and corrected addendum to *G. I. Gurdjieff, A New Life*, which was published in 2008. The two editions owe an incalculable debt to Michael Benham of Melbourne, Australia, and to Gert-Jan Blom of Amsterdam, The Netherlands, who have added to and often confirmed or corrected my own research. Benham has passed me a good deal of valuable information he had compiled about Russia in the years before Gurdjieff met P. D. Ouspensky in 1915, and revealed material concerning Gurdjieff's relations with others in the early years of the twentieth century, including the probable circumstances under which he met his wife, Julia Osipovna Ostrovska. He has provided me with printed information about Gurdjieff's activities, mentions in newspapers, places of residence, dates of steamship passages of Gurdjieff and persons involved with him. Blom has told me much about Gurdjieff's family and his activities prior to World War II that had not been revealed earlier. He has made available to me the store of photographs he has collected. Because of the large and significant contribution of Benham and Blom, this biography is a product of a triadic collaboration.

I am happily in debt to others who have shared my experience with Gurdjieff, particularly Gurdjieff's daughters Eve Chevalier and Dushka Howarth, and Madame Ouspensky's granddaughter Tania Nagro, all of whom have been generous with their oral history, written records and encouragement. My colleague Georges Nivat, professor of Russian Studies at the University of Geneva, has untangled knots in Gurdjieff's Russian. Barbara Walker Smyth of Aurora, Oregon, has given me access to Jane Heap's correspondence. Anne Orage, A. R. Orage's daughter in law, furnished photos of the Prieuré and has allowed me to quote from the letters of A. R. Orage to Jessie and members of the New

1

York group. George Kiourtzidis, the great-grandson of Gurdjieff's uncle Vasilii, has given me essential information about his family line. Of course, I owe an incalculable debt to James Moore whose biography of Gurdjieff has remained a basic reference for me. Finally, my copy editor, Bob Hunter, biographer of Ouspensky, has saved my text from scores of typos, grammatical fogginess, and misquotations, while my publisher, Siebold, has helped structure the book and has accorded me the gift of his patience, industry and tolerance.

It is appropriate, nonetheless, to justify presenting another book to the corpus of works about him, and to wonder whether there are enough interested readers to warrant its publication. The response is an emphatic "yes," for the ideas of Gurdjieff and their sources are not passing mid nineteenth century fads or fancies. Not only was he recognized during his lifetime as an important messenger of vital ideas (Taylor, *Gurdjieff in the Public Eye*), but since his death his ideas have moved in ever widening cultural circles everywhere. There are over fifty Gurdjieff groups in the Western world alone, and groups in Africa, South America and Australia. I estimate there are over forty thousand active followers of Gurdjieff's ideas, as well as countless others who are exposed to his fourth way concepts and designs such as his enneagram. Interest in Gurdjieff and studies of him are bound to continue expanding.

Contents

Introduction: Gurdjieff and the Historian

The living can sue their biographers for slander or demand correction of false, misleading and spurious "fact." The dead, however, cannot testify after the fact, and whatever autobiographical fragments they leave are subjected to biased scrutiny and adaptation. G[eorgii] I[vanovich] Gurdjieff told and wrote stories about himself without insisting on their "fact." He scattered references to events in his life in his 1924 prospectus "G. Gurdjieff's Institute for the Harmonious Development of Man" printed in 1923, the 1933 pamphlet *The Herald of Coming Good*, and in each of the three posthumously published series of All and Everything: *Beelzebub's Tales to His Grandson*, *Meetings with Remarkable Men* and *Life Is Real, Only Then, When "I Am."*

This book is "A Life," not "The Life." I cannot be so presumptuous as to think that I could relate *the* life. I believe that Gurdjieff lived many lives. He was known to travel as different persons, was seen simultaneously in distant places. Some biographers of Gurdjieff have taken incidents in Beelzebub's peregrinations in *Tales* as biographical fact, as well as Gurdjieff's putative personal history in *Meetings*. Much of the "truth" gleaned from these stories invite healthy scepticism, since until recently little evidence has been found to identify the named friends and acquaintances of the persona voice. Some readers prefer to understand whatever Gurdjieff has said of himself in his writings as parable. In effect, for the most part, the Gurdjieff we know from his writings invented himself and scripted the myriad roles he played. The best a biographer can do with the stories of his early life is to distinguish the possible from the improbable. Recourse to assumption and speculation in lieu of confirmable record, however, condemns much of the extant accounts of his early life to myth. This book is a possible life, no more.

The art or practice of determining the meaning of documents is hermeneutics. No one yet has been able to determine what is "genuine" in the stories Gurdjieff weaves about himself, and those who knew him personally can imagine Gurdjieff smiling slyly at the efforts of readers to mine ore of fact from veins of "fiction." What little we can know with some certainty about Gurdjieff's early life must be construed by means of critical hermeneutics applied to his own words along with a deep probe into the testimony of those who shared experiences with him, including Gurdjieff's stories about himself which challenge hermeneutic exegesis.

Nonetheless, as Gurdjieff would say, a chronology of events can hardly reveal a man's being. One can attribute qualities of character to someone without sensing their impact on others. Of his principal disciples, Orage was a master of persuasion, Ouspensky an exemplum of rational thought, Toomer a model of seductive charm, and Jeanne de Salzmann an engine of directed energy. Gurdjieff, despite his apparent sloppiness, rudeness and self-effacing manner, had all of these qualities and more. What is difficult for the historian to explain, however, is how he exercised such effective power over so many persons of different characters, skills, and persuasions. No one who came into contact with him came away unchanged consciously or unconsciously. Gurdjieff transferred something to everyone's being which may have wilfully rejected or unconsciously hidden beneath other impressions; but most of those who shared space with "The Old Man" bore with them for the rest of their lives an inculcated "something" of value, willy-nilly.

Seeking to discover the "facts" of his experiences that produced in him such power, I can place information about him from various sources into three chronological periods. The first, the principle time span of *Meetings With Remarkable Men*, covers the period from his birth until 1912 when Gurdjieff says he began teaching in western Russia. The second period extends from

1912 until mid 1924 when he had established his Institute in Fontainebleau-Avon and in New York City. The third and final quarter century of his life concludes with his death in the autumn of 1949.

Such chronological divisions, arbitrary as they are, facilitate inspection of materials drawn upon in extant biographical records on Gurdjieff. For the first period, over half his lifetime, we have little else than Gurdjieff's own writings and oral testimony, anecdotes if you will. Gurdjieff is his own initial historian, but the history of self he weaves offers few dates and lacks an obvious logical chronological sequence. Each of his written recollections tells a different story that seems to contradict other stories Gurdjieff told of himself orally. Consequently, the historian is tempted to supply, or invent, his own transitions to produce a logical concatenation of experiences that align the development of the man with the growth of his ideas. The task is formidable, and it has been met in a variety of ways that tend to confuse more than to clarify the man and his life.

This biography also implies ineluctably a critique of previous historical writings about Gurdjieff. Drawing upon available reliable information in them, as well as materials recently come to light, I attempt to lay out a full chronological record of his life that suggests the relation between his life and his teaching. A critical scan of current biographical writings allows me to both identify speculation and invention as well as to correct error, even those in my previous writings about Gurdjieff.

I am prepared for this multiple task fortuitously by having worked with and listened to Gurdjieff, been associated throughout my life with scattered members of his family, and indulged in countless discussions with those who followed him both in Europe and the United States. I have profited from access to the papers of A. R. Orage and Nathan Jean Toomer, and the voluminous notes of Muriel Draper, Sherman Manchester, and

Larry Morris. Dushka Howarth's *It's Up to Ourselves* (New York: Gurdjieff Heritage Society, 1998) containing papers of her mother, Jessmin Howarth, whose recollection of her own time spent with Gurdjieff and his pupils, is an important addition to current published records. Furthermore, I have consulted public sources that have appeared since the work of earlier biographers. Unfortunately, many of Gurdjieff's personal documents disappeared from his apartment shortly after he died, and in ensuing years have changed hands several times. It is saddening to see many of these documents for sale on internet sites, instead of being assembled in a single location accessible to scholars.

It has been more than twenty years since the appearance of James Moore's *Gurdjieff: The Anatomy of a Myth*, and the many works that have dealt with Gurdjieff's life since draw largely upon that work, though a great deal of new information has been made available by the opening of Soviet records, the availability of personal records of Gurdjieff pupils, and biographies of persons associated with Gurdjieff. Taking advantage of all of these, I am in the position to add to Moore's biography. In doing so, I avoid as much as possible needlessly repeating detailed information in his and James Webb's earlier *The Harmonious Circle* (1980) that is not essential to my coverage. A virtue of both those studies is the wealth of detailed historical background and interesting local color both elaborate. My own previous publications contain rosters and accounts of pupils, residents of the Prieuré, visitors and acquaintances of Gurdjieff that Webb and Moore often cite, but which are not relevant to this outline of his life.

In brief, my attempt here is to add to all current published records, and to sift out the discernible fruit of truth from the accumulation of thick husks of speculation and hopeful invention. Part of my overall strategy is a careful scrutiny of probabilities and possibilities of "fact" where certainty is not at hand. While introducing newfound fact and examining old speculation, I iden-

8

tify and erase as best I can the obvious false report and improbability put forward in current publications, a task perhaps beyond my critical capacities. Unfortunately, one can no more correct a circulating error than a cook can reseason the sauce already in a mouth.

1.

Tracing Gurdjieff: Family and Boyhood

The Gurdjieff Family

A trace of Gurdjieff's backgrounds must start with the subject himself. Putting aside for a moment what he is reported to have revealed to others in private and public talks, and what he has written of his life in his publications, the historian can begin with a number of well-documented facts and historical contexts. The official Russian form of his first name—Greek Giorgos—is Georgii, and this is what his immediate family called him. His French-Russian-Armenian language passport issued in Batumi on 29 June 1920 has his name in French as Georges Gyourdjian, and the Cyrillic form on the facing page is Георгіи Гюргжіанъ. In Armenian, Gurdjian would signify "son of Gurdji," Later documents have both French "Georges" and English "George," but he referred to himself and signed correspondence simply "G" or "Gurdjieff." If indeed as Dante insisted, nomen est omen, Georgii signifies tender of earth, "farmer" or "cultivator" if you will, and throughout his life, Gurdjieff cultivated mankind.

Gurdjieff's family name is recorded as "Giorgiades" by Moore (*Anatomy* 9), following Webb's statement that it is probable that "Giorgiades" was the original family name of Gurdjieff's father (*Circle* 26), though extant documents have his name consistently Ivan Ivanovich. The journalist William Seabrook recorded the name George S. Georgiades in an article concerning Gurdjieff's demonstrations in New York in 1924 (Taylor, *Gurdjieff and Orage* 36), possibly aware of the 1921 article printed in Germany that has his family name Gurdjiew-Georgiades. Ernest Brennecke and others followed Seabrook, though no one ventured what the middle initial stands for. Seabrook reasoned that *Gurd-* is a form of Giorgos. J. G. Bennett accepted that supposition, giving it cur-

10

rency, but were it so, we would expect that Gurdjieff's patronymic would be "Georgivich." Gurdjieff's patronymic is properly transcribed Ivanovich in conventional English transcription of Russian names, though his biographers favor the French form Ivanovitch, where the intrusive t for pronunciation purposes is dilatory in English. His mother's French papers have her first son's name George Ivanovich. Michel de Salzmann's entry on his natural father in Mircea Eliade's Encyclopedia of Religion adheres to the British-English form –vich.

Latinate European language transliteration of the Russian surname produces "Gurdjieff," pronounced in three distinct syllables; yet, following Anglophone practice, it is often pronounced Gurd-jeef, with stress on the final syllable. His niece Luba pronounced the family name in two syllables "Gyoor-jeff" (Luba 33), and this is the pronunciation Gurdjieff used in recordings. Seabrook and others, including Bennett, assumed that the family name was based on the Greek root *georgi,* not cognate with *gurdji,* a morpheme which designates "Kurd" in Turkish, and designates a Christian to Muslims. The name element Gur also designates a Georgian.

Certain things Gurdjieff has said about his family backgrounds in *Meetings with Remarkable Men* can be verified by existing records. For one, Gurdjieff writes in *Meetings with Remarkable Men* that his family emigrated to Georgia from Gumush Khaneh on the eastern shores of the Black Sea "not long before the big Russo-Turkish war, owing to repeated persecutions by the Turks" (*Meetings* 40). There were several Russo-Turkish wars during the nineteenth century, but the "big" war between these two took place in 1878, after Gurdjieff was born according to most records. There had been numerous earlier conflicts involving the Greek-speaking population of Turkey, particularly the Greek independence movement in the 1820s.

According to the Central States Historical Archives of

Georgia (File 489, Description 6, n. 2036 1807), Gurdjieff's uncle Vasilii lived in the village of Ekepad whose inhabitants were included in the village records of the larger southern Georgian village of Keivan-Bulgason, now called Velispiri, one of three villages in which Greek speaking Greeks rather than Turkish speaking Greeks settled in Georgia from Turkey. Gurdjieff's statement that the family emigrated from Turkey appears to be confirmed by Professor Rismag Gordeziani's *The Greeks in Georgia* (1990, 7) that cites Ekepad records to the effect that Ivan and his brother Vasilii emigrated from Gumush Khaneh (modern Gumushan) in Turkey and retained their Greek language. Gurdjieff's father Ivan and uncle Vasilii, then, were both born in Turkey.

Gurdjieff writes that after settling in Georgia, his father separated from his brothers (Vasilii and ?) and moved to the Armenian town of Alexandropol, "which had just changed its name from the Turkish name Gumri" (*Meetings* 40), a form of the earlier name Kumaïri. In 1837, after thirty three years of Russian occupation, Tsar Nicholas I renamed the city Alexandropol, after his wife's name. Taking Gurdjieff's statement at face value, we would assume that his family settled in Alexandropol about 1840, though Ivan Ivanovich Gurdjieff was not born until 1847.

Georgian records state that Vasilii married Politima Oprikov in November 1867, and moved afterwards to Alexandropol where the birth of their son Kiriakoz is recorded in the metric (family) book of the Church of Alexandropol. Vasilii's great grandson, George Kiourtzidis, recalls that the name of their son was Alexander. When Vasilii married, his family name was recorded as Kurdjogli. His brother Ivan Ivanovich, Gurdjieff's father, had probably lived in Georgia as well. According to the Central Archives of Armenia (File 47, Description 2, n25), he was born Ivan Ivanovich Kurchogli (Georgian form Vano Kurdji-ogli) and at the age of twenty-three, in 1871, he married eighteen-year old Evdokia Eleptherovna (b. 1852), the daughter of Elepther

Eleptheroff. Were he born in 1847, Ivan Ivanovich Gurdjieff would have been seventy or seventy-one years of age when he died on 25 June 1918, and were his son Georgii born in late 1877, when he died on the morning of 29 October 1949, he would have been almost the same age that his father had been when he died.

The Alexandropol record of local families in 1907 lists an Ivan Ivanovich Gurdjiff, his wife Eva, sons Georgii (b. 1880), Dmitri "Mido" (b. 1883), and daughter Sophia (no birth year). The appearance of the name Eva is curious, since it has no etymological relationship to the Greco-Russian name Evdokia. The 1931 French census report has Sophia born in Alexandropol in 1896. 1895 is the date on her French death certificate. Earlier municipal records mention a daughter Lukeria, a relatively common Russian name though both Georgii and his brother Dmitri mentioned a sister Luberia and Dmitri named his first daughter Luba after Luberia, a rare name. An 1885 entry on Ivan contains the names Maria and Anna, and the Alexandropol Church archives mention a daughter Melania born in 1875 (Armenia, File 47).

In Alexandropol records from 1883 to 1918, the name Gurdjieff appears often, spelled variously as Гюрджевь, and Гурджиевь. The 1907 document that lists Ivan's two sons and daughter Sophia does not mention Lukeria whose name appears in 1885 and 1887 documents. One can assume that she died before 1907. Alexandropol records have Ivan's wife as Evdokia Elepterovna, but on Ivan's death announcement, 25 June 1918, her name is given as M[unreadable] Kalerovna. The patronymic Kalerovna is given to Evdokia also on an 1885 document, and the French death notice of Gurdjieff's mother has "Evdoki Kaleroff" as her name, but I find the name Kaler only in Tyrol records from the fifteenth century. I am tempted to believe that Kaler reflects Greek kalos "good, beautiful." The given and surnames of Gurdjieff's mother have semantic convergences, since Greek

13

kalos "good" is compatible in meaning with Greek Eudoxia "Woman of Good Reputation." Since married women take their husband's family name almost always, I wonder why she was not identified as Evdokia Gurdjieff, as Gurdjieff's wife was identified on her travel documents.

In a Church Slavonic register, Ivan and his wife are identified as Orthodox Christians.

Gurdjieff's grandmother on his mother's side, Sophia, nicknamed Padji ("sister" in Turkish) was a well-regarded mid-wife who did not speak a word of Russian. His grandfather on his mother's side was Elepheriadis, a distinctly Greek form. Though Evdokia was thought by many to be Armenian, her name, Евдокия, is a Cyrillic form of Greek Eudoxia ("good thought"). The French form of the name on her death certificate is Eudoxie. Gurdjieff, who gave his mother's name to his youngest daughter, pronounced it in Russian fashion Yevdokeeya with stress on the penultimate syllable. If it seems odd that an Armenian woman would carry a Greek name, it is apparent that that Gurdjieff's mother was Greek as well as his father, confirming Gurdjieff's frequent assertion that his mother tongue was Greek. Gurdjieff's German papers, which he carried during the Second World War, identified him as Greek. (An article on the Institute in *Le Figaro*, 24 June 1939, labels him "the Armenian Gurdjieff," assuming that his Armenian passport identified his blood).

Georgii was the third born of his mother, but the first to survive more than a few days (Tchechovitch, *Tu l'aimerais* 283). The first born was probably Melania, born in 1875. One can find the names of four sisters born later: Lukeria, Anna, Maria and Sophia. Moore has 1881 as the year in which "his favourite sister" (Lukeria?) died (*Anatomy* 320), but I cannot find his source for the date. Gurdjieff writes that after moving to Alexandropol and before moving to Kars, the family was increased by "three then really charming sisters" (*Meetings* 41).

It is generally agreed that Gurdjieff's birthplace was Alexandropol, renamed Leninakan by the Soviet regime, and now restored to its Armenian name Gumri. Curiously, Louis Pauwels remarks that Alexandropol is at the foot of Mount Ararat (Pauwels, *Gurdjieff* 31), as if to suggest a Gurdjieff mythological association with the survivors of the Flood. My rough estimate has Gumri about seventy-five miles north of Ararat in Turkey. P. D. Ouspensky visited the city and Gurdjieff's home in the summer of 1917 and described what he heard and saw:

I met his family, and his mother. They were people of a very old and very peculiar culture. G's father was an amateur of local tales, legends, and traditions, something in the nature of a "bard"; and he knew by heart thousands and thousands of verses in the local idioms. They were Greeks from Asia Minor, but the language of the house, as of all the others in Alexandropol, was Armenian. . . . I liked Alexandropol very much. It contained a great deal which was peculiar and original.

Outwardly the Armenian part of the town calls to mind a town in Egypt or northern India. The houses with their flat roofs upon which grass grows. There is a very ancient Armenian cemetery on a hill from which the snow-clad summit of Mount Ararat can be seen. There is a wonderful image of the Virgin in one of the Armenian churches. The center of the town calls to mind a Russian country town but alongside it is the bazaar which is entirely oriental, especially the coppersmiths' row where they work in open booths. There is also the Greek quarter, the least interesting of all outwardly, where G's house was situated, and a Tartar suburb in the ravines, a very picturesque but, according to those in the other parts of the town, a rather dangerous place (*Search* 340–41).

Gurdjieff's Age

Gurdjieff's date of birth is a bone of contention. Though his year of birth has been given in various accounts as 1866, 1870, 1872, 1873, 1874, 1877, 1878, and 1880, current arguments center on 1866 and 1877. James Webb argues for the intermediate 1874 (*Circle* 26), and Michael Benham has told me that 1872 fits hhis chronological reconstruction of Gurdjieff's life. The bulk of Georgian and Armenian records suggest that Gurdjieff was born, as official documents later attest, in 1877. If his father died in 1918 at the age of 83, as Gurdjieff often said, then Ivan would have been born in 1835 and have been forty-two when Gurdjieff was born in 1877. If, however, Ivan was born in 1847, as Alexandropol records state, in 1877 he would have been thirty years old, an age that sounds more plausible for beginning a family, even if Gurdjieff, as he told Tchesslav Tchechovitch, was his mother's third delivery, and first live birth.

Gurdjieff's frequent mention of his age to others indicates 1866 as his date of birth, but there are no extant official documents that record his birth in that year, though all those I have scanned indicate 1877 (the 1880 date in the 1907 Alexandropol census may well be a scribal error). In the 1918 certificate authorizing the carrying of an arm, given him by the Soviet authorities in Tiflis, his age is recorded as 40, which indicates a birth date in December 1877. His 1920 Armenian passport records his age as forty-three and the photo on the passport shows a man who could be in his mid forties. The 1923 French census lists his date of birth 28 December 1877, a date repeated in the 1931 census that has his brother Dmitri's birth year as 1880. The identification he showed immigration authorities in New York in 1924 indicated 1877 as his year of birth. The 1930 United States census indicates the same. His German *Personenbeschreibung* of 1934 has 28 December 1877. In the introductory chapter "Ecstasy of Revelation" of the 1927 draft of *Beelzebub's Tales*, Gurdjieff asks: "What has this half century of my life given me?" A half century of life goes back to 1877. The term "half century" re-appears in his "Second Talk" to the New York group in 1930 in his citing "truths learned by me through my half-century's conscientious labours"; that is, would be since 1880 (Négrier, *Le Travail* 10). Gurdjieff's cousin and boyhood friend, Sergei Dmitrivich Mercourov, was born in 1881, four years after 1877 and fifteen years after the suggested 1866. It seems unlikely that Sergei could have visited the Gurdjieff family when Georgii was a young adult already out of his parents' care in 1877.

In conversation, however, Gurdjieff consistently indicated an 1866 birth date. In a talk to his French group on 28 October 1943, he remarked that he was seventy-six. In the last year of his life he was heard to say he was eighty-three. Luba Gurdjieff considered that he was 82 when he died (*Luba* 33). Since he died two months short of his December birthday, this age corresponds to an 1866 birth date. Dr. William Welch, who attended Gurdjieff on his death-bed, considered him older than a man in his seventies, and photographs of him in his last year would appear to confirm this opinion. When I was with him in the last year of his life I could have imagined him being in his mid-eighties, but not in his early seventies.

Supporting Gurdjieff's calculation of his age is historical evidence compiled by James Moore that would verify an 1866 birth (*Anatomy* 339–40). He advances three arguments for that year. First is Gurdjieff's own testimony. The second is his physical appearance in the last year of his life. The third, and most telling, is Gurdjieff's recollection of events in his early life that Moore situates earlier than 1877. For one, he cites Gurdjieff's recalling that the pestilence that wiped out his father's cattle herd a year or two after he moved from Georgia to Alexandropol would have struck in 1872–1873 (*Meetings* 40), indicating an anterior date of birth. Actually, there were several outbreaks in southern Rus-

17

sia and Turkey in the 1870s of Rinderpest, as it was commonly called. The most devastating was probably that in 1877–1878 during the Bulgarian War of Independence (that Gurdjieff probably identifies as the "big Russo-Turkish war"), mentioned in relation to Gurdjieff by Dorothy Phillpotts (*Occult Observer*, 256), and documented by C. A. Spinage's detailed history of the Cattle Plague (2003, 209). Another cattle plague struck in 1884, however, and so Gurdjieff's claim that he was seven at the time would have him born in 1877. Curiously, Gurdjieff states that at the time of the plague he, his younger brother and sister were part of the family group. If so, he would have been born before his family moved to Alexandropol.

Moore adds the November 1877 defeat of the Turks and occupation of the city of Kars by Russian forces as evidence of a birth before 1877: "Those obdurate for 1877 . . . must somehow explain why his formal education began in Kars a few months later . . . why Gurdjieff's many pronouncements on war make no mention of his own birth during the Russo-Turkish conflict" (*Anatomy* 339–40). My history books have 1878 as the date of Russian occupation and the Treaty of Berlin that placed Armenia under British protection. While the Russians were reconstructing Kars (*Meetings* 41) four years after the cattle plague—1877 or 1888—Gurdjieff's father failed in his trade as a carpenter and went to Kars "alone, and later took his whole family" (*Meetings* 41), when Gurdjieff would have been ten. In the chapter on Bogachevsky, if we assume its historical validity, Gurdjieff says that he was eight years old and younger than other boys in Alexandropol and Kars (*Meetings* 66). The statement does not make it clear that he had left Alexandropol yet, so he may not have gone to Kars until he was ten or eleven, after he had started his education in Alexandropol. Since basic school education in Russia was from the ages of eight to eleven, Gurdjieff would have attended the Alexandropol municipal school from eight to ten, and visited

Kars where his father and uncle were living. "Having settled in Kars, my father first sent me to the Greek school, but very soon transferred me to the Russian municipal school." At the age of twelve, 1889, he began private tuition under Dean Borsh.

When documentary evidence contradicts oral testimony and physical appearance, the biographer is apt to throw up his hands in despair. He can speculate that at some time when Gurdjieff was to produce papers for a passport, he pleaded destruction or loss of his birth records. This would be understood without much question if the place of birth had been over-run by warring parties, as Armenia was. Granted this possibility, a crucial question remains: why would Gurdjieff seek to extend his age by eleven years? The historian can accept the fact that documentary and oral dates of birth differ, but must base his history on one or another. Though his personal documents have his birth year 1877, I continue to envision the man I knew in 1948 and 1949 as being in his eighties, rather than in his early seventies. The 1866 date seems to accord with Gurdjieff's stories of his life. Without further evidence besides, it is difficult for me to ignore Gurdjieff's own admission of his age that indicates a birth year of 1866.

As for the day of birth, Gurdjieff celebrated both 1 January and 13 January (Gregorian calendar "new style"), or 1 January (old Orthodox style), depending on his mood, though official records have 28 December. As for his mother tongue, he said it was his father's Greek rather than his mother's Armenian (*Tales* 13), though it is probable the family spoke both indiscriminately in their household. When Ouspensky visited the Gurdjieff home in Alexandropol in 1917, the household language was Armenian (*Search* 340), though Gurdjieff admits struggling to read Old Armenian (*Meetings* 89). To American immigration authorities in 1924, he listed Russian, English and Greek as languages he reads and writes.

19

Gurdjieff's Wife and Children

At some if not all the time of his teaching in Moscow and Petersburg (the city name used familiarly by Gurdjieff, Ouspensky and its inhabitants) Gurdjieff was married to the Polish born Julia Osipovna Ostrovska. Moore assumes they were married soon after his arrival in Moscow (*Anatomy* 66). Webb does not advance a date of marriage because he suspects they were never legally wed, saying: "the woman later known as Gurdjieff's 'wife' never took the name of 'Gurdjieff' but always remained 'Madame Ostrowsky'" (*Circle* 52). Julia Ostrovsky's name on the passenger list of the *Paris* in 1924 was "Gurdjieff." She or her husband showed documents attesting to her marital status. In Russian society, married women frequently retained their maiden names after marriage for informal use. Elizaveta ("Lili") Galumnian, who took Gurdjieff's dictation for the opening passages of *Beelzebub's Tales*, was married to Sergei Chaverdian, but was known among her friends by her maiden name.

Julia did not bear Gurdjieff a child, but Gurdjieff has been credited with siring many children. In interviews he boasted of over one hundred, but the few children that are known to be his—those he himself acknowledged by name—number six: four sons: Andrei, born to a Latvian woman, Nikolai born to Elizaveta de Stjernvall in 1919, Mikhail ("Michel") born on New Year's Eve 1923 to Jeanne de Salzmann, and Sergei born to Lily Galumnian in 1927. His two daughters were Cynthia ("Dushka") born to Jessmin Howarth in September 1924, and Eve ("Petey") born to Edith Taylor in November 1928. Nikolai, Dushka and Eve are certain that Svetlana Hinzenberg, daughter of Olga Ivanovna Lazovich Milanov Hinzenberg, is their half-sister (*It's Up to Ourselves*, 220) The recent scan of Olgivanna's life in Friedland's and Zellman's *The Fellowship* reveals that Olgivanna was in Moscow in 1915 until 1917 when, married to Valdemar Hinzenberg and pregnant, she went to Tbilisi where she met Gurdjieff

(*Fellowship*, 45). When questioned many years later about a sexual liaison with Gurdjieff, she did not deny one (*Fellowship*, 424–25). Webb speculates that during his early travels in Asia he married and begot children (*Circle* 52). None have been identified.

Besides the children Gurdjieff acknowledged, many claimed him as father. In Paris in 1939, Mary Oliver, friend of Paul and Jane Bowles, claimed he was her father (Taylor 2007, 272). Colin Wilson reported that a "natural son" of Gurdjieff's was pointed out to him on an American college campus in the early 1960s (*Circle* 59). Reyna D'Assia, in Alexandro Jodorowky's *El Maestro y las Magas* (2005) is quoted saying to the author: "I am the daughter of Gurdjieff. In 1924 he came to New York and my mother brought him food that he had ordered at the Russian restaurant, my mother met him like this." The restaurant, also a speakeasy, known to have sent Gurdjieff foods belonged to Romany Marie who told Dushka that she had known him in Central Asia.

Boyhood

There is little reliable information about Gurdjieff's boyhood life either at home first in Alexandropol and later in Kars where he went to school. In his preface to *Beelzebub's Tales*, Gurdjieff recalls in detail his grandmother's last day of life when she advised him: "In life, never do as others do" (27). He told Ouspensky that when a young boy he was fascinated by the Yezidis, particularly the hypnotic state that can imprison one in an inscribed *circle* (*Search* 35–36). This phenomenon, a constraint to remain within the circle of belief of a community, only increased his interest in hypnotism. In the "Arousing of Thought" in *Tales*, he recalls several boyish episodes without noting the year in which they took place. His first tutor at the Kars Municipal school was Dean Damian Ambrosievich Borsh (*Meetings* 50–57), of the Kars Military chorus, who encouraged Gurdjieff's interest in music. His own music inspired some of Gurdjieff's early compositions (Blom, *Oriental Suite* 42 and 252, note 32).

Gurdjieff told his 1924 New York audience that his father, his "strongest intentional influence," told him stories of the lame carpenter Mustapha who invented a flying armchair (see the Nordic stories of the lame artificer Weland who flew on artificial wings and the Greek Dedalus who fashioned wings to escape from Crete to Sparta). Hearkening to his father's stories, he recalled that "he had passed his young years in an atmosphere of fairy tales, legends and traditions. The 'miraculous' to him was actual fact. Predictions of the future which he heard, and which those around him fully believed, were fulfilled and made him believe in many other things" (*Search* 36). In effect, Gurdjieff retained throughout his life the conviction that there is no essential difference between the sacred and the profane, since all things are sacred, and that there is no essential difference between story and what is called banally "reality." It is no wonder then that he took so readily to his father's instructions in manual arts and to his tutor's insistence to create new things and to turn to a new craft once he had mastered the one at hand. Concomitantly, moving from one occupation to another, he mastered the theory and practice of all crafts he touched (*Meetings* 250–51).

Before his teens, Gurdjieff had acquired exceptional aural, visual and tactile sensitivity to all things in his immediate environment. His father's songs of Gilgamesh, the Mesopotamian hero who searched the bottom of waters for secrets of life, provided him with a rich store of traditional stories under whose surfaces lay universal truths. Paying attention to his father's oral lore trained his memory and sharpened his imaginative powers. His manual training honed his powers of observation and imitation, and developed powers of concentration, and patience. Ouspensky tells the story of Gurdjieff presenting to him a mender of rugs who worked a metal hook with amazing dexterity. He would have liked to acquire the tool and study its application. A day or so later, Ouspensky found Gurdjieff sitting on the floor with a hook he had fashioned himself, skillfully repairing a torn rug.

Luba Gurdjieff, born in Alexandropol in 1915, remembers that her father, Dmitri, managed the first cinema in Alexandropol, was proprietor of a shoe shop, and served for a while as mayor of the city (*Luba* 29). Tchesslav Tchechovitch recalls that Georgii told him in 1918 that he had set up a "salle de projection" that was beginning to bring in money (*Tu l'aimeras* 134). Luba's mother told her she was born in the same house as Joseph Vissarionovich Djugashvili (Stalin) and played with him in the courtyard (1993, 3). An association of Gurdjieff with Stalin was claimed earlier by Louis Pauwels who said that the two were fellow students at the Kars Theological Seminary (*Gurdjieff* 64). This would be unlikely if Gurdjieff was thirteen years older than Stalin who was born in 1879, but possible if Gurdjieff was only two years Stalin's senior. Webb accepts Pauwels' assertion and adds without citing a source: "it is certainly true that young Joseph Dzhugashvili . . . was a boarder with the Gurdjieff family at some time . . . from 1894 to 1899," and Webb adds that he left owing the family money (*Circle*, 45). Curiously, Gurdjieff's name has not been found in the Seminary records.

Though a Stalin-Gurdjieff link is not confirmed by official records, Gurdjieff might have been signaling an acquaintance with Stalin in *Meetings* when he mentions a certain Nijeradze among other friends with whom he parted in Baghdad (1963, 191). It is known that "Gaioz Nizharadze" (or Nijeradze) was one of several aliases Stalin adopted during his early revolutionary activities. On 25 March 1908, J. V. Stalin, alias Nijeradze, was arrested and confined in Baku's Bailov prison. J. G. Bennett writes that Gurdjieff told him in 1948 that he had deleted a chapter on "Prince Nijeradze" from *Meetings* because it was too close to revealing sources in Central Asia still in contact with him (*Gurdjieff, Making A New World* 178). In her diary entry for 31 July 1936, Kathryn Hulme asked Gurdjieff if she and the other women could see the chapter on Nijeradze, and Gurdjieff replied that the women had not offered enough money for it.

The surname Nijeradze is not uncommon in contemporary Georgia. The name "Prince Vladimir Nigeradse" appears on the passenger list of the *Paris* that arrived in New York City on 2 April 1930. He was born in Kubais in 1888, which would make him too young to be Gurdjieff's friend. The poverty of extant records of Stalin's early life makes the remarks of Bennett, Pauwels and others mere conjecture. Simon Sebag Montefiore's recent *Young Stalin* (2007) denies an association with Stalin because Gurdjieff was not a student of the Tiflis Theological Seminary where Stalin studied from 1894 until 1898.

On the other hand, there is an essay by Miskha Chakaya in Miklós Kun's *Stalin: An Unknown Portrait* (2003), which quotes the author's interview with a specialist on Stalinist affairs, Olga Shatunovsykaya: "She referred to the mystical philosopher Gurdzhiev who had emigrated to the West and who has studied with Soso Dzhugashivili at the Tiflis Seminary. Gurdzhiev, she had claimed, was aware of Stalin's repulsive character and, as far as he could tell, his one-time school mate who had made it to the top of the Russian empire would have had no difficulty in reconciling the roles of self-conscious revolutionary and agent of the tsarist Okhrana." Being an agent of the Okhrana—serving both the Tsar and his revolutionary opponents—constitutes a double game Gurdjieff himself has been supposed of playing. Of course, one would like to know when and where Olga Shatunovsykaya heard Gurdjieff make this remark, which would have to have been made after Stalin's ascension, after Lenin's death in 1924.

Further, though she may have heard Gurdjieff say this, he

may have been referring to his own schooldays in Tiflis, of which no records have been advanced, and to Stalin as a co-worker.

Finally, one must take note of Lentrohamsanin in *Beelzebub's Tales* (346 *et passim*) who is responsible for the undoing of the saintly Ashiata Shiemash's good works. The element "Len" could refer to Lenin and "-tro" to Trotsky. "Ham" might be Russian *xam* "clumsy fool." San signifies "dignity." No matter what the name might suggest Stalin seems to be spared perhaps because, when Gurdjieff wrote the first series, Stalin had not been charged with the wide scale purges that began in 1927. Finally, it is probable that Gurdjieff and Stalin were aware of each other sometime or another before the turn of the century.

It is possible as well that Gurdjieff and his contemporary Alexei Maximovich Peshkov (1868–1936) whose pseudonym was Gorki ("sour, bitter," see English "gherkin"), knew of each other. It is entirely possible that Gorki met Gurdjieff in the early 1890s when the two worked in the same Georgian railway yards. Co-incidentally, Gorki's autobiographical first novel carries the title *Foma Gordeyev* (1899), and the titular hero's playmate is named Louba, the nickname of Gurdjieff's sister and niece.

This compendium of miscellaneous fact and conjecture suggests, at the very least, that in his early life, Gurdjieff was in contact with a number of diverse peoples, languages, cultures and political ideologies that would serve his career well in years to come; that is, when Gurdjieff left home on his quest for the "Great Knowledge," he was equipped with a honed memory.

N. B. Name Forms

In the pages below, transcriptions of Russian names follow, in general, the forms found in my sources. So, some patronymic forms end in *–ov*, and others in *–off*. The names "Peter" and "Pyotr" are different English transcription of the same name, as are "Georgivich" and "Georgievich." Similarly, some female names appear with either Russian –*a* or French –*e* endings, such as Lucia/Lucie, Helena/Helene, Sophia/Sophie. The maiden name of the wife of Chaverdian is recorded in extant records as both Galumian and Galumnian, and her first name as Lily and Lili. I use the form Lili Galumnian that appears in Orage's correspondence. Names of married women in written records are marked by the feminine –*a* as well as masculine –*sky*, e.g. Ostrovska and Ostrovsky, Savitskaia and Savitsky. I do not add *de* before Hartmann, Stjernvall, Salzmann, etc. unless it follows a first name.

2

1892–1912: Gurdjieff's Quest

Scanning the totality of his writings and oral testimony, one might consider that Gurdjieff spun out a good deal about his life before he arrived in Moscow and Petersburg, but it is not easy to separate fact from Gurdjieff's fiction, especially since Gurdjieff tantalized his listeners by asserting that truth is revealed by lies; that is, by stories that objectify meanings unperceived by those who take a fact as a truth. Gurdjieff said more than once that he wrote in parables, and there is no doubt of the parabolic character of the stories in *Meetings*, the second series of *All and Everything*, though much in the first nine stories of remarkable men featured there, particularly what he writes of his father and his first teacher, seem to be based upon actual events.

Furthermore, though one might complain that Gurdjieff was both careless and contradictory in dating his own life events, one suspects that his mental calendar was subjective; that he "coded" his memory purposely rather than inadvertently. He dated occurrences according to both the "O[ld] S[tyle]" Orthodox Julian as well the "N[ew] S[tyle]" Gregorian calendar without identifying to which calendar he was referring. So he celebrated both Christmases. Nonetheless, it seems obvious that the curious detailed dating in the third series, *Life Is Real,* is carefully plotted, and that his "system" of chronology, if system it is, is an envelope chronology.

1892–1895

In *The Herald of Coming Good*, for another example, Gurdjieff writes that it was in 1892, after a period of research trying to understand the essence of things with which he had come into contact, he decided to "abandon everything and to retire for a definite period into complete isolation" (16). He would turn from his studies of the physical nature of things to a study of their metaphysical aspects. The gap between the time of his decision and his putting it into operation is confused almost immediately by the statement that "this took place during my stay in Central Asia" in a Muslim monastery, though this must have occurred later. It would appear more likely that he was twenty-five rather than fourteen years old in 1892.

In his Institute prospectus of 1923, Gurdjieff cites 1913 as the year when he and a small number of others returned to Russia, specifically Tashkent. It seems hardly possible that he was but seventeen at the time. This twenty-one year gap between 1892 and 1913 is, then, the period Gurdjieff spent gaining the lore he sought in the East. Within this numerically symbolic envelope of time Gurdjieff gained the apparent totality of knowledge that he carried westward to impart to Europe and America, conjoining, as he was wont to say, the wisdom of the East with the energy of the West. All the other dates Gurdjieff mentions in connection with his "revelation" of truth fall within this twenty-one year stretch of events.

His memory of incidents dated within this or any other chronological frame is subject to "mutation," as current neuroscientists might say. Memory shifts as it adjusts to fresh contexts of recollection. It orders and reorders, expands and contracts time, dis-members and re-members events. The "reality" of an event is as mutable as the memory of it. Gurdjieff wrote about "involuntary" memory that causes negative emotions (*Tales* 1204). Perhaps alluding to Proust's madeleine as an ancillary to memory, Gurdjieff recorded many associations stimulated by a meringue (*Tales* 1206). He told his New York pupils in 1948 that they would remember his teaching each time they smelled something that reminded him of their meals with him. For the neuroscientist, memory is determined by the last thing remembered of an event. For Gurdjieff, the axial date 6 November 1927 evoked the memory of things he experienced as a young man, and in particular his epiphanic revelation of the conjoining of his inner and outer worlds (*Life Is Real* 20 et passim).

Gurdjieff measured out life events in cyclical pulsations of time rather than in a linear chronological flow of measured segments. His written recollections are quite purposely *not* fitted into a contiguous flow of a total life experience. Gurdjieff remembers his acquisition of esoteric lore in spots of time when he became aware of an inner world that had been hidden beneath the accoutrements of his outer world. Gurdjieff told an audience in New York in 1949: "Consciously erase all you have been taught and you will discover the essence knowledge you have been born with." At another occasion he added: "you are born with innate powers in your self."

Trying to fit between Gurdjieff's *terminus post quem* of 1892 and the *terminus ante quem* of 1913 the adventures he recalls in his various writings is comparable to trying to fit together misshaped jigsaw puzzle pieces to find a hidden pattern. The first piece in the puzzle is Olga de Hartmann's history of the origin of the Seekers of Truth in 1893 which she recited at his demand to Gurdjieff and his pupils in Essentuki in 1918:

Twenty-five years ago in Egypt, near the pyramids . . . three tourists met accidentally and from their ensuing conversation it was clear that all three had nearly the same world outlook and understanding of the meaning and aim of life.

One of them was a Russian prince, another a professor of archaeology and the third a young Greek guide. The Russian was wealthy and from an ancient lineage. In his youth he had lost his wife, whose death so strongly touched him that he pulled himself away from ordinary life and began to occupy himself with spiritualism. He began to travel and met some exceptional people who were interested in esoteric teachings.

He went to India many times and lived in the temples. His unhappiness over his wife's death pushed him to travel all the time. His meeting with the professor and the Greek took place on his second trip to the Egyptian pyramids. It was science and only science that brought the professor to the pyramids.

Before their meeting, all three had spent many long years searching, and that is why they had all arrived at the same conclusion that 'something' absolute existed, but they did not have enough knowledge to come to an understanding of it . . . To know all was too much for just three men. All religions, all histories, all special knowledge about life was too much for three people to arrive at during their short lives. But without this knowledge, they would always encounter obstacles on their way.

So the idea came to them to draw to themselves people of different knowledge. Again, another difficulty arose because if the new people they attracted did not have the same interest in, and aim for, something higher, even their special knowledge would not help. Different specializations would bring them nothing without this. They made a plan to find these necessary people, and to direct and prepare them with their advice in their material as well as spiritual lives. With this aim, the three men parted and went different ways, and the final result was that about fifteen people came together.

She continued with a description of the places they traveled at the start of their search: Persia, then in 1899 to India, Tibet, and Ceylon. Some went to Turkey, Arabia and Palestine before all met at Kabul in Afghanistan.

There are few records in other sources for Gurdjieff's travels in this period. Pyotr Kuz'mich Koslov, 1862-1935, a Russian Army captain, explorer and naturalist, led an expedition to the East, Mongolia, Gobi, Altai, Uzbekistan, Afghanistan 1899-1901 (recorded in 1927, Putshestvennik "The Traveller," and in the Geographical Journal, 34, London Royal Geographical Society, 384-408.) Koslov was an assistant to and successor of Nikolai Przhevalsky, friend of Sven Hedin and, probably, of Aurel Stein. In his account of the expedition, Koslov mentions Gurdjieff on a raft going down the Kunar River towards the junction with Kabul River: The text in a history of Afghanistan reads: "In the year 1900 the Russian mystic George Ivanovitch Gurdjieff traveled by raft down part of the river as part of the expedition led by Professor Kozlov in search of the ruins of ancient Shambala" (*Uddiya Until the 8th Century: A Short History Overview*). The claim that Kozlov was looking for Shambala seems illogical, given his status in the Army and the scientific purpose of his voyage. Nevertheless, it is not unlikely that the return of Kozlov's group did pass the Pamirs and Uzbekistan. Gurdjieff writes that he planned to travel up the Amu Darya in the year 1900 (*Meetings* 252), and he had been on the banks of a "tributary of the river Chitral, which flows to the river Kabul, and in its turn flows into the Indus" (219). He was not looking for Shambala, but for the Sarmoung monastery.

Many—J. G. Bennett, James George, James Webb, Idris Shah and David Hall among them—have proposed several locations for the monastery, from Tibet to Hindu Kush without citing convincing evidence. I assume that Gurdjieff visited an Essene/Sufi monastery, and that the name he gives it may be Tocharian for "self-consciousness," in accord with the Mt. Athos Hesychast and Gurdjieff belief in a natural grace through consciousness of one's own spirituality. Magical monasteries like Sarmoung and cities like Kitezh and Belevode were a commonplace in Russian imagination in the nineteenth century (Figes, *Cultural History* 308). In the Altais in the 1920s, Roerich met peasants who still believed in them. Gurdjieff recounts as well his adventures in the Gobi Desert (*Meetings* 164-75), which had been one of the destinations for Kozlov's expedition. There is no reason to doubt that Gurdjieff was a member of Kozlov's group.

31

In Gurdjieff's story to Olga, after "many years" twelve remained of the original fifteen and only four reached Chitral in Hindu Kush (Pakistan). Three years later, they returned to Kabul where they drew "corresponding people" to them. "This was the beginning of our Institute." Five years later they transferred activities to Russia, but because of the political situation there, returned to Kabul (*Our Life*, 1992, 70–73).

When Gurdjieff gave a talk four years later at the Dalcroze school in Paris in 1922 on the origins of the Institute, he told the same story with some added details. He said then that "the earliest beginning of the Institute can be considered to have been in 1895, when three tourists met by chance in Egypt by the pyramids. Finding that all three were Russians they became very close friends." The first was "Prince L." who had set off on his travels in Asia after losing a loved one ten years earlier (if L. is the Lubovedsky" of *Meetings*, it is appropriate that his name signifies "carrier of love"). The second, an archaeologist and assistant curator of a museum who had made expeditions to Hindu Kush, Armenia and Babylon, prefigures the Professor Skridlov of *Meetings*. If his name derives from skrivat, "to hide, conceal," it fits a searcher for hidden things. The personage Skridlov might have been based on Kozlov. The third, youngest of all, was Gurdjieff himself (only seventeen if born in 1877), whose interest was magic.

The impulse for the search, then, arose in Egypt, and was "formalized" shortly after in Alexandropol. The historian can attribute the coincidental tourist attraction to Egypt that sparked the search to the recent founding in Russia of a Department of Egyptology at the Institute of Oriental Studies, where Russian scholars were incited to make independent expeditions to Egypt. In the prospectus for the Institute in France, edited by Orage and printed in 1923, Gurdjieff adds that in Alexandropol he joined a society founded in 1895 under the name of "Seekers of Truth" that set out eastward on an eighteen-year quest.

It is obvious that Gurdjieff was not absent from home for that entire period. Dmitri Gurdjieff told his daughter Luba many years later that his brother "was all the time going somewhere. He used to come home for one or two weeks and get clothing and money and then he would go. Sometimes it was a couple of years— nobody heard anything." Luba remarked that "nobody knew if he was alive or dead, and suddenly he would appear again" (*Luba* 28). Gurdjieff told an interviewer in Boston in 1924 that he had studied medicine at the University of Athens, but quit his studies to go to sea as a sailor (*Gurdjieff and Orage* 58). The "National and Capodistrian University of Athens," formerly the "Othonian University," the first University in the newly established Greek State and in all the Balkans had an excellent Faculty of Medicine. The sea voyage he took after leaving the university may be the one that brought him to Egypt where he met the Russians.

Where some stories in *Meetings* fit into chronological gaps is difficult to determine. Biographers have strained to extract "fact" out of the fictions in *Meetings*, and indeed many stories seem to derive from actual occurrences. For one, the final chapter, "The Material Question," a verbatim record of a New York City talk in April 1924 recorded by his interpreter Boris Ferapontoff and edited by Orage, fills with events some of the period of twenty-one years. James Webb despairs of finding fact in the "allegory" of *Meetings*, and cautions his reader that it is best from a historical point of view to "treat each character as if he were an aspect of Gurdjieff himself" (*Circle* 30).

James Moore calls Gurdjieff's stories of his pre-European period "auto-mythology" (*Anatomy*, 7) and admits in reference to *Meetings*, that "we possess not one shred of independent evidence to confirm his extraordinary account (*Anatomy*, 24). Reading those stories as probable truth, he projects an imaginative rendition of Gurdjieff's progress through a twenty-four year period from 1887 to 1911, the putative chronological spread of his search for hidden truth. In doing so, he occasionally belies Gurdjieff's own dates in the period from 1892 to 1913.

Despite his wide travels and the broad contacts he must have made throughout those areas he says he visited and studied, official documents from the East made public in the last decades inexplicably fail to mention the name "Gurdjieff." How many different nominal identities he adopted during his quest is speculation. Rom Landau's identification of Gurdjieff with Agwan Dordjieff, based on the testimony of Achmed Abdullah (*God is My Adventure*) is easily argued away by Webb (*Circle* 49–51) and Webb's identification of Gurdjieff with Ushé Narzunoff is put in doubt since Gurdjieff was comfortably ensconced in France putting what he hoped were the final touches on his magnum opus while Narzunoff and Dordjieff were together at the All-Soviet Congress of Buddhists, 20–28 January, 1927. In the first decade of the century, Dordjieff was in contact with Kozlov concerning Russia's interest in Tibet.

It is certain that Gurdjieff adopted fictive identities during his travels because, as Webb points out, "it is certain that any traveler, however innocent, who ventured into so sensitive an area would be under suspicion and have his name pass into the files of the Great Game at Delhi, Simla and Whitehall" (*Circle* 50). The records of Russians in India and Tibet at the time Gurdjieff would have been there—Agwan Dordjieff, Ushe Narzunoff, and Esper Ukhtomsky—reveal remarkably similar adventurers to what we know of Gurdjieff. It is no wonder that it is widely thought that he assumed a multitude of aliases and disguises throughout his Asian travels.

Besides being mentioned as a member of Kozlov's expedition, no extant testimony of persons with whom he might have traveled mention Gurdjieff's name during his quest for esoteric lore. There is no good reason, however to dismiss the general outlines of the stories Gurdjieff tells about himself, with the possible exception of the bulk of *Meetings* identified by its author as a "mesoteric" text that calls for particular interpretation in the context of all three series of *All and Everything*. I have no qualms against using the term "history" for Gurdjieff's recollection of events in his other works, despite his apparent indifference in his dating. One can hardly attribute alternate dating to loss of memory, when one considers the prodigious feats of memory displayed in the text of *Beelzebub's Tales*.

It seems reasonable to suppose that his assignment of a particular date to a particular event is purposeful. It is senseless, then, to construct an alternative chronology with imagined events fitted to it. For example, Moore offers the date 1883 for Gurdjieff's going to work in the Tiflis railway yards after being refused entry to the Theological Seminary (*Anatomy* 18, 22), when by his reckoning, Gurdjieff would have been only seventeen years of age. Tiflis, the Russian form of Georgian *Tbilisi* ("warm place") was the administrative center of Turkestan, and the Trans-Caspian railroad he would have worked on would reach Tashkent, the later capital, only in 1889. Both date and occupation are not confirmed in Gurdjieff's text. Moore cites 1887 as the year when "the entire continent of traditional knowledge . . . summoned Gurdjieff" (*Anatomy*, 25). It is the date he gives for Gurdjieff's setting off to the East after he and Pogossian discovered documents [in 1886?] mentioning the Sarmoung Brotherhood (*Meetings* 1963, 89–90) an event and date uninformed readers are liable to take as fact.

Webb, with a different birth date in mind, calls 1892 a watershed year in which Gurdjieff, at the age of eighteen and eligible for military service, disappears from official sight and becomes involved in political intrigue (*Circle*, 47). What Webb overlooks is that Gurdjieff, an elder son of a family he supports, would have been exempt from military service, and in fact, Gurdjieff was registered as a "reservist." At the time, he was contributing to the family's keep by making and selling artificial flowers (*Tu l'aimerais*

201–202). Moore speaks of a "shadowy grouping" in Alexandropol in 1889 that coalesced in 1895 into the formation of the group know as "Seekers of Truth" (*Anatomy* 25), both dates lending support to the hypothetical 1866 as the year of Gurdjieff's birth.

Though the stories in *Meetings* and Gurdjieff's scattered references to Seekers of Truth suggest a traveling company of *searchers*, in his own accounts, he is consistently a single quester, which makes sense considering that his quest is ultimately to discover himself. Moore says Gurdjieff met Prince Lubochevsky in Egypt while exercising his job as a tourist guide to the pyramids and Sphinx in 1887 (*Anatomy*, 29), though that is not a date advanced by Gurdjieff himself. More likely is a date posterior to Gurdjieff's decision to alter the course of his studies in 1892, perhaps even just a year later when he might have left medical studies to go to Egypt. He told Orage that, lacking funds to pay for the journey, he took a job as servant to a Russian-Greek duke who was on his way there. The trip took two months during which, as servant to the duke, he served his food, and stood by while it was eaten. Most of the time, it was not, but just thrown back in his face, spiced with insults. He took this and other mistreatment with patience and tolerance, for he was eager to get to Cairo (*Gurdjieff and Orage* 30). He was probably in his mid-twenties at the time, though he says that when he was twenty-one, he decided to travel to India and Tibet.

He later said that at the same age he read the works of Madame Helena Petrovna Blavatsky and took her indications seriously. He traveled to every place she mentioned in *The Secret Doctrine*, but he found that nine of every ten of her references were not based on first hand knowledge. This cost him nine years. "I finally arrived in India, at its center of development," he told Orage in 1923. "I would gladly spare any human being the fruitless efforts I have gone through" (*Gurdjieff and Orage* 30). Were he twenty-one two years after his return from Crete in

1896, his birth date would have been in the mid-seventies; but this calculation does not fit other indications of age and time. Blavatsky (1831–91) did not publish *Secret Doctrine* until 1888, and it was not translated into Russian until the second decade of the following century, though Gurdjieff might have heard of the book as well as of accounts of her travels and discoveries in India described in her earlier *Isis Unveiled* (1877) whose contents were widely known to Russians interested in India and Tibet in the years Gurdjieff was there. Orage told his New York group that "Gurdjieff in his youth read Madame Blavatsky's Russian letters published in 1892 under the title *From the Caves and Jungles of Hindustan*" (unpublished Larry Morris notes 44). It is currently thought by many that Blavatsky plagiarized and embellished material she had found in an English guidebook to India. Nonetheless, if Gurdjieff had been born in 1877 and set off at twenty-one on the traces of Blavatsky for nine years, he could not have been in Egypt in 1900 as he said elsewhere, and not in Petersburg in 1901 as has been thought likely. Were he born in 1866 and set off in 1887 for several years, one can fit in his other adventures including his joining of the Seekers, for Gurdjieff's nine years involved other activities besides searching for Blavatsky's sites.

On his way to follow Blavatsky's traces in India, Gurdjieff paused for over two years in separate stays in a Muslim Dervish monastery somewhere in Central Asia. He would have converted to Islam while there if his claim is true that he visited Mecca, and then Medina where he found the Muslim religion better preserved. He spent time elsewhere in Central Asia and India before he arrived in Tibet shortly after the turn of the century. Either he passed himself off successfully as a Buddhist or had converted to Buddhism to study there, since Tibet was closed to non-Buddhists at the time, though Blavatsky said she had been able to "sneak in."

1896–1901

Gurdjieff writes that in Crete in 1896, one year prior to the fighting between Greek patriots and Turkish occupiers, and the first year of his search, he was struck by a stray bullet (*Life Is Real* 7). Intermittent fighting had already broken out in 1896 after autonomous Crete adopted a new constitution which favored Greek Christian residents. Turkish forces landed in Canea shortly thereafter and battled the Christians. When on 4 February 1897 Greece claimed sovereignty over Crete in the name of King George, there was a large scale massacre of the Moslem peasantry. Crete was accorded certain autonomy when it joined a union with Greece in the course of 1898. So, Gurdjieff was wounded when he found himself, as he would often in the twenty years that followed, between two religious and national interests.

After being carried to Jerusalem during his recovery, he walked home to Russia. If we give credence to his exposition to his New York group in 1924, in 1898 the "Community of Truth Seekers" decided to undertake an expedition through the Pamir region and India. They agreed to assemble at Chardzhou in the Transcaspian region on 2 January 1900, and then move up the Amu Darya (*Meetings* 252). During the two year interval between 1898 and 1900, Gurdjieff might have divided his time between Alexandropol and Baku, where he was a member of a society studying ancient magic. He bought an Edison phonograph which he put to work in Krasnovodsk and Kizil-Arvat in the Transcaspian region recording local songs and anecdotes which he played to the locals for a fee.

According to his exposition of his money-making projects to the New York group, on the way to continue his trade in Ashkhabad he met Madame Vitvitskaia, with whom he wagered that he could earn a certain amount of money by a definite date. To do so, he set up in Ashkhabad an "American Traveling Workshop,"

and earned a substantial amount of money in repairing everything brought to him—from typewriters and sewing machines to
watches and corsets—often by exaggerating the problem and his
personal difficulty in solving it. "As most of the articles they sent
for were either worthless to begin with or went to pieces almost
at once, and as there was not a single repair shop in the locality,
each family accumulated stacks of broken things [. . .] All these
I repaired" In short, Gurdjieff played the American who repairs
European faulty goods (*Meetings* 254–64).

1900–1901: Gurdjieff, Russian Medicine, and Julia Osipovna Ostrovska

Despite the information Gurdjieff gave in Essentuki and Paris concerning the founding of the Institute, he seems to have
been elsewhere during several periods of time rather than traveling with the other "seekers" across Asia. There is reason to
believe that Gurdjieff was back in Egypt in late 1900, resting
from his work in Turkestan where he was known for treating the
alcoholism of human machines as well as repairing mechanical
ones. This is an inference gleaned from apparent autobiographical
references in the story of Beelzebub's visit to Egypt in the chapter "Russia," where by the pyramids he met an elderly "power-
possessing" Russian associated with "The Trusteeship of People's
Temperance" in Saint Petersburg. In his first Talk in New York
in 1930, Gurdjieff refers to the financial crisis in his life brought
about by these "Russian power-possessing people" (*Life Is Real*
79–80). After exposing the problems of the Trusteeship in fulfilling its mission, the Russian invited "Doctor" Beelzebub to accompany him back to Russia to contribute to its organization.
They arrived two weeks later after the Building of the Trusteeship
was completed but not yet inaugurated (*Tales* 592–95).

If this episode has a base in historical fact, the person Beel-
zebub/Gurdjieff met in Egypt would have been Prince Alexander

Petrovich Oldenburgsky (1844–1932). After the death of his father, Prince Peter Georgievich, in 1881, Alexander inherited the trustee's responsibility for Oldenburgsky Charity House, Asylum Care House, Nurse Community of St. Trinity and, in 1897 the Antiplague Committee, of which he was chairman. His major achievement was the founding in 1890 of the first scientific research institute in Russia, the Imperial Institute of Experimental Medicine (in 1917 the adjective "Imperial" was dropped), of which he was the trustee. The *Chicago Daily Tribune* issue of 23 January 1893 contains an article mentioning the work on Cholera in the "bacteriological laboratory at the Institute of Experimental Medicine which belongs to his Highness Prince Oldenburg."

When Beelzebub arrived in Petersburg, he felt out of place, for he appeared to be neither Russian, nor even European (*Tales* 609). That is, Beelzebub like his maker Gurdjieff was an alien. He set up a chemistry laboratory despite troubles with "hereditary power-possessing beings." Nonetheless, he was invited by a High Excellency to the inauguration of "The People's Building of the Emperor Nicholas II" (*Tales* 613–14). This High Excellency was probably Alexander Petrovich, and the building is the subject of an article in the *New York Times*, 9 December 1900, headlined "St. Petersburg New 'Palace of the People'; Immense Building for the Masses to be Opened Dec. 19. Dining Room to Seat 2,000 Concert Hall, Opera House, and Other Attractions—The Work of the Committee of Temperance." The article names "His Royal Highness the Prince Oldenbourg" as the chairman of the St. Petersburg Committee of Temperance. In *Tales*, Beelzebub's function in relation to the Temperance committee is the curing of alcoholics, something for which Gurdjieff himself had proved adept. A *New York Times* article of 2 October 1904 notes that Prince Oldenburg, the brother-in-law of the Tsar, and chairman of the St. Petersburg Temperance Building, was involved in new and unusual medical treatments.

An important factor in the development of experimental medicine in Petersburg was the scientific interest—and the Tsar's personal interest—in Tibetan medicine. Many persons associated at one time or another with Gurdjieff were involved in the study and application of Tibetan and Mongolian medical traditions. The painter and scene designer Nicholas Roerich took part in studies of Tibetan medicinal psychological practices. Agwan Dordjieff held the post of Head of Tibetan Doctors of Buryatia. Pyotr Alexandrovich Badmayev, whose father was the godson of Tsar Alexander II, had left the Oriental Faculty of Saint Petersburg to study Tibetan medicine, and then returned to be associated with the Imperial Institute. It is easy to imagine Gurdjieff working with these persons, all of whom he knew personally at one time or another.

A few days after the inauguration of the Palace, Beelzebub was finally presented to the "Great Autocrat" (*Tales* 618), and the following day he received an official permit to operate his chemistry lab (*Tales* 619–20); but instead left Petersburg for other parts of Europe (*Tales* 621). Were this adventure inserted into Gurdjieff's life chronology, it would figure in early 1901. Were Gurdjieff in Petersburg in late 1900 or early 1901, he may have made other important contacts there during his stay. His "elderly Russian friend," Alexander Petrovich, was married to Eugenia Maximilianovna, daughter of Grand Duchess Maria Nikolaevna (the Tsar's sister) and Prince Maximilian of Leuchtenberg. It is not impossible that Julia Osipovna was lady-in-waiting to either Eugenia or Maria, and that Prince Alexander brought Gurdjieff into contact with her. Born on 23 April 1889, she would have been only eleven years of age at the time, but she may have made such an impression upon him that he sought her out years later. One caveat attends these speculations, no matter how likely they seem: Gurdjieff's name has not been found in the court and municipal records of Saint Petersburg of the time.

1901–1904: Gurdjieff's Second and Third Gunshot Wounds

In 1901 or early in 1902, Gurdjieff served the thirteenth Dalai Lama as collector of monastic dues, a service that gave him access to every monastery in Tibet. He said to Orage in 1923. "I will truthfully say that it is true I discovered extraordinary developments. I did not discover one single being with universal development, only monsters. A particular variety of the monstrous, but with no attainment of objective reason, no more than in the West, only different" (*Gurdjieff and Orage* 31).

In Tibet in 1902, a year before the July 1903 English incursion into Tibet led by Younghusband, Gurdjieff was struck by a second stray bullet which required some six weeks for recovery (*Life* 9). It is reasonable to suppose that during the English invasion in the summer of 1903, Gurdjieff fled with the Dalai Lama north into the Gobi Desert from Lhasa before making his way back to Central Asia, probably to Turkestan. To get back home from there, he joined a group of topographers working for the Turkestan Topological Administration among whom was a distant relative of his. It was then 1904 (*Life Is Real 28*). Little else is known of Gurdjieff in Tibet, or even how many visits he made there. Louis Pauwels accepts the assertion that he was an agent of the Lama (*Gurdjieff* 30–31), and makes the rather incredible suggestion that in Tibet he recommended the Swastika emblem to the German Karl Haushofer who in turn passed it on to Himmler (*Ibid* 62).

Back close to home in 1904, Gurdjieff found himself once more caught between warring factions. Local populations in Georgia had risen up sporadically against the Russian piecemeal annexation of the province, and in the area north of Tiflis there was fighting between Cossacks working for the "imperious" laying of the "foundation stones of the groundwork of . . . 'great Russia'" and people of Gori (birthplace of Stalin) near the rail tunnel of Chia'tura. There Gurdjieff, though he does not explain what he was doing, was struck for the third time by a stray bullet (*Life* 9). Webb speculates that he was operating as a double agent (*Circle* 75–76).

The "year before" formulaic dating of the first and second wounds is applicable here as well, since in the year after his third wound, a number of events crucial to the course of Russian history occurred. January 1905 marked the workers' march on the Tsar's Winter Palace in Petersburg to demand civil rights. Tsar Nicolas II was absent at the time, but the Imperial Guard fire on the crowd killed over one thousand persons. The October strikes throughout Russian later in the same year forced the Tsar to grant many of those rights (in 1896, the year of Gurdjieff's first stray bullet wound, 30,000 workers had struck in Petersburg for equal rights). Each of Gurdjieff's three "accidental wounds" was suffered not long before massacres in three popular uprisings. His body served as a barometer of coming storms of blood letting.

The third wound almost caused Gurdjieff's death. He was brought unconscious in a cart to a mountain cave in the east by an old man who fetched a barber to staunch his wound. The barber and two Khevsur clansmen conveyed him higher into the mountains to a larger cave which served as a burial place for these Georgian highlanders (*Life* 10–11). Not fully recovered, Gurdjieff fled the "political psychosis" of hostile groups, traveling toward the Transcaspian region, and being careful to avoid both Armenians and Tartars, each of which would consider him the other (*Life* 12). Already trained to play roles and adopt disguises, he managed to find repose near the Persian border in Ashkhabad, the principal city of Turkmenistan. There he discovered a distant relative exiled to the area who warned him about imminent identity checks. Not yet in full health, Gurdjieff set out alone for Central Asia and arrived in Yangihissar on the edge of the Gobi desert, east of Pamir in Chinese Turkestan, where he had recovered from his second bullet wound two years earlier (*Life* 16).

Gurdjieff's 1909 "Lodge"

Though Gurdjieff had been, undoubtedly, in Western Russia earlier than 1912 when he says he arrived in Moscow, he does not mention an earlier presence there in his own writings and talks. So 1912 is generally accepted as the time of his arrival and earliest teaching in a European cultural milieu. There is, nonetheless, evidence for a probable stay in Petersburg and Moscow in the first decade of the century, besides the reflections in Beelzebub's account of his work in Petersburg in 1900–1901. The fallacious Stalinist purge confession of G[leb] I[vanovich] Bokii (1879–1941) in 1937–1938, mentions a Masonic lodge in 1909 that had been founded by Gurdjieff. Other persons he named were N. K. Roerich and his wife, Dr. K. N. Riabinin, B. Stomoniakov, I. M. Moskvin and Gurdjieff's cousin S. D. Mercourov (Grekova, 1998, 290–91). The official text reads:

At his interrogation the accused confessed that he became a mason in 1909. The Lodge he joined was created by the well-known mystic Gurdjieff who after the Revolution emigrated to the West. His successor was Dr. Barchenko. In addition, Bokii confessed that he was the head of an anti-Soviet spiritualist circle whose members were occupied with foretelling of the future.

In the depositions of the SPEKO collaborators arrested after their chief is mentioned a commune organized by Bokii in a country house, whose members, men and women, got drunk together, practiced communal bathing, sang dirty songs. In a word, behaved indecently outside working hours. As is well-known, Gurdjieff organized in emigration an "Institute for the Harmonic Development of Man" whose members tried in every way to reach the depths of "one's own I," including in "sessions"—briefly in collective drinking orgies. It is possible that the use of alcohol, removing the psychic safety barriers, actually was practiced in Bokii's commune, who was to an extent a follower of Gurdjieff.

What is curious in this confession—though confessions made during the purges cannot be taken as unequivocal "facts"—is that the lodge named in the deposition as "The Unique Work Brotherhood"—obviously not "Masonic" since women were not admitted to the Masons—was in operation while Gurdjieff is assumed to have been in Central Asia. The obvious pejorative slant of the language, the charges of singing dirty songs and drinking to release one's "I" could very well be used to characterize Gurdjieff's later practices. Nevertheless, Gurdjieff's rituals and other Institute exercises, including the toasts to idiots, have been related to Mason rites (Négrier 14–17).

The *Modern Encyclopedia of Russian and Soviet History* (MERSH) has entries for the members of that "lodge" that suggest Gurdjieff's involvement. Bokii was born in Tiflis and grew up in Georgia before studying in Petersburg. In 1921 he became associated with Soviet security organizations Cheka, OGPU and the NKVD for which he was Deputy Commissar of Foreign Affairs. The Bulgarian born Boris Spiridonovich Stomoniakov (1882–1941) was Soviet Trade representative in Berlin from 1920 to 1935. Ivan Mikhailovich Moskovin (1890–1939) was a member of the Presidium and chief of the personnel section of the Supreme Sovnarkhov of the USSR. All were arrested and tried in 1937–38. Coincidently, the MERSH entry for "Ouspensky" includes the statement: "Study circles, if not societies, exist in the Soviet Union. Notes of Gurdjieff's lectures in Essentuki were circulated in the 1920s and 1930s and are alleged to have influenced such writers as Andrei Platinov, Sergei Budantsev and the émigré novelist Ovadiya Savich, who had been a member of the St. Petersburg group. Kasmir Malevich participated in the work in Petrograd."

It is also possible that Gurdjieff was in Petersburg in 1909 in connection with the new Buddhist temple established there by Dordjieff at the behest of the thirteenth Dalai Lama, or perhaps, as James Webb supposes, in association with Shamrazan [Nikolai] Badmayev, the adviser on Tibetan affairs to Tsar Nicolas II. Webb asserts that Gurdjieff and Badmayev, a Buddhist by origin and Christian by conversion, were not only acquainted, but worked together. If so, then Gurdjieff's treatment of alcoholics by hypnosis, as Badmayev's, may have been practiced in association with the Petersburg Temperance Society. It is possible that Gurdjieff made contact again at this time with Julia Osipovna, now twenty years of age, and may well have married her. In 1927, a year after her death, he recalled that eighteen years earlier—that is, 1909—Julia in Petersburg had been remarked for her beauty (*Life Is Real* 38). The information he supplied to American immigration officials in November 1930 had his age twenty when first married. That would suggest that it was 1897 when he married Julia, if not another woman earlier.

1909–1912: Continuing the Quest

It is likely that between 1901 and 1909, and after that until 1912, Gurdjieff continued his solitary search in the East, though he said that he pursued his quest in company with others. In his Institute prospectus of 1923, he mentions the return of others to Russia in 1913. Ouspensky recalls asking Gurdjieff about the others, but Gurdjieff did not identify any of them (*Search* 15–16). At another meeting in Petersburg, Gurdjieff said that his group of searchers was once in Hindu Kush (eastern Afghanistan, northwest of today's Pakistan). In his earliest publication, Gurdjieff implies that he had been in contact with a number of other people, and that after some years, satisfied with what he discovered, and having organized three groups of people according to their "types," he felt that he should "originate" an institution to prepare others to put into the lives of people what he had learned. So, he founded an Institute for Man's Harmonious Development (*Herald* 24). He decided on Russia for the enterprise, and in Moscow in 1912 he organized "The Institute for the Harmonious Development of Man" (*Life* 28).

The place and date of the first "Institute" are different in other writings of Gurdjieff. In his brochure prospectus for the Institute, he gives the date 1913 when he and other searchers returned to Russia, stopping on the way in Tashkent which had been seized by Russia in 1886. James Moore writes that Gurdjieff arrived in Tashkent in 1905 after his recovery from his third wound, and then in Moscow on 13 September 1911 (*Anatomy* 36–38). Gurdjieff's Paris talk about the origin of the Institute mentions a stay in Kabul in Afghanistan before proceeding on to Moscow. Later he said that he was in Russian Turkestan in 1911, moving from one town to another on his way toward Moscow.

Sometime along his route, though he does not say where or when, he sent twenty-seven men and twenty-seven women to a monastery "in the heart of Asia" (*Herald* 59–61). There is circumstantial evidence of the survival of a group of Gurdjieff followers in Siberia according to the account of Olga Kharitidi, a Soviet psychiatrist from Novosibirsk who visited Kuiya just north of the Nenia River on the north-western slopes of the Altai in the last quarter of the twentieth century, and there heard that Gurdjieff followers still survived in the area (*Invention* 231).

Nonetheless, in Gurdjieff's oral and written accounts of his travels after 1892 when he decided to embark on a quest for esoteric lore, and before he arrived in Western Russia, there are a number of gaps in the history of his activities, particularly between 1905 when he recovered from his third bullet wound, and 1911 when he moved piecemeal toward Moscow. During this time, he also "carried out private and government contracts for the supply and construction of railways and roads," before liquidating his affairs. Near the end of 1913 he arrived in Moscow with a million roubles as well as valuable collections of carpets and porcelain. During these years, he must have acquired the greater part of the knowledge he exposed later to groups in Moscow and Petersburg.

It should be kept in mind that he started on his quest for the "Great Knowledge" with well-developed faculties of concentration, memorization, reading both natural and artificial signs, knowledge of philosophy and science and medicine. He was acquainted with the deterministic philosophical trends of his day: social, sexual and evolutionary. He knew of various philosophical reactions against determinism such as Brahmanism, Theosophy, and *fin de siècle* humanism. He absorbed these ideas, as he had the phenomena of his immediate social and natural environment, with a will power of Nietzschean intensity and proportion, as well as with a capacity for relentless self-examination. He could play a number of musical instruments and understood much of Western as well as Eastern musical theory.

Most important of all, perhaps, is the fact that he had a well-cultivated sense of humor, and this sense was inherent in his extraordinary pleasure in all natural human functions. Right into the last year of his life, Saturday baths were occasions to exchange ribald tales which were expected to contain deep meaning. From an early age, thanks to his father's and others' stories of Mullah Nassr Eddin, he knew aphorisms that commented humorously on the foibles of mankind. As he set off for the East as a young man, Gurdjieff was comparable to the receptive capacities of the blank phonograph rolls upon which he had recorded story and song, he was ready for the totality of impressions he would acquire consciously in Sufi, Essene, Esoteric Christianity, Yoga and Shaman schools, and ready to transform experience into knowledge, and knowledge into wisdom.

Gurdjieff told different stories about his travels and acquisition of knowledge and powers in every publication. Gurdjieff "invented"—if you will—a history of self that resists confirmation in assumed facts. In effect, Gurdjieff lived several lives with several identities. He was, admittedly, a shape-shifter, a shaman—if you will—and there is much evidence in his stories to suggest this identity. He never spoke of himself as one, though he did display powers that are known to be particular features of shamanic powers: exceptional sight and hearing, communication with animals and a voice that can paralyze beasts. The shaman, functions out of time—Gurdjieff's unique subjective— and traverses worlds with the vehicle of spirit. The shaman, or "Holy Fool," reconstructs his own being in rituals of death and rebirth that entail physical pain—torture, if you will (Eliade, *Myths, Dream* 59-98).

The three wounds that he suffered, if not in supranatural existence, are described in terms reflecting shamanic ritual deaths and rebirths of life. He locates the first in 1896 in Crete, the second in 1902 in Tibet and the third two years after in Chiatura in the Transcaucus. The eight-year span from first ritual death to the third reflects the harmonic octave with an interval "shock." When close to physical death due to the third wound, he is transported on a donkey to a cave where he slowly recovers his health. The cave is the dark womb where the Shaman is born to his new life, and the donkey that carries him there is the collaboration between humans and animals that Shamans achieve. Those who knew Gurdjieff at the Prieuré remarked on his communicating with the animals there, notably Philos, his dog, a cat and two peacocks (*Life Is Real*, 37). In a second cave to which he is brought, he finds himself in company with "mummified" dead (*Life Is Real* 11).

Earlier in his youth, he risked his life in a contest with Piotr Karpenko that consisted of each lying in a shell hole during firing at nighttime on an artillery range. The risk of death is a form of self-torture during which "there arose in me for the first time the 'whole sensation of myself', which grew stronger and stronger, and a clear realization that . . . I had put myself in a situation of almost certain annihilation, because at that moment my death seemed inevitable" (*Meetings* 205). The experience is typical of shamanic initiation, including an association with an animal, since Karpenko means "little carp" in Russian.

Gurdjieff's extensive travels in Central Asia would have brought him into contact with Shamans who demonstrated magical powers. In recalling his sense of self during recovery from his gunshot wound in a womb-like cave, Gurdjieff writes:

". . . keeping watch over myself, I could attain almost everything within the limits of man's possibilities, and in some fields attained even to such a degree of power as not one man, perhaps not even in any past epoch, had ever attained.

For instance, the development of the power of my thoughts had been brought to such a level that by only a few hours of self-preparation I could from a distanced of tens of miles kill a yak; or, in twenty-four hours, could accumulate life forces of such compactness that I could in five minutes put to sleep an elephant. (*Life Is Real*, 20)

These powers, real or constructed, are common to the Shamans with whom Gurdjieff had been in contact on occasion and from whom Gurdjieff acquired particular hypnotic powers and a capacity to put himself into trances (*Meetings*, 23) and absorb negative energies. By the time he arrived in Western Russia to begin his professional career as a master of rugs, dance, and music, Gurdjieff was a man of many parts and many roles.

3

1912–1917: Moscow and Petersburg

Glimpses of Truth

By the time he arrived in Western Russia to begin his professional career as a master of dance, Gurdjieff was a man of many parts and many roles. He declared often that he started his teaching in Moscow in 1912/1913 and, if so, for obvious reasons he could not have begun his teaching right away. He needed to gather an audience, and he did this in Moscow in the same manner he did later in Petersburg, by advertising. He placed announcements in papers to the effect that G. I. G., a well-known Orientalist, was to present a ballet entitled "The Struggle of the Magicians." Further, he distributed here and there a prospectus for a center for the study of esoteric knowledge. The ballet was never performed and the centers of study and their supposed teachers did not exist. Gurdjieff could not stage a ballet without a cast, and it would appear that he arrived in Moscow without an accompanying troupe. He needed a cast for the roles in the ballet and a group of followers to train as teachers of the "system" he had brought back from his work in the East.

He also needed money, and he exercised uncanny skills in earning it. As Ouspensky remarked after first meeting him: "He was an extraordinarily versatile man; he knew everything and could do everything." As an example he relates how Gurdjieff bought carpets in Moscow and sold them at a higher price in Petersburg. "The sale of these carpets was in itself remarkable. G. put an advertisement in the papers and all kinds of people came to buy carpets. On such occasions they took him, of course, for an ordinary Caucasian carpet-seller." Ouspensky noticed that Gurdjieff could play on the weak side of his clients. He felt that Gurdjieff's selling technique was "acting" (*Search* 34). Ouspensky was to discover that an integral part of Gurdjieff's relations with

51

others consisted of play acting that exposed "weak sides" he could exploit.

The earliest record of Gurdjieff's teaching appeared in an essay Gurdjieff circulated among his Moscow pupils in 1915 entitled "Glimpses of Truth." The purpose of Gurdjieff's circulating this narrative among his followers and his asking Ouspensky to edit it was to publicize a synopsis of what his teaching consisted. Though it was probably composed by Gurdjieff himself, it appears as a narrative of someone who had read Gurdjieff's ballet advertisement in *Golos Moskvi*, and was told about the master of dance by an acquaintance who told him that Gurdjieff had wandered about the East many years before arriving in Petersburg and Moscow (*Glimpses* 8), a detail that seems to confirm suspicions that Gurdjieff had been in Petersburg before arriving in Moscow.

The essay is as follows: In mid-November 1914, after the Great War had begun, a certain "A" (Andrei Zarahoff?) brought the narrative persona by train and sledge to a dacha many miles from Moscow. After arriving about nine in the evening, he met and listened to Gurdjieff for a considerable amount of time. As the narrator listened to Gurdjieff explaining the structure of the universe as a reflection of the statement in the *Emerald Tablets* of Hermes Trismegistus—"as above, so below"—he realized that Gurdjieff's Russian, that was halting to begin with, had become more and more fluent, comprehensible and exact (*Glimpses* 12). A difficulty in understanding Gurdjieff's speech before it becomes perfectly clear is a phenomenon many others have reported over the years.

Gurdjieff's talk that night revealed the unity of the laws governing the maintenance of the universe. Microcosmic man reflects the Macrocosmic totality of the universe. Those laws can be understood as the musical octave with its seven notes separated by two gaps, adding up to nine, the number structure of all things (*Glimpses* 18). The musical octave, whose every note constitutes an "inner" octave, is the key to understanding the Unity of all things, including the anatomy and physiology of the human body. The seven days of Creation referred to in the Bible are an octave, and the number eight in Christian symbolism stands for a new beginning just as the *do* of each octave is a new beginning.

What I tell you, Gurdjieff indicated to his listener, you already knew. I order and systematize your knowledge. Learning this by yourself is self-initiation, the first step toward realizing the meaning of the Socratic "know thyself" (*Glimpses* 28). When questioned about his ballet scenario "The Struggle of the Magicians," Gurdjieff replied that there is a certain sense in the sacred dances he adapted from what he saw in the East (*Glimpses* 31). Bad art, he said, is a product of bad knowledge, contrary to the objective art, for example, of the Sphinx and the music of Orpheus that transmit knowledge to those who can understand it (*Glimpses* 32–34).

When the narrator asked his traveling companion the hour, he was told it is nine pm; that is, Gurdjieff has exposed his ideas in a matter of seconds. "Time does not exist here, he concludes" ("Glimpses" 37). This closing statement seems so much a Gurdjieffian ploy that it is hard to imagine that he did not write the scenario himself, for Gurdjieff repeated frequently that there is no significant measure of time in the transcendent world, except in changes in states of being, much as the Christian concept of "Grace" is a state in which one has moved beyond time as a duration of life to a timeless state. It is no wonder, then, that Gurdjieff called time the "unique subjective" (Taylor, *Philosophy* 67). In the story context, the clock-time measure "nine"—twenty-one on a whole-day clock—reflects what Gurdjieff had said about the musical octave and its gaps. Twenty-one is the multiple of [the laws of] three and seven.

The importance of "Glimpses of Truth" as the first written record of Gurdjieff's teaching in Moscow is its exposition of the musical octave as a mathematical code of the macrocosm of the universe as well as of the microcosm of the body and mind of man. Of course, Gurdjieff would have known the Western philosophical concept of the music of the spheres produced by a force moving across the orbit-strings of the seven celestial bodies visible from our world. Gurdjieff's exposition to his anonymous visitor identifies the principle behind the creation and maintenance of the universe and all things on it. This is the "Great Knowledge," and no greater knowledge is necessary to understand one's inner and well as outer worlds of being.

Prince Ozay

Not withstanding the implications of this introductory lesson to Gurdjieff's "system," James Webb has speculated that there is a written record of an even earlier Gurdjieff teaching in Petersburg: "One account which seems to describe Gurdjieff—on a mysterious errand, accompanied by a 'slant-eyed friend'—in St. Petersburg during the winter and early spring of 1913–1914," he proclaims, "is contained in the autobiography of Sir Paul Dukes" (*Circle* 84–87). He refers to Dukes' account of meetings with a certain "Prince Ozay." Following Webb, James Moore takes the identification of Gurdjiefff with Ozay as a certitude (*Anatomy* 74, 341).

Here is the evidence. In *The Unending Quest* (1950), Dukes described his travels from London to Holland, Latvia and Petersburg as a teacher of English. In Petersburg he studied the piano with Anna Essipova whose interests in the supernatural led Dukes to read Blavatsky's *Secret Doctrine* and to participate in several spiritualist séances, leading to encountering a hypnotist healer named Lev ("Lion") Lvovitch (Webb's form is *Levovitch*) who takes him to a master he called "Prince Ozay." Dukes describes his visit accompanied by Lvovitch to a person in hiding, "of whom there are but few in the world." I have questioned in detail Webb's and Moore's arguments that Dukes' Ozay could have been Gurdjieff in disguise elsewhere (Taylor 2004), but similarities and differences between Ozay's and Gurdjieff's expositions of "higher knowledge" should be briefly reviewed.

Ozay, who speaks good English compared to poor Russian, is interested in sound, like Gurdjieff in "Glimpses," particularly in the sound that has hyper-kinetic force. He tells Dukes that the "Lord's Prayer" contains particular power that can be exercised only when properly recited, or chanted, "especially the Name which is above every name, as your scriptures express it. That is why the Name must be hallowed. An overdose might easily kill you before you're trained for it. . . .Young man," he said sternly, "I could kill you in an instant, sitting here, without either of us moving a muscle. . . Understand this clearly. No man can acquire this kind of knowledge without risking death." Gurdjieff vaunted much the same power in his mind, saying that he could kill a yak tens of miles distant by the power of concentrated thought, and even put to sleep an elephant (*Life Is Real* 20). What Gurdjieff and "Ozay" both vaunt is logokinesis, the material force of word.

Webb conjectures that Dukes' "Prince Ozay" mirrors Gurdjieff of "Glimpses of Truth," on the grounds that "it seems difficult to believe that there were two such teachers in the same area at the same time" (*Circle* 87), but one could argue that Gurdjieff's Moscow and Dukes' St. Petersburg, had their share of teachers of this sort. The name "Prince Ozay" is a pseudonym; and, although Gurdjieff must have used many pseudonyms in his travels, he is not known to have used another name than "Gurdjieff" in Russia and the West. Moore observes that *Ozay/ Odzay* in Tibetan is "ray of light" and that "Ozay" sounds close to "Ushé," the first name of Narzunoff, (*Anatomy* 341), but Ozay is a not uncommon Turkish name (*oz* means "power" in Hebrew).

55

Finally, what marks a significant difference in the two teachers, despite their common interest and instruction in sound—sounding words and song in Ozay, and the mathematics of the musical octave in Gurdjieff—Gurdjieff's octave demonstrates the ultimate totality and harmony of all created things, while Ozay's word is an individual kinetic force.

For Moore, Dukes was in 1913 Gurdjieff's "first foreign pupil—significantly enough, an Englishman" (*Anatomy* 71, 74, 167, 350). That claim has been challenged by the New Zealander Rolf Alexander, who wrote on the back fly-leaf of his book *The Power of the Mind: The System of Creative Realism* (London: Werner Laurie, 1956), that he had been a personal pupil of Gurdjieff in 1913. Moore writes that after Dukes, Gurdjieff's next "convert" was the Finnish doctor Leonid Robertovich de Stjernval (*Anatomy* 76), though it was not until the late spring of 1915 that Stjernvall met Gurdjieff.

Moscow and Petersburg 1915–1917

When Gurdjieff gathered his first pupils in Moscow and Petersburg is not known. Ouspensky (b. 1878) says that he was urged to join them after Easter 1915 in Moscow by a musician and a sculptor (*Search* 6), who was most likely Sergei Dmitrivich Merkurov. Merkurov, perhaps Gurdjieff's first Moscow pupil, had brought into the group Vladimir Pohl who, according to one record, introduced Ouspensky to Gurdjieff (*Hartmann* 1964, v). Soon after his joining Gurdjieff's group, Ouspensky told the psychiatrist Dr. Leonid Stjernvall (b. 1872) in Petersburg of an exceptional person, to whom a certain Caucasian sculptor, Merkurov, had introduced him in Moscow. Ouspensky assured Stjernvall that Gurdjieff was undoubtedly the only one who could provide an answer to the different questions which preoccupied the doctor. Ouspensky said that Gurdjieff, a boyhood friend of Merkurov, would soon make an appearance in Saint Petersburg.

When Stjernvall and his wife Elizaveta arrived at their first meeting, "we found the room already full, and we noticed, looking about us, a man of middle age, medium build, tanned either by race or the sun, with a particularly penetrating gaze. Gurdjieff greeted each of us very warmly and courteously. Then he joined us in listening to one of his disciples read the first lesson intended for us" (Val, *My Dear Father 83-89*, my translation from the French). Besides Stjernvall, Ouspensky knew the mathematician Andrei Andreivich Zaharoff, who was also among Gurdjieff's first Petersburg pupils.

Webb reports Bennett's saying that Gurdjieff told him he had met Rasputin and Nicholas II while he was in Petersburg (*Circle* 82). That he had met the Tsar much earlier has been suggested above, though Gurdjieff may have crossed paths with Grigori Yefimovich Novy (known popularly as Rasputin "the debauched") at this time. Nikolai de Stjernvall says that his mother, who had known both Rasputin and Gurdjieff in 1916, does not associate the two (Val *Daddy* 137–45). Nevertheless, Rasputin, who suffered from drug addiction, had been treated in 1915 by Pyotr Alexandrovich (Zham-Saran) Badmayev with Tibetan medicine. Gurdjieff had known if not worked with Badmayev earlier in his medical practice. Rasputin's murder during the night of 29–30 December and its impact on the court of the Tsar are detailed in the French Ambassador Paléologue's journal entries for 30 and 31 December 1916 and 3 January 1917 (vol. 3).

What Gurdjieff taught his early pupils is only vaguely suggested by "Glimpses of Truth." Ouspensky's record, *In Search of the Miraculous*, is a detailed record of twenty odd months of listening to and questioning Gurdjieff in Moscow, Petersburg and Essentuki. Ouspensky makes the point that everything Gurdjieff taught, including physical exercises, can be understood by the axiom "as above so below." This is not only a hermeneutic precept but a philosophical and religious principle explained eloquently by the archangel Raphael in Milton's *Paradise Lost* in reply to Adam's request for a "full relation" of God's creative purpose:

...what if Earth
Be but the shadow of Heav'n, and all things therein
Each to other like, more than on Earth is thought
(*Paradise Lost* V, 574–76)

The image suggests the harmony of all things from Plato's divine *idea* to the earth's substantial form, from Gurdjieff's macrocosmic *all* to his microcosmic *everything*, from universal unity to human diversity. The laws that govern the one also govern the other; that which maintains the structure of the universe maintains the human body, just as William Blake's world is contained in a grain of sand. Gurdjieff, as others before and after him, saw mankind blind to its own anatomy and physiology. Man could not exercise his innate capacities to anywhere near their potential. He offered a method to perfect the self by raising its consciousness and creative energies, while insisting that his pupils should not follow him, but follow the direction he points, a direction leading from outer worlds of illusory appearances (the Hindu's *maya*) to inner worlds of consciousness and conscience. He expressed the same idea allegorically when he said: "I am like a coachman. If the horse goes to the left, I pull the right rein, and if to the right, I pull the left one" (*Hartmann* 1964, 19). The destination of the coach is higher body being and its passenger higher consciousness.

What makes Gurdjieff's teaching distinct from much of the self-work he observed in his travels, is its "fourth way." "Absolute" control of the body—the fakir's way—is one way toward self-perfection (and "immortality"); control of feelings—the monk's way—is another; and control of thought—the way of the yogi—is a third. Each of these ways demands exclusive singular purpose; that is, exclusion of other ways. Gurdjieff's "fourth way" joins all three ways in a harmonious relation and operation. The fourth way does not demand withdrawal from habitual patterns of mundane life, but indicates a method for a person to use it to reach the goals he already has (*Search* 99).

While working toward perfection in the world of the inner self, one can remain what one was in the world at large. A most important factor to control in the work is non-identification, withdrawal of the self from external influences of thought and feeling, like those of school and church that block rediscovery and liberation of the uncontaminated essence one is born with. "Self-discovery" is a goal of the method. "Be an entity, not an identity," Gurdjieff insisted.

Gurdjieff's pupils in Moscow and Petersburg—renamed Petrograd at the beginning of the Great War because of its German-sounding name, though Gurdjieff and his pupils referred to the city by its earlier and now restored short form— represented the elite of Russian society, the *intelligentsia* among the high echelon of professionals who mixed with and often had pretensions to aristocracy. Gurdjieff was an alien, a rustic from the provinces. Whatever his powers of altering his appearance, for Russians in the North he was a provincial much as Rasputin was in the eyes of the local citizenry. Gurdjieff exploited to his advantage how he was seen and judged by the public. Seeming to be a traveler from distant civilizations suited his role as a bearer of esoteric lore and master of exotic dance and transmitter of traditional ethnic music. Class differences did not seem to intrude into the relationship between teacher and pupil precisely because of the understood difference in cultural and ethnic backgrounds.

There is one place in Ouspensky's record, however, where Gurdjieff inserts the issue of "class" into the discussion of one's capacity for self-development. In an evening explanation of the "objective way" of living, Gurdjieff suggests that even a "simple *obyvatel* may sometimes do such work within him that he will overtake a monk or even a yogi." Gurdjieff's use of the word *obyvatel* seemed to disturb his "high class" audience, and sparked a lively discussion. Aware of the effect of his statement, Gurdjieff, though not a native speaker of Russian himself, offered an explanation of the term that aroused class-conscious questions from his pupils such as: "Can it be said that an *obyvatel* is a good citizen?" (*Search* 363). For them the term designated a "common" man, one without class or education. The Russian scholar Georges Nivat has explained to me that: "*Obyvatel* is a citizen, and inhabitant of a town, and also a petty bourgeois. It was a sort of depreciatory word along with *obyvatel'chtchina*, odious pettiness of the bourgeois—or mechtchanstvo, from mechtchanin, the lower rank of a town's inhabitants—what the Russian intelligentsia hated most." In effect, Gurdjieff is shaking his pupils out of the illusion that their class is privileged as far as work toward self-perfection is concerned.

Ouspensky, a prominent writer who worked in Moscow and Petersburg as a journalist, was a member of the "intelligentsia" but did not have the social connections of Thomas Alexandrovich de Hartmann, an esteemed composer and officer in the Tsar's Reserve Guard, or of Doctor Leonid Robertovich Stjernvall, a noted psychiatrist. Hartmann wrote later of the disadvantages of his class pride when he found himself out of the context of his habitual society (*Our Life* 1964, 34). Ouspensky, on the other hand, seemed to others always to carry himself with the bearing of a member of the aristocracy. After all, he came to Gurdjieff with a well-established reputation. He had lectured to audiences in Petersburg and Moscow in the winter of 1914–15 about his travels in the East before his return to Moscow in 1914. Before meeting Gurdjieff, he had published two books, *The Fourth Dimension* (1909) and *Tertium Organum* (1912). Both had brought him considerable fame.

Gurdjieff knew of Ouspensky's work and it is quite clear from the first conversation the two had in a small café in Moscow, that Gurdjieff, having gleaned Ouspensky's demonstrated intelligence and knowledge, had lured the journalist into his group. Andrei Andreivich Zarahoff played intermediary for Gurdjieff in mid-December 1916 to bring Hartmann, a renowned composer at the age of thirty, and a member of the Reserve Guards, to the disreputable Pushkin Restaurant on Nevsky Prospekt to meet Gurdjieff. After a brief exchange with him in the company of Stjernvall, Gurdjieff told Stjernvall to get Hartmann in touch with Ouspensky and read "Glimpses of Truth." Hartmannn met and was introduced to the work by Ouspensky, and with his wife, Olga Arcadievna, saw Gurdjieff twice before February 1917, when he was ordered to duty on the front near Kiev and Gurdjieff left Petersburg forever.

After Gurdjieff had quit Petersburg after the abdication of Nicolas II, Ouspensky was conscripted into the guards, but only attended military assemblies (Moore *Anatomy* 91–92) until he was released from military obligations because of his poor eyesight. About this time Ouspensky married Sophia Grigorievna Maximenko (born 1878 in Kharkov) and brought her, her adult daughter Helene ("Lenochka") and her husband Mikhail Pavlovich Savitsky into his household. Although Sophia joined Gurdjieff's group and became an important teacher in her own right in later years, Ouspensky does not mention her presence in the Petersburg group. It is curious as well that Gurdjieff's wife Julia Osipovna Ostrovska, Olga de Hartmann and Elizaveta de Stjernvall are not named in Ouspensky's account of the work in Petersburg, though all attended Gurdjieff's talks.

The internal political strife during 1916 and 1917 disturbed the continuity of Gurdjieff's teaching. In November 1916 he remained in Moscow. On 2 March 1917 the Tsar Nicholas II abdicated, and after a one-day titular rule by his brother Mikhail, Prince Lvov assumed the head of government until Alexander Kerensky took over. In April Lenin arrived in Petersburg from

Switzerland and Germany and preached the revolution that was finally achieved when the Winter Palace was stormed and Kerensky's caretaker government overthrown on 25 October 1917 (for an excellent day-by-day description of the progress of the Revolution see Paléologue).

Gurdjieff had left Petersburg for the last time in February. Ouspensky and others who saw him off witnessed an extraordinary scene. The Gurdjieff on the Nikolaevsky Station platform was not the same Gurdjieff who came to the window of his compartment to wave goodbye. He looked at them "with a quite exceptional importance and dignity in every look and movement, as though he had suddenly become a ruling prince or a statesman of some unknown kingdom." A journalist who travelled with him wrote an article about this supposed "oil king" from Baku with a French novel under his arm (*Search* 324–26). After a short stay in Moscow, Gurdjieff went south to an exile and a new stage in his work, back to his geographical matrix.

4

1917–1919: Essentuki to Tbilisi

The events in Gurdjieff's life between his departure from Moscow and his arrival in Constantinople three years later are documented in a number of accounts. First is Ouspensky's narrative in *Search*, and second is Gurdjieff's talk given to the New York Group in 1924 entitled "The Material Question." Hartmann and his wife's *Our Life* is a detailed recollection of their trials with him during this time and Elizaveta de Stjernvall wrote an account in Russian of the same period. Jeanne de Salzmann's unpublished memoirs undoubtedly cover the Tbilisi period in 1919 and 1920, as do the published portions of Olga Ivanovna Hinzenberg Wright's memoirs in Friedland and Zellman's *The Fellowship*.

It all began for Gurdjieff's pupils when the master summoned them from Petersburg to him in Alexandropol. Elizaveta de Stjernvall recalls that her husband received a telegram in September 1917 reading: "Terminate all your affairs and your goods right away and head for the south of Russia this month" (Val *Daddy* 1997, 98). Ouspensky writes that in June 1917 he received a telegram from Gurdjieff with the brief message: "If you want to rest come here to me." Ouspensky arrived in Alexandropol after a journey of five days, when the usual trip would have taken but three days (*Search* 340). Two weeks after Ouspensky's arrival, Gurdjieff said they would go back to Petersburg. A few days later, after passing through Tiflis, at Mineralni Vodi (Mineral Waters), Gurdjieff sent Ouspensky ahead to Moscow and Petersburg with his news for others, while he would go to Kislovodsk.

On 28 August 1917 Hartmann, who had been assigned to military duty at Rostov-on-Don, went straight through with his wife and chambermaid to Essentuki to join Gurdjieff, and were met at his door by Andrei Zaharoff. Webb and Moore recapitulate their story as well as Gurdjieff's in "The Material Question," and I need not repeat those details, but Elizaveta de Stjernvall's account entitled "Across the Caucasus with G. I. Gurdjieff," translated from Russian into French by her son Nikolai and included in his *My Dear Father* (61–80), appeared only in 1997 and adds to the others.

1917 Sochi

The Stjernvalls left in November to meet Gurdjieff in the Black Sea resort of Sochi. Gurdjieff had left Essentuki earlier to go by train to Tuapse with Julia, the Hartmanns, Lenochka Savitsky and Zaharoff. A few days later, after the Hartmanns returned from the military garrison in Rostov with his papers signed, the group walked over the southern Caucasus chain to Uch-Dere to the south, where they were joined by Ouspensky and the Stjernvalls, who had been told by Gurdjieff to meet him there. It is obvious that Gurdjieff had plotted this curious convergence of pupils, as if the geography involved was a pattern only he could read, or rather design. In Uch-Dere, Gurdjieff went down daily to the shore to read the movement of ships on the Black Sea as indicators of the progress of the war. When he sensed the approach of the Bolsheviks, who had occupied Tuapse by this time, he sent the Hartmanns, both tired from the journey to Uch-Dere, back to Essentuki by train and marched north to Oghlniki with the remainder of his group. Again, as the Bolsheviks were closing in, Gurdjieff scouted for another location on the coast, but finding nothing satisfactory, in mid-December, he moved his group of some twenty persons back to Essentuki.

1917–1918 Essentuki

Arriving a week before Christmas, according to Moore, he settled his group comfortably in quarters large enough to accommodate families in separate quarters, assigned household tasks for each, then directed the group to do what Ouspensky complained were exhausting physical exercises, including Dervish dances and "psychic tricks." Gurdjieff suggested finding a name for the colony, something like *Sodroojestovo* "Union of friends for common aim" (*Search* 372–73). In her memoirs, Olga de Hartmann says that the name finally decided upon by Gurdjieff, though it did not sound like proper Russian to Ouspensky, was "Essentuksky Obshcheznitiye Mezhdunarodnavo Ideino-Trudovovo Sodruzhestva" which the Russian scholar Georges Nivat, questioning the form of the Russian, translates as "The Communal House of the International Philosophico-Worker Union of Essentuki," and adds that *Obshchezniti*, or *obscehzjitie* is a usual term for a student's dormitory of residence. In her memoirs, Elizaveta de Stjernvall recalls that the sign painted on the wall of their residence read "International Alliance of Ideological Workers" (*My Dear Father* 58). The name was formulated to assure Bolshevik authorities of the community's worker character.

Not only had Gurdjieff taken upon himself heavy financial obligations to house and feed some twenty persons, before the end of 1917, he reported:

> One rainy morning, while sitting at the window looking out at the street and thinking how to obtain this, that and the other. I saw two odd-looking conveyances pull up at my door, from which a number of shadowy forms emerged.

> At first it was even difficult for me to make out what they were, but, as my agitated thoughts grew a little calmer, I gradually began to realize that these were people, or more exactly skeletons of people, with only their burning eyes alive, clad in rags and tatters, their bare feet covered with wounds and sores. There were twenty-eight in all, among them eleven children between the ages of one and nine.

> These people turned out to be relatives of mine, among them my own sister with her six children (*Meetings* 278).

65

The relatives included his mother, his brother Dmitri, his wife Anna ("Asta") and infant daughter Lukeria ("Luba"), his youngest sister Sophia with her fiancé Georgilovich Kapanadze, his sister Anna Anastasieff, her husband Feodor and their daughter and two sons. His father had refused to leave his home in Alexandropol. Moore writes that Anna and her family had stayed behind with Gurdjieff's father (*Anatomy* 107), but Valentin Feodorovich Anastasieff ("Valia"), who was six at the time, writes that his whole family went together in 1917 to Essentuki where they stayed for eight months (1973). They had walked first from Alexandropol to Tbilisi, but learning that Gurdjieff was in Essentuki, they procured carts and traveled a military road to arrive at his doorstep. In all, at that moment in Essentuki, Gurdjieff was fulfilling voluntarily a paternal responsibility for some eighty-five persons.

Where Gurdjieff had gotten the money or the credit to rent the houses along the coast no one seemed to know, or perhaps care. A few days after his arrival in Essentuki, he ordered the engineers, lawyers and accountants to go look for work in the enterprises of the town, already under Bolshevik control. The authorities received them well, appreciating their individual talents and, assuming from the name of their commune, they were brothers in revolutionary spirit.

Twice a week, Gurdjieff received the public in the evening to explain the work of his *Ideino-Trudovovo Sodruzhestva*, or philosophical working community. The audience included a number of teachers, scholars and other professionals who were also in exile in Essentuki. Ouspensky and others gave talks. Gurdjieff paid special attention to his own pupils whose work he supervised and for whom he assigned tasks. For an example, he sent a young man of the group away with a small amount of money with orders to find another city in which to stay for a week before returning. The man, who had always been in his mother's close care, had no practical sense whatsoever, but returned a week later with an awareness of the realities of his situation. Many in the group were treated similarly in order to become conscious of and master their weaknesses.

In effect, Gurdjieff used the perilous situation in which they found themselves as a laboratory to exercise his work of transforming the potential of his pupils into actuality. The march with the Hartmanns from Tuapse toward Sochi earlier was a similar exercise. In February 1918, Gurdjieff had letters sent to Moscow and Petersburg inviting his remaining pupils to join him. As time passed, however, basic commodities became difficult to acquire, a situation of which Gurdjieff knew how to take advantage. In his scouting outside the town, he came across a large amount of entangled silk threads, brought them to the house and had the women disentangle and put them on home-made spools. It took almost two weeks for the work to be done, even with the aid of those who had arrived recently from Petersburg and Moscow, but the result brought in a good deal of money from local merchants. Hartmann sold a boxful in Kislovodsk nearby.

The "curriculum" of the community included a variety of daily physical exercises, both gymnastics and dance routines. There were evening musical recitals given by Gurdjieff and pupils as well as talks. Men and women were directed in cooking and housekeeping tasks. Throughout this Essentuki interlude, Ouspensky was feeling less and less comfortable with the "work." It is clear that he did not appreciate the routine of strenuous exercises, and though Gurdjieff's ideas were still of primordial importance to him, he felt the direction the man himself was heading was not. Though he does not go into detail, he indicated in his recollections that Gurdjieff seemed to be leading his pupils in the way of the monk; that is, over-weighting work on man's emotional center. When Gurdjieff started a program of rigorous physical training in preparation for a move westward across the Caucasus to the coast, Ouspensky stayed apart with his wife, her daughter and her husband Mikhail Pavlovich Savitsky (Webb gives his name as Sventitsky). I suspect that Gurdjieff felt he no longer "needed" Ouspensky. In Petersburg, Ouspensky had been a valued intermediary, one who could screen potential members of the group, and lead discussion during meetings. Curiously, though Ouspensky moved away from Gurdjieff several times since arriving in the South, he kept coming back, even without Gurdjieff's invitation.

The region of Essentuki was suffering increasingly what Gurdjieff called "war psychosis." In "the district of Mineral Waters," he explained to his New York group in 1924, "towns passed from hand to hand: one day to the Bolsheviks, the next day to the Cossacks, and the day after to the White Army or to some newly formed party . . . . What made me most anxious was the situation of about twenty of my pupils . . . who were of military age. Young and even middle-aged men were being conscripted every day. . . This constant tension could not be endured any longer; cost what it might, some way out had to be found" (*Meetings* 271–72).

As an added protection for the travels he intended to undertake with his group in the coming summer, Gurdjieff acquired a document from the National Soviet of the Transcaucasus of Tiflis identifying him as a refugee from Alexandropol authorized to travel in different regions of Russia with two men. It was dated 20 May 1918. The names of the two men are not noted on the document.

In late July, Anna and Feodor Anastasieff and her children returned to Alexandropol where they learned that her father, who had refused to accompany her to Essentuki, had been killed by Turks. The Alexandropol hand-written certification of his death has the date 26 June 1918 on it. Moore writes that in July 1918, Anna, her husband and children arrived [in Essentuki] with the news that, Gurdjieff's father had been killed by the Turks in May as he defended his house (*Anatomy* 109). Anna's family decided then to move to Feodor's home in Baytor on the Turkish border near Mount Ararat.

Meanwhile, Gurdjieff announced to his Essentuki pupils that they would trek across the mountain range to Tuapse where they would walk to Sochi and continue one way or another to Tbilisi, a city Gurdjieff knew well when it was still known by the Russian name Tiflis, the capital of Georgia (the country had declared independence on 26 May 1918, after leaving the Caucasian federation with Armenia and Azerbaijan). Tbilisi was for the moment calm and remote from the fighting. While both men and women pupils underwent intense physical training, carrying sacks of stones up and down stairs and around the grounds, Gurdjieff announced to local authorities that he needed materials for an expedition to search for dolmens and gold in the mountainous regions northwest of Essentuki. He had Pyotr Shandarovsky, who was working for the Bolshevik authorities, procure passports for his group, and present a requisition for horses, mules, carts, shovels, pickaxes and alcohol to wash gold ore. Gurdjieff strained the denatured alcohol through loaves of warm bread and baked onions to produced drinkable eau de vie, a practice that was used in military units through World War II. When all things were in place for the exodus, Gurdjieff assembled the volunteers together and demanded absolute obedience to his direction. To add life-value weight to his demand, he placed a revolver on the table in front of him.

August–October 1918 Across the Caucasus
In the memoirs of Elizaveta de Stjernvall, it is recorded that at eight in the evening of August seventh, 1918, after a long wait for local political activity to calm down, Gurdjieff led seventeen pupils, two horses, two mules, four dogs and two cats from Essentuki in two cattle cars en route to their supposed goal of Tuapse. Dmitri and his family stayed behind to guard the valuables Gurdjieff and his group had hidden in the basement of his

house. Ouspensky also stayed behind, caught for the time-being in the Bolshevik web of control, but he managed to support his household as librarian of the local library until the White Russians liberated the town early in 1919. In June of that year, he was able to escape north.

Three men and two women occupied the first train wagon with the horses, dogs, bench carts and tools. Another cart and baggage were loaded into another wagon. The arrival and stay overnight in Armavir were without incident. Gurdjieff assigned specific tasks to all, particularly finding and preparing food and caring for the animals. The group spent three days there on a siding waiting for the train to move again. Meals were made outside near the wagons, and pupils slept where they could after a guard had been assigned. After a three day wait, the route onward was still blocked. Finally, Gurdjieff moved his people into a deserted military barracks, then to small houses near the Belaya (White River), where they slept on the floors. Everyone rose at six, the horses were led to grazing, and pupils took the liberty to go swimming. The weather was warm. There were abundant fruits and vegetables for the picking, so the wait was not without some consolation and comfort.

While they stayed frustratingly in place, three hermits looking for spiritual nourishment visited. They had heard of Gurdjieff's presence and asked him many questions, the answers to which they seemed not to understand. As the days passed, artillery and rifle fire resounded from the direction of Maikop ("Valley of Apple Blossoms") about twenty miles to the northwest. Armed patrols passed close by but paid no attention to the group. Another visitor who came by a few times was a half naked Buddhist monk with red hair and bare feet who, when fording the river, cried out to the women watching: Don't look, don't look!" Though he identified himself as a Finn and former officer of the Guards, Stjernvall, who was Finnish by nationality, had difficulty communicating with him. When he learned Gurdjieff's destination, the monk joined the group.

News came that Maikop had fallen to the White Army. Gurdjieff hid the young men of the group under the river brush to escape notice of the Bolsheviks who were conscripting all the manpower they could find. Two days later, after increased noise of combat, Armavir fell to the Cossacks, and Gurdjieff with his group were able to proceed on to Maikop where, on 31 August, he procured a White pass written on the back of his Bolshevik pass with the same authorization, including the right to carry a revolver. On 1 September, the group left Maikop on foot, horse and carts for the mountains. They passed through ruined Cossack villages to Kumichki, beyond which there were no passable roads (*Meetings* 276). They left behind the carts there and loaded their material onto the horses and mules, and began the westward trek toward Sochi. It was impossible to identify the armed patrols that passed them as either White or Red. All depended upon Gurdjieff's judgment. If he pulled the left end of his moustache, the others were to assume the patrol was Red and the appropriate side of the pass paper would be shown; if he pulled on the right, the right side would be shown.

In the midday heat, the group set out and by evening had found a village where they camped for the night on the grounds of a Cossack who also offered fodder for the horses and mules, and supplied the tired marchers with milk and bread. They spread straw on the grass for beds, and at dawn Gurdjieff roused the company for departure. They followed a grassy trail and made good time until two in the afternoon when they paused for a rest. They were climbing toward the Mariisky Pass or the Klukhor Pass leading toward the Black Sea, both within sight of Mount Elbrus.

About five in the afternoon, after an ascent that forced them to unload the carts and carry the tools and baggage, they caught sight of Kammenolomsk where they spent the night sleeping on the floor of a deserted schoolhouse. In the morning the women were sent out to look for food. Some peasants gave them bread, and after a breakfast of bread and fruits they set off again. They came again to the Belaya river and, in the town of Dohovskaya, Hartmann was sent to acquire safe-conduct passes. Unfortunately, the official who was authorized to issue them had disappeared. After a fruitless wait of an hour or so, the group went on. During their first stop, four Cossacks approached and insisted on searching their luggage. Gurdjieff produced the white side of the passport and the Cossacks rode off after explaining that they had been fooled earlier and had let pass some apparently inoffensive persons who turned out to be Bolsheviks. They added that some townspeople had told them that Lenin and Trotsky were hiding among Gurdjieff's group. Staying in place for the night, they feasted on chickens they had been able to buy in Dohovskaya, and later came upon a number of youths who invited them to join them roasting maize.

The next morning they forded the White River which was not very wide, but whose bottom was rocky and current strong. They forded the river one by one, with Gurdjieff going last on the mule cart. When the mules balked in the water and seemed about to bolt, several of the men jumped back into the water to secure the cart. Gurdjieff jumped in the river, and held onto the mules until all the baggage and materials were unloaded safely. Then they proceeded upstream over rocky terrain, pushing the cart now being pulled by the horses. It was late in the afternoon when they paused again, having covered less than ten miles. They spent the night in a shed beside a small building occupied by a deranged forest guard. He left them alone but swarms of fleas did not. Some of the group built fires and roasted potatoes to pass the night.

Early during the next day's trek, the cart had to be abandoned because of the rough terrain. The search for foodstuffs occupied much of the trekkers' attention until in a small village they found the entire population drying sunflower seeds. They spent two days there, sleeping in an old schoolhouse, and left carrying the material that the overloaded horses could not. The next day they slept on the tent tarpaulin they carried, then went on the next morning through marshes that mired the horses. When they stopped on dry ground, Gurdjieff doubled back with four men to fetch more of the material the horses could not carry and to rejoin the members of the group who had stayed with it.

Over the next few days a system of relays was established. One part of the group would go ahead while another would join it a day later with the horses. The terrain became more difficult to traverse and the cold increased in intensity the higher they went. They were consoled by places of rest which offered splendid panoramas of the mountain chain. One day, Gurdjieff somehow found flour with which he made a hundred Greek cakes to feast his companions. Finally they began a descent that proved even more difficult on limbs and muscles. After pausing on a plateau, the group lost direction in the mountain brush, then split up to find a path, but it took eight hours of walking with heavy loads before they regrouped in the evening.

If no one else did, Gurdjieff knew where they were and led them toward a group of huts they could see below in the distance that he said were occupied by Armenians. The group reached them at nightfall, only to find them recently deserted, judging by objects left hastily behind. The group paused two days there, where there was little to eat besides potato soup and mushrooms. The horses lacked forage. Gurdjieff went on with one group while the other tended the horses. One of that group, while trying to adjust the pack on a horse fell on an axe and cut himself badly. Tending to his wound delayed their departure, but they finally rejoined Gurdjieff five miles further on.

It was a short descent from there to the foot of the mountains where they came across a hunter's hut decorated richly with animal hides. The hunter, about thirty years of age, welcomed them and fed the entire group sour milk, cheese and cornbread. He had a herd of five hundred cows and a large store of cheese. They left with his parting gift of twenty five pounds of fresh goat meat.

The group made their way along the slope of the White Mountain and stopped for the night in a small hamlet of dairy farmers. Gurdjieff told the others to take the next day off from tasks in order to rest for the ascension of Mount Belotschenki. Leaving four men to watch over baggage and materials they could not carry, the others left in two groups, heading for Babouk, but fatigue, heat, and rocky terrain slowed them and the horses considerably, though they managed some fifteen miles. The first group stopped for the night in a clearing, but the second did not arrive. While waiting for them, Gurdjieff sent Stjernvall ahead to reconnoiter. He came back near noon to say that he had found a village a few miles away whose chieftain promised them a hearty welcome.

After they arrived, the chieftain put grass at their disposal for the horse and an unlimited supply of fruit for the people. A number of them then retraced steps back to the dairy hamlet with the horses to fetch the remaining material and the four guards. Gurdjieff volunteered, but none of the others wanted to accompany him. Finally, the man with the cut arm took the initiative, and took the trail with Gurdjieff and two women, one of whom was Elizaveta de Stjernvall, who found the going so arduous that she mounted one of the horses under the eyes of Gurdjieff's disapproving look.

After gathering the material and loading the horses and leashing the dogs, the group started back, but the horses lost the trail in the dark. The women urged Gurdjieff to return to the hamlet for the night. Gurdjieff agreed and the group went back. They were off again early the next morning, and as they neared their goal they saw Stjernvall running toward them, worried that they had gotten lost or waylaid. They pitched tents on the grounds of the chieftain, and washed clothes in the river not far away. It was the first time the group had changed clothes in three weeks. When they arrived, the villagers were making arak from softened dried pears boiled with yeast. When the mix was distilled, the vapors gathered in an alembic, and produced a sort of vodka.

Gurdjieff had his people gather pears and apples which he made into a fruit stew. Toward evening the second group that had been left behind straggled in, announcing that they had been attacked by bandits who stole their goods, including their rifles and pistols. One woman in the group had talked the robbers out of some of their loot, but not the firearms. Gurdjieff decided that henceforth a leading group would not leave a stopping place before the arrival of the second.

They rested four days in Babouk recovering from various wounds and ailments. Stjernvall was very ill. Gurdjieff, hale as ever, promised the others he would reduce the length of their treks forward, and he helped lift Stjernvall onto their second-best horse when they left Babouk. The best one had disappeared. Soon after, when the group was approached by a gang of brigands brandishing weapons. Gurdjieff calmly walked up to them and began a conversation in a local dialect that none of his companions understood, but during which he learned that the brigands were for the moment without a leader. Gurdjieff persuaded them to join his group and they all sat down together and shared a roasted pig, before each group went its own way (Tchechovitch, *Tu l'aimerais* 108).

In just over one day's march further, the expedition reached Solohov where a Polish engineer offered them three rooms in which to sleep. He treated them with chicken and eggs and his servants served them with extraordinary courtesy. Solohov was on a road and, though Sochi was not very far away, without a cart and with hostile peasants accusing them of going to Sochi to restore the old regime, Gurdjieff thought it prudent to rest there for six days. He profited from the pause to search for dolmens, which peasants in the area had put to a variety of uses, such as cooping chickens. Almost all the dolmens were hollow with stone lids.

One afternoon, the servants told Gurdjieff that their employer, Philipovich ("Pan"), had frequent fainting spells from which he recovered without remembering what had happened. They added that he had consulted specialists without success. Gurdjieff suspected what might be the cause of this narcolepsy and went to Pan's bedside where Pan told him that he had been maliciously hypnotized years earlier. Throughout the following day, Pan's servants were astonished to remark that their patron did not once fall asleep. He was so thankful to Gurdjieff that he refused any payment for food and lodgings and asked if he could join the group. Gurdjieff assented, and Pan followed him from that moment on all the way to Constantinople and France (Tchechovitch 109–12). On the road once more, with one of Pan's carts the group reached Sochi, occupied now by Circassians. Comfortably installed in various hotels in Sochi, members of the troupe relaxed and recovered their physical and moral strength. After Gurdjieff disbanded the group, Andrei Zaharoff and Alexander Petrov left for Essentuki.

The record of this same journey by Thomas and Olga de Hartmann differs little in the main, but is not quite as detailed as Elizaveta de Stjernvall's Russian account. In his New York recollection of the adventure, narrated in a combination of Russian and broken English, with interpreter on hand, Gurdjieff said that the expedition took two months, but offered no further details, saying that the story "has already been written and will doubtlessly be published by certain members of this singular scientific expedition, who subsequently returned to Russia and are now cut off from the rest of the world" (*Meetings* 276).

One wonders why Gurdjieff took this route and this manner of movement to get from Essentuki to his ultimate destination Tbilisi. With his passes, and his extraordinary facility of getting authorities on both sides of the conflict to give him aid, he could have gone by way of rail the some five hundred miles or more between the two cities. Obviously, he planned the expedition as a "will task," an exercise in operational relations between pupils and a master. The trips he would take with pupils in France later were similar. For Gurdjieff, such voyages were occasions for him to observe pupils responding to imposed conditions.

Gurdjieff, well past mid-life in the second half of 1918, had undertaken an extraordinary risk, but taking risks was the principle way of developing a higher being. What seems remarkable to one viewing this adventure from a distance is that Gurdjieff knew exactly what he was doing and what materials he needed to do it. None of his pupils died, though some were women not at all accustomed to trials much more strenuous than hosting receptions in Moscow and Petersburg salons. They lost weight, suffered bruises, sprains, and debilitating fatigue, but gained precious knowledge of and confidence in their strengthened being. Remarkable is it that, apparently with neither map nor compass, Gurdjieff could traverse such rough terrain. He seemed at every moment to know where he was, and how to take advantage of the terrain. He even demonstrated to the group how to walk safely over rocks and along precipices by testing the ground foot by foot in daylight and dark. Every step taken was an exercise in what he called "intentional suffering," doing what one does neither necessarily want to do, nor understand punctually the purpose of the doing.

Gurdjieff and a handful of his faithfuls remained in Sochi for several weeks. He stayed with a distant cousin who died of tuberculosis while he was there. Hartmann occupied himself giving piano lessons, while his wife sold for clothing pieces of the tarpaulin they had carried from Essentuki. Gurdjieff played cards in a local Circassian Officers Club where he and local merchants kept up with the political and military news. In January, the White Russian General Anton Deniken had captured Essentuki, and elements of the White Army were moving down toward Sochi. It was the moment for Gurdjieff to lead the way to safety. They found passage on a small ship, and two cold days later disembarked in Poti, boarded a train and arrived a day later in Tbilisi, a city now again in the hands of the old regime.

5

1919–1922: Tbilisi to Fontainebleau

Tbilisi 1919–Paris 1922

Gurdjieff, still suffering from a fever of 104° due to an illness contracted during the crossing of the Caucasus, found lodgings with a cousin Turadzhev (*Anatomy* 125), and set about with Julia in surroundings familiar to him from the century before to find a way to earn money. He sold the ring of one of his women pupils for food, and then, drawing on his experience with Caucasian textiles, he entered the flourishing local carpet trade. His fever subsided and in three weeks he gained enough money to support his group with enough left over to invest in a new venture (*Meetings* 279–80). The city was at the time also home to British troops, stationed to "protect" the new nation.

Meanwhile Hartmann had found no trouble in securing an appointment as teacher of composition in the local Conservatory which boasted some two thousand students. Whereas, in Essentuki Gurdjieff had played a guitar for his music, in Tbilisi, with a piano available, Hartmann played for Gurdjieff's dances and gymnastics. As a member of the state opera with a wife chosen to sing the lead role in a production of "Carmen," Hartmann came into contact with the scene designer Alexander de Salzmann, whom he had met years earlier in Munich. Salzmann (b. 1874), a native of Georgia, was back in his homeland with his pregnant wife, Jeanne Matignon Allemand, who taught a Jaques-Dalcroze class in the city. Salzmann was also part owner of a local cabaret, "The Peacock's Tale." The co-owner was a Latvian named Valdemar Hinzenberg who, two years earlier on 31 January 1917 in Kursk, near Moscow, had married Olga Ivanovna Lazovich ("Olgivanna"), the daughter of a Montenegrin general. They were living with their infant daughter Svetlana (Friedland and Zellman, *The Fellowship* 47–48).

In Munich before the war Hartmann had known of Salzmann before he moved to Hellerau where he met and married nineteen-year-old Jeanne Allemand, born in Reims and raised in Geneva, where she studied with Emile Jaques-Dalcroze. When the war broke out Jaques-Dalcroze returned to Geneva, while Salzmann and his wife went to Moscow and Petersburg where he designed stage scenes. After the war they went south to where she taught a class in Dalcroze "eurhythmics" in a local Military School. When Gurdjieff met the Salzmanns, he found him "fine" and her "intelligent." Jeanne, after hearing from Hartmann about the "Sacred Dances," invited Gurdjieff to watch a demonstration of her eurhythmics class. He did so, and a few days later returned and took command to teach his gymnastics (*Our Life* 77). Hartmann surely knew of the favour and use of peasant myth, song and dance in opera and ballet. Stravinsky, Roerich and Nijinsky featured the machine of the human body much as Gurdjieff did in his dance and movement gymnastics (Figes, *Cultural History* 274-87).

Olgivanna Hinzenberg was in a small audience watching a few of Jeanne's students doing Gurdjieff's "Sacred Gymnastics" and, impressed by what she witnessed and what she had heard of this charismatic Armenian, she returned the next day and offered to work for him. He asked her if she had a wish, and she replied: "Georgivanich, most of all I want immortality. There is so much injustice in the world and Christ speaks such marvelous things. If it is that way, through his words, that I can reach immortality, could you help me?" He said yes. Gurdjieff had her fire her servants and set her to work in his kitchen, first supervising her preparation of a lavish feast for him, the Hartmanns and the Salzmanns. A few days later she started training in gymnastics, what Ouspensky had called "numbers" (*Fellowship* 52). Olgivanna flourished in the "work" though she did not earn the affection of the more experienced women. Jeanne de Salzmann gave birth to a daughter Natalie ("Boussique/Boussik," "Bouska" to Gurdjieff).

Soon after, Elizaveta de Stjernvall announced to her husband and to Gurdjieff that she was pregnant.

In that spring of 1919, Dmitri appeared in Tbilisi and gave his brother details about the death of his father and the moving of his sister with her family to Baytor. He also reported that White Army troops had found the cache where Gurdjieff had stored his and his group's goods before leaving Essentuki. The Whites had assumed that they were Bolshevik goods and confiscated some and destroyed others, including Gurdjieff's Petersburg porcelain collection. When Dmitri filed a complaint, the White Army leader said that he would hold the goods for the proper owner. Gurdjieff decided to attempt to regain them. To avoid the problems that a young or middle-aged man would face crossing battle lines, he sent Olga de Hartmann with letters to his sister-in-law and Ouspensky, both of whom he assumed were still there. He had Olga carry a little box with a single pill "in case of extreme necessity" (*Our Life* 81).

After a harrowing trip by water from Sochi to Novorossisk one hundred and fifty miles westward, and by train from there, she arrived in Essentuki to find Ouspensky with Lenochka's baby son Leonid ("Lonia") in his arms. The biological father was a Petersburg lawyer and Gurdjieff pupil, A. Y. Rachmilievich. Where Lenochka's husband Mikhail Savitsky was at the time is not reported (Webb 166 has her with two children). At the local commander's bureau, she found only a few valuables, including two carpets. After another uncomfortable voyage, she arrived back in Tbilisi. Then Gurdjieff dispatched her and Hartmann to Armenia to give concerts and study Armenian music. What Gurdjieff had in mind was a production of his oft-advertised "Struggle of the Magicians" with new music.

Back in Tbilisi, the Hartmanns joined other members of the group in the summer mountain resort of Borjom. Gurdjieff set Olga to work remaking an old favorite coat of his. When she found difficulties sewing, he demonstrated to her his skill with needle and thread. In the fall of 1919, when Gurdjieff decided to re-establish his Institute, he challenged his pupils to come up with a suitable name for it. They failed to come to a consensus, and Gurdjieff, who had the name already in his mind, declared that he would call it "The Institute for the Harmonious Development of Man," a name hardly improvised at the moment, for he had already used it for an earlier group in 1912 (*Life* 28, *Herald* 24). On 6 October 1919, the Ministry of Education of the Republic of Georgia authorized the opening of the Institute. He managed to lease a large hall and set to work with inventive skill in carpentry to adapt it for his "gymnastics" and for a spring 1920 production of "Struggle of the Magicians," with music by Hartmann. It was doubtful that Gurdjieff ever intended to stage the ballet, but the preparation for it was a group "work task."

Unexpectedly, one day Gurdjieff called Hartmann to him and told him to renounce his music. Hartmann replied that he would do anything for Gurdjieff, but he would use his free time as he wished (*Our Life* 90). No more was said at the moment. The demand was preposterous in its form, but its intent was to challenge Hartmann's sense of self. It was also a covert signal that Hartmann should think of the time when it would be right for him to go back to his musical career and leave the "work" behind him. Coincidentally, on 28 September a new member joined the group when Elizaveta de Stjernvall gave birth to a son. Leonid, who had not been able to give his wife a child, greeted the newcomer, and may have suggested his name, Nikolai, after the late martyred Tsar.

The gymnastics and sacred dances attracted many local young men and women, among them Elizaveta ("Lili") Galumnian Chaverdian, a skilled dancer whom Gurdjieff welcomed as a pupil. Work continued on the stage properties for the ballet, and Gurdjieff demonstrated his expertise in electricity by fashioning a rheostat to alter brightness. Several members of the artist colony in Tbilisi were attracted to the activities of Gurdjieff's group, including the "rayists" like Ilia and Kirill Zdanevich who were followers of Mikhail Larionov whom Ouspensky had called the "modern Prometheus," a "magician who sees what others do not" (Anthony Parton, *Mikhail Larionov and the Russian Avant Garde* 135). They championed the visual art aspects of Ouspensky's fourth dimension when they met Gurdjieff in Tbilisi. Kirill made a portrait of Gurdjieff in January 1920.

Gurdjieff also received interesting visitors associated with the British forces. One was Carl Bechhofer Roberts who arrived with a letter of invitation. Gurdjieff showed him the sights of Tbilisi rather than entice or bore him with work ideas. The polyglot polymath Frank Pinder, attached to the British Economic Mission to Deniken's White Russian Army, who had spent time with Ouspensky in Ekaterinodar, and had put Ouspensky in touch with the editor A. R. Orage in England to publish "Letters from Russia," visited Gurdjieff on Ouspensky's recommendation and watched a rehearsal of "Struggle" (*Circle* 166).

As winter turned to spring in 1920, the coherence of the Institute seemed to dissolve. The Turks had once more penetrated into Armenia. Gurdjieff heard that in January they had razed Baytor and slaughtered his sister Anna, her husband and children except for Valentin ("Valia") who had been able to hide. After being rescued by the Red Army in June, Valia walked and hid on trains from Baytor to Tbilisi, some hundred and fifty miles away. His cousin Luba recalls Valia walking into her garden, crying out "I am Valya. Where is Mama?" He told his aunt Asta that the Turks had raped his mother, and that he had escaped with a baby, who died on his way to them (*Luba* 18).

When summer arrived, Gurdjieff told his pupils to pack up to leave for Constantinople immediately. Webb and Moore report that the group went by foot and mule cart the some two hundred miles from Tbilisi (*Circle* 180, *Anatomy* 139), but that mode of transport was unlikely, considering the goods and children they had with them, as well as the length of time it would have taken to travel that far by foot. At any rate, neither Hartmann nor Gurdjieff made this claim. About this time, Gurdjieff's cousin Alexander Gurdjieff left Kars with his family, and took ship from Batum for Greece where they settled and took the name Kiourtzidis, a Greek cognate form of the family name.

Leaving dancers Olgivanna Hinzenberg and Lili Galumnian behind, the group arrived in Batum to leave the Caucasus. Moore dates the departure 7 June (*Anatomy* 140), Webb has the group arriving in Constantinople in late June (*Circle* 180). Neither date fits the facts. Hartmann gave a concert in Batum on 2 July 1920. A few days before that, though Batum was in Turkish hands, Gurdjieff had managed to procure an Armenian passport dated 29 June 1920 on the French page (the last digit is not clear on the Armenian page) with an expiration date on the Russian page of 29 June 1921. Gurdjieff's timing was propitious. Soviet forces had marched into Azerbaijan in April, annihilating the government, and they arrived in Batum a few days after Gurdjieff and his party left. Unfortunately, his good luck could not save many of the goods he had carried with him to the port. He was able to carry off only two of the many carpets brought from Tbilisi, and he arrived in Constantinople with only two small diamonds in his pocket to sell for money (*Meetings* 282).

July 1920–August 1921 Constantinople

The move to Constantinople did not have the desired axial effect that the move two years later to Avon, near Fontainebleau, France would have. Apparently, Gurdjieff knew the city well. In *Meetings* he writes that he met Ekim Bey there and dived for tourist coins in the Bosphorus to sustain himself while investigating Mevlevi Dervishes (*Meetings* 178–81). If there is a factual core to the story, he would have been there after returning from Tibet and before he was shot in northern Georgia in 1904. Gurdjieff spoke Turkish fluently from his boyhood, and from the moment of his landing in the summer of 1920, he knew where he had to go to live and what to do to earn money.

At that time, in some respects, Constantinople must have resembled Algiers and Lisbon in 1940, that is, it swarmed with refugees from war zones on en route to safety and, hopefully, a new life. I suspect that for Gurdjieff, the city was a weigh station, a place to measure the value of the music and sacred dances he had composed in Tbilisi, rather than reap riches out of the sea. He had no intention of settling there permanently, though he may have hoped for a pleasanter atmosphere in which to work. The allied occupying forces and the sudden influx of foreigners incited popular resentment, if not outright hatred of Armenians, Greeks, Russians and the British and French occupiers. On 10 August, a scant few weeks after Gurdjieff's arrival, the Treaty of Sèvres stripped Turkey of all her European territory except for Constantinople, established Armenia's sovereignty and Kurdistan's autonomy. Undermining morale further, Greek forces had landed in Smyrna and threatened seizure of parts of the Turkish coast. In the autumn of 1920, some hundred and thirty thousand exhausted remnants of Baron Wrangel's Crimean White Army, having abandoned Sebastopol on 15 November, arrived looking for room and rest.

Gurdjieff took up residence in the packed Beyoglu European quarter of Pera on the north-eastern side of the Golden Horn, and set about finding money to feed, clothe and house his group. A few days after his arrival, Olgivanna Hinzenberg showed up with her daughter and a husband who made it clear he would rather be elsewhere. Three months later, he left alone for the United States (*Fellowship* 57–60).

From the moment Gurdjieff arrived, he was under surveillance by British Intelligence in the person of John Godolphin Bennett, a twenty-three year old specialist in Oriental languages who had before him a dossier on Gurdjieff forwarded from India, but that file was on Agwan Dordjieff whose name was confused with Gurdjieff's because the graph d was represented in Russian of the day by the graph g with a superscript line above it. Bennett came face to face with Gurdjieff himself quite by accident six months later in July 1921, when both were attending a dinner hosted by Prince Mehmet Sabaheddin (*New World* 90), just before Gurdjieff left the city.

In the late summer of 1920, Gurdjieff established his "office" at the Black Rose, a café gathering place of White Russians in Pera, and he worked in both Constantinople and Kadiköy across the Bosphorus as a healer of pathological and psychological ailments. He visited Ouspensky in Prinkipo (Princes Island), on the Asian side of the Sea of Marmar, attended his talks at the YMCA known as The Lighthouse, and strolled with him through the local bazaars. He took him to the Mevlevi Dervish dances outside the Khanen Gate and explained that the whirling of the Dervishes was based on counting patterns. During one excursion, Ouspensky confided to Gurdjieff that he was compiling his Petersburg and Essentuki notes into a volume tentatively entitled "Fragments of an Unknown Teaching," and Gurdjieff nodded assent (*Search* 382–83).

Meanwhile, Hartmann had met with the Turkish composer Ali Rifat Bey who was a member of a commission charged with writing the repertory of Sufi Turkish music, both Bektasi and Mevlevi. Gurdjieff and Hartmann visited the Pera mosque and watched a number of performances of Dervish dances. Dervish dances were given often in a number of tekke, or religious centers in Constantinople. During their period of observation, Gurdjieff and Hartmann added Dervish music and dance gestures to their sacred gymnastics (*Our Life* 97–98). Large numbers of Greeks and Turks attended Gurdjieff's demonstration, and those familiar with Sufism and the Dervish brotherhood were aware that the enneagram reflected the various significances in Islam of the number nine.

He attracted new pupils in Constantinople, most notably Tchesslav Tchechovitch, a deserter or escapee from the White Army, a former sculls champion, circus strongman and wrestler who had been listening to Ouspensky's talks and Gurdjieff's monopolizing of the question period. When he paid a visit to the man he had thought "ridiculous," Gurdjieff put him to work on the spot arranging furniture in his demonstration hall while he lectured him on the necessity of understanding the deep meanings of individual words (*Tu l'aimerais* 144–45). Tchechovitch recalls that Gurdjieff kept an "open house" in Constantinople, receiving all comers to his table. One was the German Alphons Paquet, who had known Salzmann in Munich. Another was Boris Mouravieff (1890–1966), a native of Petersburg who followed Ouspensky's teaching. Mouravieff visited Gurdjieff later in Fontainebleau, after which he founded a center for the study of Esoteric Christianity in Geneva where he wrote a "continuation" of Ouspensky's system entitled *Gnosis* (1965). He was fond of telling his listeners that when he asked Gurdjieff where he had found his ideas, Gurdjieff replied: "I stole them."

In October 1920, Gurdjieff moved to Prinkipo where he rented a hall and staged a number of well-received demonstrations of Eastern dances and new gymnastics that displayed the grace of the whirling Dervish dances (Hartmann *Our Life* 97–98). He re-established the Institute there and started rehearsals once again for a production of "Struggle of the Magicians." Bennett saw both the gymnastics and the "stop" exercises (*Witness* 68, 120). Curiously, at this time, Gurdjieff once more demanded that Hartmann renounce his music. Hartmann agreed to give up his conducting, but insisted on continuing to give piano lessons (*Our Life* 98).

Gurdjieff was increasingly discouraged and oppressed by the political unrest incited by an increasing revolutionary mentality, and decided to move on. He transferred his classes to Kadiköy and put some of his new pupils in charge as he prepared his departure. At this time his demonstrations were reviewed in the local press (see Zarcone, *La Turquie*). A dance critic, Yakup Kadri wrote an article for the journal *Ikdam* in February praising a Gurdjieff performance he had seen on 10 February 1921 in the Apollon theater in Kadiköy. He not only admired the dances, but described the psychological principles involved in the work of the Institute. In the pages of the same journal two weeks later, the philosopher Mehmet Ali Ayni, a specialist on Sufism and occidental mysticism, wrote that Gurdjieff's dances were not associated with any religious system and lacked the force of sacred dances. In a second article Ayni said that it was obvious that Gurdjieff had borrowed much of his dance gestures from Sufi rituals. For Ayni and other Sufi experts, Gurdjieff's sacred dances were both projections of planetary movements and demonstrations of universal laws, whereas the Dervish dances played out a cosmic drama experienced by the human soul descending from the Absolute down to the material world (see Petsche, Johanna M. *The Gurdjieff/de Hartmann Piano Music and its Esoteric Significance*).

Whether Gurdjieff's dances represented the values of Dervish dances accurately or not, his use of Dervish dance and music was instrumental in preserving the sacred rites of the brotherhood founded by Djalal al Din Rumi in the thirteenth century. Not long after Gurdjieff left Constantinople, Kemal Ataturk banned Islamic religious rites, including the Dervish dances. They were revived in the mid-fifties, when they appeared more as dance spectacle than cosmic play. Ataturk also adopted the Roman alphabet for the Turkish language, and banned the wearing of the fez, a sign of loyalty to Islam.

It may well have been that Gurdjieff was thinking already of an eventual move to the United States. Olgivanna Hinzenberg's and Olga de Hartmann's family contacts there might have encouraged him. His intentions might explain Associated Press dispatches that were sent from Constantinople to America in the spring of 1921. Though they may not have reached many interested eyes, two of them found their way into small town newspapers. The earliest, brought to my notice is dated 16 May 1921 and appeared in the Maine *Daily Kennebec Journal* on 9 June 1921, headlined "New Gospel of Health, Man is Three in One, From Middle East" and read:

A new gospel of health, that man is not one but three, and that he cannot function fully until his three personalities are in harmony, has come here from the Middle East on the tide of Russian and other refugees from far countries.

This gospel is proclaimed by a small, dark man of mystery, a Greek Tartar G. I. Gurdjieff. He has contributed to the meager intellectual life of the city in a new throb.

The outward and primary form of his teachings begins with dances borrowed from the Mosques of Persia and the temples of India. He puts some of his patients on bread and water for months at a time but requires them, all the while, to carry on the most violent exercises which conform to the music of a piano.

Gurdjieff's teachings have some similarity with the ancient Greek conceptions of the development of mental force and bodily grace and activity.

He is persuaded that his teachings will change the art of living. He has gathered about him a group of converts who say they are going to spread his theories westward, some going to the United States. He says that he was taught by Russian physicians and psychologists.

The same dispatch with added text appeared in the Pennsylvania Wellsboro Gazette on Thursday, 1 September 1921. The headline read "GREEK TARTAR PREACHES NEW GOSPEL OF HEALTH, Says Man Has Three Personalities, Seeks

Fourth to Control the Other Three." The added text was:

In harmony there is health declared Gurdjieff. The western world of medicine and psychology has never grasped the truth that man is not controlled by one personality but by three and when these three are not in harmony a man says he is sick. A sick man, a man with that tired feeling, is like a horse and carriage without a driver. The man is not master of himself.

Civilization has led man away from himself physically and spiritually. Too much use of the head has deharmonized him. Man is composed of three parts, just like a machine. One part thinks, one part feels, and one sleeps and eats. If man thinks too much, or eats too much, or sleeps too much he falls ill.

My plan is to first put man back into a common unity and then gradually develop a fourth personality which controls the other three. If this fourth personality or dominating consciousness is not developed, the three men in the same body will never establish control with each other and the anarchy we call (undecipherable) destroys him.

Those who are familiar with Gurdjieff's ideas may smile at this presentation of his ideas, but the basic idea behind the tripartite consciousness of man is recognizable. This was probably the first view in America of Gurdjieff's "fourth way."

Though he was determined to move on, Gurdjieff was short of funds and necessary papers for his pupils. He sent the Stjernvalls to Finland to liquidate their assets there, and Olga de Hartmann's brother in America responded to her plea and sent three hundred dollars from New York City, enough to cover current expenses. Bennett wrote later: "I was also then able to help Gurdjieff in one of his amazing business deals. He had cured a Greek youth of drunkenness and drug addiction, in return for which he received a half-interest in a ship that had been requisitioned by the British Navy. As the navy no longer required it owing to the changed situation in Anatolia, I was able to get it released, and Gurdjieff sold his share for a large sum of money that he used to get his group away to Germany, for which he had no difficulty getting visas" (*New World* 131).

He did have difficulty getting papers for all. When enough visas arrived (the Nansen passports designated particularly for Russian and Armenian refugees were not issued until September 1921), he left with others on 13 August 1921 by rail for Berlin (*Meetings* 283–84), leaving behind several pupils who were not yet ready to leave, including Tchesslav Tchechovitch ("Tcheko") and Alexis Merslioukin. Gurdjieff told them they could follow him to Berlin once they acquired proper papers.

The Constantinople interlude had lasted just over a year. Ouspensky left in October for London alone two months later after receiving an invitation from Lady Beatrice Rothermere who had earlier commissioned the English translation of his *Tertium Organum*. Ouspensky's wife Sophia, her daughter Helena ("Lena" or "Lenochka"), with her husband Savitsky and her son Leonid ("Lonia") were then with Gurdjieff in Germany.

August 1921–July 1922 Berlin

The long and tiring journey by train from Constantinople included stops in Sophia, Belgrade and Budapest before terminating in Berlin. Unfortunately, there is little extant record of Gurdjieff's activities in Germany. Hartmann wrote that "when we arrived in Berlin even Mr. Gurdjieff did not know what would occur there and in which directions we would have to turn our efforts. He always waited for the right moment for the next step" (*Our Life* 100). Hartmann realized later that Germany was but a preparation for the later move to France, though others thought that Gurdjieff chose Germany because of the country's proximity to Russia where he still maintained contacts. Gurdjieff, however, would never allow a hiatus in the progress of his work, and went to work right away with his inimitable energy: "I immediately

91

began to travel about Germany," he said, "going to different places where various acquaintances had found possible buildings for the Institute" (*Meetings* 284). He set up his business office at the Cristal Café in Berlin.

Webb speculates on the possible contacts Gurdjieff had made with influential Germans during his Tibetan interval, but they remain only in the realm of speculation (*Circle* 186–87). Of course, Alexander and Jeanne de Salzmann both knew Germany and spoke fluent German (raised a francophone, Jeanne's family name was Allemand "German"). Olga de Hartmann had numerous family connections in Germany, and old friends and acquaintances of the Hartmanns and Salzmanns were in the audience when Gurdjieff gave his first Berlin talk on 24 November 1921. The Salzmanns had also spent time at the Dalcroze School in Hellerau before the war, and were friends of Harald Dohrn, the present owner of the property. When Salzmann took Gurdjieff to Hellerau to view the property, Gurdjieff made an offer to Dorhn (*Circle* 188–89). Moore says that Gurdjieff had a letter from Dalcroze to lend support to his offer. The property, however, had already been promised, and despite Dorhn's susceptibility to Gurdjieff's hypnotic urging, the deal fell through (*Anatomy* 157–58). Webb errs in assuming that at Hellerau the pianist Rosemary Lillard and dancer Jessmin Howarth "were so impressed by Gurdjieff's gymnastics that they abandoned Eurythmics to follow the new master" (*Circle* 189). Neither was in Germany. Finally, from Berlin Gurdjieff procured the necessary visas to free Tchechovitch and Alexis Merslioukin from incarceration in Budapest where they were suspected of being either Soviet or White Russian spies. Alexis had been tortured.

Gurdjieff had a pamphlet advertizing the Institute published in Berlin in late 1921, when he was still hopeful of acquiring the Hellerau property. Its front page read: "Das Institut für harmonische Entwicklung des Menschen" and continued "Nach der

Methode von G. J. Gürdschiejew-Georgiadis." The strange name form may have been fashioned for a German-speaking audience, but it looks strange indeed.

In early 1922 Gurdjieff decided to visit England. One can only speculate on the reason. He did know of Ouspensky's success there and had met many English in the Caucasus and in Constantinople. He may have supposed that England would be an appropriate location for the Institute. From the moment he arrived in Berlin, he had Boris Ferapontoff give English lessons to him and his pupils, perhaps in anticipation of such a move. When he arrived in London on 12 February 1922 with Olga De Hartmann as his secretary-interpreter, probably with a Nansen passport in hand, he received an invitation from Ouspensky to attend his meeting (*Search* 384). He did so the next day and gave a talk outlining "the Work" to Ouspensky's group in Kensington. That night, at a dinner with Olga, Lady Rothermere and her secretary, Dorothy Ireland, the meeting broke up when Ouspensky made inappropriate remarks to Dorothy Ireland. Gurdjieff agreed to return to Germany the next day and, to appease Olga, they stopped in Paris to visit one of Olga's cousins, married to a wealthy Frenchman named Bienaimé.

The moment they returned to Berlin, Gurdjieff began buying all manner of household materials and electrical equipment. When asked the reason, he replied that it was not a question only of the devalued Mark, but the machinery would make his future patients feel he was up to date. They were not to heal, but to impress (*Tu l'aimerais* 44–45). The electrical equipment was probably an electrophone invented in 1919 by the Saint Petersburg Russian, Lev Sergeyevich Theremin (1896–1993) which consisted of a box with antennae and activated by hand movements about the antennae which altered frequency, or pitch, and volume.

Gurdjieff returned to England to give talks on 5 and 15 March. In summing up his impressions after these visits—the last of which featured an angry exchange between Gurdjieff and Ouspensky—Gurdjieff "came to the definite conclusion that the best place for the foundation of the Institute would be neither Germany nor England, but France . . . . England, owing to its insular situation, would not have allowed any development in this respect; an Institute founded there would have taken on the narrow character of a local institution" (*Meetings* 284–85). There were other reasons, of course. One was the reluctance of the English Foreign Office to give him a visa, despite urgent interventions to the Home Secretary by Kenneth Walker and Maurice Nicoll on his behalf (*Anatomy* 164–65). Secondly, Ouspensky let it be known among his people, who had passed a good deal of money to Gurdjieff for an eventual move to England, that: "I had decided for myself that if the Institute opened in London I would go either to Paris or to America." Nonetheless, Ouspensky went on to express an intention himself to establish an English branch of the Institute at some future time (*Search* 385). A final consideration was financial, but with money passed to him in England, and thanks to the connections of Olga de Hartmann and others, he had some expectation of financial support in France.

In the spring, Olgivanna's husband, Valdemar, asked her to accompany him with Svetlana to the United States. She refused, and in April, her brother Vladimir Lazovich came to Berlin, picked up Svetlana and took her to Hamburg where they boarded the *Orbita* on 26 April 1922 for New York, arriving on 8 May 1922. Olgivanna was free to go alone to France with Gurdjieff.

Unlike England, France had already integrated many thousands of Russian refugees, and felt no necessity to impede the arrival of more who would compensate somewhat for its horrendous loss of manpower in the trenches. England preferred not to know that just across the channel was a man they considered a staunch opponent of their former interests in India and Tibet. Nonetheless, Gurdjieff, still considering his chances for England, made an appeal on 28 July 1922 to a certain Mr. Page (Russell?), an acquaintance of Ouspensky who had influence with the Home Secretary, for a visa for himself and Julia.

Without waiting further for a favorable response, early in the morning on 13 July 1922, Gurdjieff saw the Salzmanns and others off on a train for Paris, and the next morning he and the remaining pupils followed. He was met at the station in Paris by Salzmann as crowds thronged the streets to celebrate the one hundred and thirty-third anniversary of the storming of the Bastille.

6

14 July 1922–31 December 1923: Paris and Avon

1922 Paris

A story that circulated about Gurdjieff's arrival in France appeared in the "Guide de Fontainebleau Mysterieux," stating that Raymond Poincaré, the former French President and current Minister of Foreign Affairs (not Prime Minister as I have him, 2001, 25n and Moore 367), ignored English requests to ban Gurdjieff's entry into France because Poincaré was duly upset at British intentional over-evaluation of the pound at the expense of a lower French franc value. The collapse of the German mark rate from May to June 1922 was a not insignificant factor influencing Gurdjieff's decision to leave Berlin, and the low value of the franc against the pound promised to be beneficial to Gurdjieff who had collected a substantial sum of pounds during his three trips to England. He said later that "France gave me the impression of a country which was then politically and economically more stable than the others . . . . Consequently to my eyes it appeared to be the most suitable base for the diffusion of my ideas" (*Meetings* 284).

The day following his arrival in Paris, Gurdjieff knew what he had to do. He required lodging for his pupils and for himself, a hall to practice his dances and contacts for money-making enterprises. He could profit from the fact that whereas Constantinople had been swarming with unwanted and uncultured Russian émigrés, Paris welcomed a higher class Russian immigrant who had little problem adjusting to Parisian social and business life, waiting tables and driving taxicabs on one level, and managing restaurants, cafés and nightclubs on another. In the early 1920s, one Russian cabaret after another opened and did good business. On 22 October, the Château Caucasien on the Rue Pigalle, renamed the Caveau Caucasien, featured the gypsy choir of Dmitri

Polyakov and the voice of Nastia Polyakova. The Yar, a few doors higher and the Troïka on the Rue Fontaine opened their doors in 1923. Estimates of the numbers of Russians in exile in Paris in 1922 range from 45,000 to 100,000. There was place for even more.

Hartmann found an apartment for Gurdjieff on the Rue Miromesnil, not far from the presidential Palais de l'Elysée. Ouspensky came over to Paris with Lady Rothermere and Ralph Philipson, a Yorkshire industrialist, a few days after Gurdjieff's arrival. At meetings at the Hotel Solferino and Hotel Westminster, with Ouspensky acting as mediator, Gurdjieff secured a commitment of funds to finance his short term projects. Ouspensky stayed on in Paris as Gurdjieff's secretary to screen the English who were already in Paris or intended to come there. Americans had been in the audiences of Gurdjieff's talks in London in the late winter of 1922, and Paris was the preferred expatriate refuge for innumerable Americans, mostly artists fleeing an increasingly isolationist mentality in the United States, the extreme example of which was the refusal of the United States to join the League of Nations that its own president, Woodrow Wilson, had a major hand in founding. A not inconsiderable motive, perhaps, was the passing of the Volstead Act, the 18th Amendment to the American Constitution known familiarly as "Prohibition" that went into effect on 6 January 1920 banning the sale of alcohol for any but medicinal purposes. The act was not repealed until 4 December 1933, almost fourteen years later.

Gurdjieff taught that one who had perfected his being was largely immune from accident, and one who achieved a unity of being was less likely to suffer from accidents than ordinary beings. Gurdjieff relied on his own will and heightened sense of purpose to direct his activities, and what could be called "accidents"—unplanned or circumstantial phenomena—seemed to spare him in Paris as they did in the Caucasus. Dushka Howarth tells the story that a few days after the arrival of his group in Paris, Alexander and Jeanne de Salzmann strolled down an alley in the Jardin de Luxembourg past Jessmin Howarth, a Dalcroze instructor and ballet director at the Paris Opera, who was sitting on a bench. She realized after they had passed that the two were pre-war colleagues of hers at the Dalcroze School in Hellerau. She had assumed they had perished in the war.

They were out of sight before she could accost them. That evening, when she related her vision to Louis Jouvet, he told her that Alexander had come to him already to offer to manage the lighting for *Pelleas and Melisande*. Jouvet had mentioned Jessmin's presence in Paris to Alexander and told her now to come to the Opera to see him. She did so the next afternoon, and Alexander told her that his wife, Jeanne, was looking for a hall to practice Gurdjieff dances. The Dalcroze studio on Rue Vaugirard was empty during the summer break, and Jessmin offered it to them. Alexander told Jessmin that she should meet and get the approval of Gurdjieff. When she did at the Café de la Paix, he approved of the offer, and so work on the dances started once more.

An "accident" of ever greater purport was the decision of A. R. Orage (b. 1874), owner and editor of an influential London cultural weekly, *The New Age*, to abandon his career as journalist and cultural taste-maker, and go to Paris to follow Gurdjieff's way. Orage, known as the finest critical voice in England, had been instrumental in bringing Ouspensky to England and was a faithful listener to his talks, but when he heard Gurdjieff in February 1922, he proclaimed that he was "going to find God" (*Gurdjieff and Orage* 19).

After Ouspensky gave him Gurdjieff's address, Orage sent a letter on 22 July asking permission to "work for the Institute." He admitted that he had little financial support to offer, £250 per annum, but he would sell *The New Age* if accepted.

Ouspensky wrote him back on 1 August, saying that Gurdjieff had no quarters for the Institute, and if Orage wished to come over to observe the work in the Dalcroze School, he would have to live apart. Gurdjieff advised the selling of *The New Age* right away. One hundred pounds—the figure Orage had supposed the journal would bring—would be sufficient for a year's study with him (*Gurdjieff and Orage* 24–25). There were several other English drawn to Gurdjieff's work. One was the Jungian psychiatrist Dr. James Carruthers Young, who witnessed Gurdjieff's "movements" (the word "gymnastics" was dropped since the word in French designated another kind of physical exercise) and became a follower.

Meanwhile, Olga de Hartmann, who was staying with her cousin Bienaimé in fashionable Neuilly, went reconnoitering in the countryside about Paris for a suitable place to house all of Gurdjieff's pupils and yet be close enough to Paris for him to ply his varied trades. One occupation that brought a good deal of money right away was his medical practice. As he explained: "One of the best sources of income during these months was the psychological treatment of certain difficult cases of alcoholism and drug addiction. I was widely considered one of the best specialists in this field, and the families of these unfortunates sometimes offered me very substantial sums . . ." Gurdjieff also opened two restaurants, then sold them, traded oil shares (*Meetings* 288), and established the Grand Café as his temporary business office. He operated illegally, in effect, for his demand on 1 August for a "carte d'identité" had not been approved yet.

Near the end of September 1922, Olga de Hartmann reported that she had located an ideal property, a château in Avon in the Forest of Fontainebleau that could house up to a hundred pupils. There were scores of fir trees on the property, outbuildings, and acreage enough for large gardens. Gurdjieff agreed to acquire the property sight unseen. The château was called Prieuré

("Priory") des Basses Loges, because the property had once housed a religious order. The main building had been constructed, he was told, in the seventeenth century and given by Louis XIV to Madame Maintenon, his second wife. It was owned later by the family of Alfred Dreyfus (1859–1935), the French officer falsely accused and imprisoned as a German spy. After his acquittal in 1908, Dreyfus and his brother Matthieu gave the property to his lawyer Fernand Gustave Gaston Labori (1860–1917) in lieu of a fee. After Labori's death early in the war in which Dreyfus distinguished himself, the widow Labori moved to Paris. Neither of the Dreyfus brothers wanted the property, unoccupied since 1914, so she put it up for sale, despite the objections of her son and a poor postwar market for large properties.

After some haggling during which Olga de Hartmann played negotiator, Gurdjieff acquired the property on a one-year lease with an option to buy that was to be exercised after six months. Tchechovitch reports that Gurdjieff was advised and represented in the transaction by a bright young businessman who turned out eventually to be a thief (*Tu l'aimerais* 49–51). The fee for a year's rent was 65,000 francs (*Meetings* 285), and the sale price has been estimated at 700,000 francs (Webb 233, Moore 170), a price in keeping with the usual ten times rental charges. According to statistics at the time, there were eighteen francs to the dollar, ninety to the pound, so the figure of 700,000 francs would approximate $40,000 or £8,000, figures that appear very low for the amount of property involved. Considering that the money was to come from England, and the franc was losing value throughout the period, it was to Gurdjieff's advantage to postpone full payment as long as possible.

On 30 September, Gurdjieff signed the lease, and moved to the Prieuré the next day, heavily in debt but confident that he would make the best of things. "When I walked through the gate of the Château du Prieuré, it was as though, right behind the old porter, I was greeted by Mrs. Serious Problem" (*Meetings* 285–86). His major problem remained money, though he had some assurances from Rothermere, Philipson, and perhaps from Bienaimé, Olga de Hartmann's wealthy cousin. A second problem was language: "When I arrived in Paris I spoke no Western European language" (*Meetings* 286). Speak, understand, what have you, this is a slight exaggeration, if only because Gurdjieff could wend his way commercially within any linguistic environment. A third problem was more urgent. He needed to get his property ready in a hurry to receive the group he had brought from Berlin as well as numerous new-comers hanging about Paris. He says that he succeeded in getting his needed loan from London, that is, from Rothermere, Philipson and a money-lender travel agent named Thompson—"various persons interested in the Institute." Tsjechovitch writes (*Tu l'aimerais* 35) that a certain "Thomson" was a visitor to the Prieuré.

1 October 1922 marks a major axial turn in Gurdjieff's fortunes, considering the succession of events that followed his application of conscious labors on the Prieuré property. He had a list of priorities. First was the necessary refurbishing and maintenance of the Prieuré, two tasks reflecting the cosmic laws of three and seven in the "system." Second, he needed to increase the number of paying pupils. The entourage he was directly responsible for numbered some two dozen or more. Third, he needed to receive visitors who would carry news of his venture abroad. He had need of adequate room for his dances, movements and talks. Finally, he intended to expand his musical repertory by singing and playing music for Hartmann to transcribe.

Among those who moved onto the property in the weeks that followed were Gurdjieff's wife Julia Osipovna Ostrowska ("Yulievna"), Olgivanna Hinzenberg, Salzmann, his wife Jeanne and their daughter Natalie ("Boussique" or "Buska"), Stjernvall, his wife Elizaveta and their son Nikolai, the Hartmanns, Boris

Ferapontoff ("Starosta," the old one), Olga Vachadze, Patchuli, Dr. Hambachidze, Dr. Kisilov, Elizaveta ("Lili") Galumnian Chaverdian, Adel Kopcinte, Andrei Andreivich, Valerian Merkurov, his wife Nina and their son Anatole ("Toly"), Tchesslav Tchechovitch ("Tcheko"), Philipovich and Adamovich, the three Polish brothers Kozlonski, Alexis Merslioukin, Yevgeny Schvetchnikov and his wife Elizeveta, the Petersburg lawyer Alexei Yakovlevich Rachmilievich ("Rachmoul"), and the young Irène and André Lapina. A distinguished resident in October 1922 was Russian Baroness Marie ("Mitzi") Rausch von Traubenberg who was recommended to the French authorities by the Soviet embassy. She and her husband, Russian artist Baron Constantin Rausch von Traubenberg (1871–c. 1935), were acquainted with Boris Mouravieff and had known Gurdjieff in Petersburg. When the baron chose to remain in Russia to serve Soviet art, his wife took exile in France where she learned of Gurdjieff's Institute.

To fulfill his immediate financial obligations, Gurdjieff kept his Paris jobs, which he would exercise until the end of 1923. This division of labor meant that he would have the Prieuré population, including those who were living in the dependence adjacent to the château called the Paridou, start early in the day on projects he had assigned the night before while he went to Paris where he might remain for several days at a time, spending nights in his Miromesnil apartment.

To facilitate his travel between Fontainebleau and Paris, Gurdjieff bought an automobile. He refused driving lessons, but insisted on teaching himself to drive on the property. Some of the English residents of the Prieuré assumed he would teach himself by "inspiration," but the noise of gears shrieking and wheels spinning went on for some time before he mastered the elements. Though he requested a *permis de conduire* on 6 June 1923, it was suspected that he never obtained it (Young, *Experiment* 38). Gurdjieff's driving behavior was a casual topic of conversation and a cause of anxiety for those who rode with him. Gurdjieff's decision to drive to Paris and back instead of taking the train would eventually change the course of his life.

Within days of moving into the Prieuré the arrival of two persons from England made a dramatic mark on his work in France and beyond. A. R. Orage and Katherine Mansfield moved into the Prieuré in mid-October. The New Zealand-born writer Mansfield had been "discovered" and her talent honed by Orage in London. Now, a few days before her thirty-fourth birthday, she was at the pinnacle of her career and reputation, having seen *The Garden Party and Other Stories* in print earlier that year. She was suffering from incurable tuberculosis. Earlier that year she had experienced Dr. Ivan Minoukhin's experimental x-ray treatment without improvement. Knowing her case to be hopeless, through the intervention of Orage, she had listened to Osupensky late that summer and had an interview with him on 30 September (Moore, *Gurdjieff and Mansfield* 139). Two weeks later she was examined by Dr. Young, already in the Gurdjieff fold. Gurdjieff knew of her desire to come to him. He would not promise her a cure and advised her to go to the south of France, but he told her she was welcome to come to the Prieuré for a short stay. She arrived on 17 October.

Orage was already there, and had daily talks from the first day with Katia (as she was called at the Prieuré). Orage's own abandoning of his career as editor of *The New Age* baffled his friends and drew condemnation from literary circles. The critic John Gross concluded in hindsight that "high literary ability can co-exist with the most dubious doctrines, and survive exposure to the most extravagant kinds of nonsense" (*Gurdjieff and Orage* 19). Others were even less kind, but Orage was impervious to their criticism, perhaps because he had kept from them and his reading public a particular motive known to Gurdjieff that concerned "Social Credit," a social scheme promulgated by Major Clifford

Douglas and championed by Orage. Social Credit is a scheme whereby work is rewarded not by money that ends up inexorably in financial institutions to be hoarded and exploited, but by public credit for the individual workers who earn it. Though he had been promoting Social Credit in the pages of *The New Age*, Orage could not get it advanced as a viable economic policy by those in power. Despite whatever else he hoped for from Gurdjieff, he wanted to reinforce the expression of his economic ideas, and Gurdjieff assured him that his work was dedicated to helping pupils achieve their personal aims.

Gurdjieff made life as comfortable as possible for Katia Mansfield. He had Adele Kafian and Olgivanna tend to her, and Katia wrote letters back to her husband Middleton Murry expressing her ecstatic joy in being part of the work. After a few weeks, though, Gurdjieff advised her to go to a rest home. When Tcheko found her in tears one day, she told him that she was being expelled. Tcheko convinced her of Gurdjieff's charity and, although he knew little English, coached her on articulating a plea to remain. It worked, and Gurdjieff told her she could stay as long as she wished.

Gurdjieff had raised the question to Stjernvall and Salzmann, saying that if she died at the Prieuré, "dirty tongues will slander us and say that we are the cause of her premature death." They replied that he was used to calumny, and he had always been able to put up with it. He said: "we will put up with it" (*Tu l'aimerais* 36–37). At Christmas, Lady Rothermere was assigned the task of making an English Plum Pudding, and Mansfield helped her. After she died on 9 January, Gurdjieff's name did circulate about Paris and London as the man who killed Katherine Mansfield. Mansfield's husband, the literary critic Middleton Murry, was lax in setting the record straight that his wife had written him letters expressing her almost ecstatic happiness during her stay. Murry would not, or could not, pay for her funeral, and she was buried temporarily in a pauper's grave. Today she rests close to the Gurdjieff plot in the cemetery of Avon.

Several English besides Orage and Mansfield arrived after the settling of the Prieuré, including Francis Pinder, Dr. Maurice Nicoll and his wife, Dr. James Carruthers Young and his wife, the brothers Bernard and Louis Metz, Antoine Finch, Edith Gladys Alexander, Ethel Merston, Elizabeth Gordon, Dulcie Leggatt, Barbara Craster, Eleanor Crowdy, Bea Rothermere, Dorothy Ireland, Jessmin Howarth, and a Mr. Page (Russell?), closely associated with Ouspensky in London. The first two Americans on the scene were Grace Potter and Jessmin's American pianist friend and associate Rosemary Lillard. The red-haired Irish dancer Doris Tyndall was there until the fall of 1923 when Gurdjieff told her to leave because her flirtatious behavior disrupted work. Her accidental or suicidal death at a nursing home four years later was frequently blamed on Gurdjieff's having "forced his sexual attentions" on her (*Moore* 196).

Olga de Hartmann's parents, the Schumachers, arrived during the year, having found living conditions in the Soviet Union uncomfortable. Gurdjieff had told Olga earlier to invite them (*Our Life* 125). Olga's brother, Leon, had left for the United States directly from Russia after he was permitted in 1916 to change his name to Schoumatoff because of his German-sounding name. The same antipathy toward German names had changed the name of Petersburg to Petrograd two years earlier. Olga's father, Arkady, however, thought himself too old to change, and kept his name.

It is difficult to calculate the amounts Gurdjieff charged individuals for accommodation. It is known that he usually announced charges that were more that his pupils could afford, and then accepted less. As he had explained to Ouspensky in Petersburg, it is necessary for people to make the effort to pay more than they think they can afford (*Search* 13, 165–66). In all, there seems to have been some fifty to sixty persons residing at the

Prieuré at one time or another in the year following its purchase. Some came and went, according to their work schedules in Paris or elsewhere. J. G. Bennett estimated that in 1923 there were twenty-five to thirty Russians there, the same number of English, but no French or Americans (*Witness* 106). The French literary critic Denis Saurat, an acquaintance of Orage and a specialist in the mystical poetic strains in Blake and Milton, came down to visit in the summer of 1923, and he calculated in his article about the Institute that there were some seventy Russians and an equal number of English, but no French (*Nouvelle revue française*, 1 Nov. 33). One Russian family notably absent was Ouspensky, his wife, Sophia Gregorievna, her daughter, Lenochka, and husband Savitsky and son Leonid ("Lonia"), all of whom remained in Paris for the time being.

Meanwhile, during the last months of 1922, the refurbishing of the château, its outbuildings and ground continued at an almost frantic pace. There are several well-known pupil accounts about the early years at the Prieuré. It is superfluous to cite them here, but the recollections of Tchesslav Tchechovitch add a rare view of Gurdjieff as a jack-of-all-trades and lover of nature. For one thing, Gurdjieff never went to bed before the others and never got up in the morning after them (*Tu l'aimerais* 15). He directed his work to have his pupils become conscious of their faults as well as their virtues. Though he was away in Paris often during the day, in the evening he would survey all the work he had assigned carefully. When Tcheko once showed Gurdjieff proudly the cement drain he had constructed for the baths, Gurdjieff criticized his judgment of the work and destroyed it with a trowel, then sent the disheartened pupil off to tend to the manure in the stables. The next morning Tcheko saw that during the night the work had been redone perfectly (*Tu l'aimerais* 16), but by whom and when?

This strategy of shocking pupils into self-observation is what

Gurdjieff called "stepping on corns." Those who couldn't tolerate the pain of ego-destruction were welcome to leave. Gurdjieff's technique was not meant to expose superiority in knowledge of certain matters, but to bring to life latent skills of observation in his pupils. Gurdjieff explained that one cannot claim superiority over another unless he demonstrates that he can do what the other does and do it better.

The understood covenant of understanding among the pupils was willful collaboration. Working together on tasks assigned by Gurdjieff required a great deal of patience and tolerance. Pupils were crowded two to three in rooms on the third floor "Monk's corridor." Princes and paupers shared the same space, sights and odors. Gurdjieff, Julia, and honored guests resided on the second floor "Ritz." Members of the family and some close associates lived in the "Paradou," once it was made habitable. Work crews were a motley mix of artists, doctors, lawyers, teachers and what Tchesslav called "clochards," beggars or bums. Each had a specialty that Gurdjieff found he could exploit for the benefit of all.

Within a week of moving to the property, Gurdjieff had Stjernvall buy two cows and Salzmann prepare a pig pen. During Gurdjieff's absence in Paris, one of the cows calved. A new pupil who vaunted his agricultural training, despite Julia's objection, milked the cow immediately, explaining that the first milk was indigestible for the calf and might cause damage to its digestive tract. Unfortunately, the calf died the day after. When Gurdjieff returned from Paris and heard of the calf's death, he explained that the quality of an animal's first milk was essential to clean out the digestive tract (*Tu l'aimerais* 246–47). The agriculturalist left.

The Prieuré had a large collection of fowls, chickens, guinea fowl, ducks and two peacocks. Madame Stjernvall was responsible for their care, but during a long absence of Gurdjieff in Paris,

107

she and the others noticed several mornings the bodies of chickens and ducks killed by an unknown intruder into their coops. Despite careful locking of the cages, each morning, remains of fowls killed and eaten were found. When Gurdjieff arrived and looked over the scene, he had all the cage doors left wide open during the following night. Before going to bed, he noticed the gathering of ducks and chickens on the grass. The next morning, he and the others witnessed a parade of proud fowls, led by the peacocks, with a duck dragging the tattered body of a weasel that had been nearly pecked to death (*Tu l'aimerais* 249–52).

Despite the physical strain involved in some of the tasks Gurdjieff assigned his pupils, he seemed to sense when limits were reached. After Orage had dug an irrigation ditch, filled it in and dug another, Gurdjieff came by and said, "Enough, now we coffee drink." Hartmann recalls Gurdjieff, noting Hartmann's strain at a job, saying "Thoma, now go and burn some leaves." Hartmann realized that "every activity in the Work showed clearly that the aim was never for outer results, but for the inner struggle." That inner struggle had to do in these instances with "attention" (*Our Life* 106–107).

At the end of November 1922, the sauna was completed, but Gurdjieff was unhappy with the humidity and uneven distribution of heat. He moved the lower bench tier forward toward the stove of rocks, and installed a sort of thermostat that reduced the vapor cloud while evening the temperature. Gurdjieff had his guests pay for the bath with two stories. When a story failed to entertain, or repeated an earlier one, Gurdjieff would ask Salzmann to retell it, and he would do so with comic gestures, movements and voice (*Tu l'aimerais* 243–44).

In this respect, Gurdjieff was an industrial psychologist. He measured efforts and found ways intuitively to save time and increase productivity without increasing physical effort. For a simple example, if one carried water in a pail from one place to another for a task, then the pail would be filled on return with something else. Efforts serve efforts, he said. In the summer of 1923, when a group of men tried to break apart a large boulder they had unearthed in digging to make the Turkish bath floor, Gurdjieff observed their futile efforts, then told them to turn the boulder over until he found the right spot. He had a hammer blow directed there and the boulder broke in two. He did the same with the parts until the stone was reduced to small pieces.

There are numerous examples of Gurdjieff's exceptional respect for natural life. His treatment of horses and mules during the crossing of the Caucasus range is one example. For another at the Prieuré, when pupils cleared away old boards, rats and mice fled, and were dispatched quickly with sticks and boards. Suddenly, Gurdjieff cried "Stop"! When the others looked at him with surprise, he pointed to a mother mouse with babies clinging to her back. After she departed, the pupils went back to their killing.

1923

In the spring of 1923, Olgivanna's husband, Valdemar, contacted her from Paris, apparently to make a further attempt at reconciliation. After Olgivanna failed to respond, he set sail on the *Paris* on 14 April 1923. Arriving in New York, he declared himself an engineer, named his brother-in law, Lazovich, as a local contact, and his wife, Olgivanna, at the Prieure as a relative from the country he was coming from. Undoubtedly, he had a happy reunion with his six-year old daughter, Svetlana.

On 28 May 1923, Gurdjieff received official permission to receive members of his family from Russia. Soon after, Gurdjieff's mother, his sister, Sophia Ivanovna and her husband Kapanadze with their daughter, Lucia, and Valentin Anastasieff arrived. At the end of the summer, Dmitri, his wife Asta Gregoria, and their three daughters, Luba, Genia and Lida, landed at Marseille where Stjernvall met them and brought them by train to the Gare de

Lyon in Paris, then by train to Fontainebleau, and finally by fiacre to the Prieuré. They all moved happily into the newly refurbished Paradou. Gurdjieff hosted a feast that evening with whole lambs roasted over an outside fire set in the stump of a tree.

It should be remarked that throughout this period Gurdjieff was under surveillance by the local authorities who had heard that he was a Mason who practiced hypnotism. His petition asking to have his family join him bounced about different offices before being approved. Throughout the winter, the French Ministre de l'interièur received letters denouncing him and the operations of the Institute. The local police were ordered to check on the Institute operations and the validity of the papers of its members, as for Gurdjieff, he was noted to have unfavorable antecedents. In February 1923 the police filed a negative report on the population of the Institute.

The major construction project of the winter of 1922–1923 was the "Study House," constructed out of an unused French Airplane hangar Gurdjieff had bought, had disassembled and trucked to the Prieuré where it was re-assembled. It was a feat of memory for Gurdjieff to recall where pieces fitted or, more likely, he refitted it to his mental blueprint. Work began in February around a center pole holding up a ceiling consisting of canopies under a metal frame roof. The walls were fashioned of mixed mud and leaves pressed between slats. Windows were set in the walls, carpets were strewn on the leveled floor, and iron stoves set in place for heat. There was a low dais at one end upon which a chair was set for Gurdjieff. Anxiety mounted as the moment arrived to remove the supporting center pole. Even Gurdjieff seemed not to be sure the canopy structure would not collapse without it. As the workers got ready to flee the structure in case of disaster, the pole was removed. The Study House ceiling held!

Cloth hung from the roof was painted and embroidered with aphorisms. The windows were covered with designs Salzmann painted. With the completion of the Study House, movements, sacred dances and readings could be performed with room to spare (Hartmann 107–108). Lights and fountains followed, and Gurdjieff was ready to receive visitors to watch demonstrations. Reports had already circulated in the Paris press about the strange behavior observed at the Prieuré. The *Paris Excelsior* showed photos of the Study House, which it called "un temple mystique en pleine forêt de Fontainebleau." It mentioned G. S. [sic] Gurdjieff as the founder of an Institute for the Harmonious Development of Man.

A journalist acquaintance of Orage, E.C. Bowyer, published a four-part series in the 19 February 1923 issue of the *London Daily News* with Orage's brief exposition of the ideas of Ouspensky and Gurdjieff. "By his elaborate combination of appeals to the senses," Bowyer wrote, "Gurdjieff believes he is providing many aids to meditation." At the same time, the writer Clifford Sharpe published a two-part description of the Institute, calling its members "The Forest Philosophers," an epithet that became popular in Paris. Coincidentally, Gurdjieff shared the front page of the Daily News with the news of the discovery of the tomb of Tutankhamen.

It is clear from such articles that the presence of Orage at the Prieuré brought the Institute rapidly to the notice of English and French readers, though, as Saurat remarked, there were no French pupils to be seen. Orage was also influential in getting the word about the Institute across the Atlantic to America. A reporter, Ernest Brennecke, visited the Institute and, after being shown about by Orage, wrote a full-page article for *New York World* in the autumn of 1923. Another reporter, Maud Hoffman, a former pupil of Ouspensky's in London, visited the Prieuré during the summer of 1923 at Orage's instigation and wrote a two-column article that filled a page in the *New York Times* in early 1924.

One article that had not been noted in earlier studies was

entitled "Romantic Search For Life's Secret," and subtitled "Salvation in Dancing." The anonymous writer, an acquaintance of Ouspensky, was better informed than others. Despite inevitable exaggeration, the article displays sober objectivity in reporting the scope and gist of Gurdjieff's teaching. It is noted, for example, that "'The Company of the Harmonious Development' under Gurdjieff . . . comprises doctors, lawyers, artists, scholars, scientists, and society women wearied of inane rounds of butterfly life. . . . Katherine Mansfield, most brilliant woman writer of her generation, spent her last years [sic] in the Fontainebleau community. The famous editor of a famous journal resigned and disappeared from the world to seek the secret of perfect development among the trees in this strange community of mystics. Has this extraordinary man Gurdjieff the secret of perfect happiness? Has he wrested from those remote and fantastic priests of Thibet some knowledge long since forgotten by the Western world?" The article concludes with a statement by Gurdjieff deploring the waste of life among those who know not how to embark on a search for happiness.

Due to reports like these, Gurdjieff became an "item" in the rumor and gossip mills of Paris. An example of typical gossip was reported by the American novelist Kay Boyle, sitting at a café in Paris near two American writers and publishers, Harold Loeb and Robert McAlmon. She heard them discussing a turbaned man sitting further away: "The cult has been spreading," she heard, ". . . It's mass hypnosis . . . Gurdjieff started some years back in the East as a hypnotist . . . .Anyway, out there in Fontainebleau he gets people of various nationalities . . . to repeat numbers and words in their own languages, to repeat them over and over." The conversation continued with amazement at the ridiculous behavior of Gurdjieff's pupils. Actually, the turbaned man they were looking at was not Gurdjieff at all (*Gurdjieff and Orage* 40–41), but that does not alter the fact that wild rumors circulated about him. Another American woman reported hearing from someone who had seen him in Tiflis that he was an Armenian rug merchant. "He was clever enough to have gotten out of Russia during the Revolution with about forty followers. Since that time he is being considered a kind of god." After revealing that he operated some clubs where opium could be bought, she continued: "He has a château where human derelicts and sex-starved old maids went hoping to save their souls" (*Shadows* 67). Not long after the same woman joined the Institute.

From springtime 1923, visitors from Paris visited the Prieuré, though many did not succeed in getting through the gates. Others met Gurdjieff in Paris. The American poet Ezra Pound, whom Orage had promoted in London, was in Paris on his way to a new life in Italy when he met and talked with Gurdjieff. They enjoyed each other's company, and Pound volunteered to judge a cooking contest between Gurdjieff and the Romanian sculptor Constantin Brancusi, awarding the crown to Gurdjieff. In his *Guide to Kultur* (1938), he wrote: "Brancusi ed. Cook on occasions and G made Persian soup . . . If he had more of that sort of thing in his repertoire he ed. had he supposed it, or desired it, have worked on toward at least one further conversion" (*Gurdjieff and Orage* 27).

It seems that soon after getting the Institute in working order Gurdjieff anticipated putting the Institute on the road westward. After all, Gurdjieff was wont to say, America is the backdoor to Asia. He cultivated American visitors and others who had spent time in the United States as if to gather impressions of the "American psyche." The photographer Man Ray, novelist Djuna Barnes, American painter Eugene MacCown, sculptress Thelma Wood, poets Charles Henri Ford and Alan Ross McDougall, poetess Edna St. Vincent Millay, art patron Peggy Guggenheim, and poet-editor Robert McAlmon all visited. Sinclair Lewis, author of *Main Street* and America's first Nobel Laureate for Literature, was spending the summer of 1923 in Avon, when he wandered to the Prieuré five minutes away, talked with Orage and others and stayed to watch the dances that night in the Study House. In a letter he wrote to his father the next day, he observed: "The dancing is very interesting, some of the dances are imitations of Oriental sacred temple rites, some of the stunts requiring a high degree of muscle control . . . . But it must be a hell of a place to live—they sleep only four hours a night, and eat almost nothing, with occasional fasts of six or eight or ten days!" (*Gurdjieff and Orage* 20). It was said that Gertrude Stein motored down as well, but no record of her visit is extant.

A notable guest at the Prieuré during the summer of 1923 was Imogene ("Ima") Hogg, daughter of "Big Jim" Hogg, former governor of Texas. Ima, forty years old, had been Rosemary Lillard's sponsor in Houston, and had sent her to Paris to continue her music studies. She and a friend, Estelle Sharp, were on a European tour and decided to visit Rosemary at the Prieuré. Ima, an oil heiress and a woman of strong will and fortitude, was so impressed by what she saw that she stayed and joined the work for a few days before rejoining her travelling companion to continue the tour. She returned to the United States in October 1924, having promised to continue supporting Rosemary's studies, if not money for the Institute. Estelle Sharp, the heir of her father's share in the Sharp-[Howard] Hughes Tool Company after her husband's death in 1912, was also in the position to help if she wished.

Gurdjieff moved into a new flat in Paris on the Rue du Commandant-Marchand in the sixteenth arrondissement between the Etoile and the Bois de Boulogne, and for the remainder of 1923 he selected and trained pupils for future dance demonstrations. He taught them also what he called "tricks and half tricks," mostly feats of memory. The comment Kay Boyle overheard about numbers and words was not far from the truth. Gurdjieff taught mnemonics, a technique of associating numbers with proper nouns. He had pupils remember, for example, one hundred words in numerical form: 18 miracle, 42 thank you, 67 electricity, and so forth (*Tu l'aimerais* 160). Pupils also learned to associate words with notes played on the piano, so that they could read sequences of notes as words and phrases, even in languages of which they knew not a word. A spring visitor from England, Mary C. Bell, later wrote of the preparation for performing tricks: "We had to learn a sign language of numbers, so subtly constructed that when skilfully done, we could communicate numbers to one another in the middle of a large crowd without being observed" (*Bell* 1949). She revealed that they also used the Morse code to communicate code words and names, usually by having someone in the audience convey the word-numbers to Tchechovitch who remained out of sight of the audience, but who could transmit the numbers to Hartmann at the piano. These and many other "tricks" were displayed with great effect in later American demonstrations.

It was during this period in France that Gurdjieff introduced his "toasts to idiots," a feast ritual typical to the Caucasus region. The Georgian toast tradition, consisting of toasts given in a fixed order, survives to this day. At Gurdjieff's table, the toasts were offered by the tamada or "director," a person who sat to Gurdjieff's left. Gurdjieff explained that there were twenty-one levels of idiocy, by which he meant individual idiosyncrasies, and each toast was dedicated to one of them, though rarely did the number of toasts with armagnac or vodka exceed eight. The first might be "toast to ordinary idiots," then proceed to square and round idiots, though the order of toasts was not fixed. Gurdjieff's own rank was "unique idiot" and Orage was just below him as "super idiot." Children were "candidates for idiocy." In a privately circulated paper, John Bennett explains that that the "Toast Ritual" is a scientific and symbolic representation of human destiny that expresses the secrets of our inner life. In an unpublished "After-dinner discussion," he elaborated:

115

"There are twenty-one gradations of "Idiots"—of identity, of kinds of beings. This gives you the picture of the going out and the returning, but it also adds something more, which is very important, and that is that there can be a kind of false returning, a returning which has not got the potential for totality. This is what Gurdjieff was anxious to get over to people with his Science of Idiotism: that every kind of effort produces an integrative effect—a soul is made whenever there is an act of decision— something is integrated. But integration is not enough."

Integration has to be such that it can reach completion.

Gurdjieff explained that the unique opportunities for self-understanding which the toasts presented would be destroyed by interpretation outside the moment they were presented at his meals. Gurdjieff refused to discuss the toasts except at the table.

By the end of autumn 1923, Gurdjieff had a select troupe prepared to perform his demonstrations, and he let it be known that the Paris demonstrations would be a rehearsal for the United States. He had two motives for going to the United States. First, he hoped to raise money there for the Institute; and secondly, while doing this he thought he could attract a large number of Americans to join his pupil population. Once in New York, he admitted that he deemed "a tour through the different states of North America, with constant travelling and change of environment, far from the usual surroundings and consequently always with new impressions, will create the necessary conditions—in accordance with my established subjectivity—for a complete rest" (*Meetings* 291).

Orage was the linchpin in the operation. First of all, he spoke and wrote perfect English; secondly, he had influential literary contacts in New York; thirdly, he had the advantage of a seductive charm and wit. Finally, it should not be ignored that he and Gurdjieff had forged a close friendship over the past year. In many respects, Orage was the closest friend Gurdjieff had since leaving his homeland. Ouspensky might be all right to drink vodka with, Gurdjieff had said, but not for more. Orage could play language games with Gurdjieff, exchange puns and jokes. They laughed together, though neither spoke the other's language well. Orage had acquired only a passive command of "work" Russian. Further, Gurdjieff trusted Orage to present the Work. In short, they "hit it off."

Many pupils who would not be part of the presentation group had left the Prieuré during the summer to return to occupations elsewhere. Despite the exodus, or perhaps because of it, Gurdjieff's finances were in poor shape. He hoped that the demonstrations would bring in enough money to pay the travel fares for his group. Lady Rothermere and Philipson were unwilling to advance more money to him. "Bea" Rothermere had pledged to help Krishnamurti in England, and she was still committed to continue her financial support of Ouspensky. Gurdjieff found it necessary to borrow money for the rental and decoration of the Theatre of the Champs Elysées for ten performances between December 13 and Christmas Day, including two matinees as well as evening performances. Hartmann, who orchestrated music for the movements, some of which were new, hired an orchestra of thirty-five instead of the hundred he wanted, and so had to adapt what instruments he had to the task. Gurdjieff himself had to do without a full troupe. Orage and Stjernvall would be absent—though perhaps neither were assigned roles—and one of his lead dancers, Jeanne de Salzmann, was in her final month of pregnancy.

The night before the dress rehearsal, Study House materials were brought to the theater, whose foyer was transformed into an Oriental palace. Pupils not used for the dances, outfitted in costumes from "The Struggle of the Magicians," received and ushered spectators. Fountains poured out champagne. The program for the demonstrations printed in *The Echo of the Champs-Elysées* two weeks earlier and edited by Orage, announced three parts of "The Art of the Ancient East." Part 1 announced the Gurdjieff work and a performance of gymnastic exercises derived from an esoteric school in Kafistan on the heights of Kidjera, followed by the piece known as "The Initiation of the Princess," and concluding with the famous "stop exercise" accompanied by explanations of its function.

Part 2 offered the "Movements," derived from the Kisiljan Monastery in Chinese Turkestan, followed by movements from Afghanistan. Then there were movements from a monastery in Khavar in Kafiristan, devotional exercises identified with Kashkar, a Dervish funeral ceremony, ritual prayer movements from Sari in Tibet, movements from a Christian monastery in Transcaucasia and, finally, movements of the Whirling Dervishes. Part 3 offered a variety of dances and concluded with a ceremony, according to the program notes, that Gurdjieff had witnessed himself in the Hudankr Sanctuary in Chitral (The complete orchestral music of the Paris demonstration is presented on CDs attached to Gert-Jan Blom's *Oriental Suite*).

A supplemental insert announced future demonstrations of the "The Art of the Ancient East," grouped under three programs: Movements, Music, and Religious Phenomena. On the back page of the program was printed an essay over the name H. Br, "What the Gurdjieff Institute has sought to present to us." Inserted in the folio program was the Institute prospectus.

When the curtain fell at the end of the first night, Hartmann asked how it had gone, and Gurdjieff answered: "Never think of results, just do" (*Our Life* 111). In effect, the doing was fine, and press reports were enthusiastic. Some in the audience might have sensed a Mevlevi Dervish character to many of the dances. Philip Mairet, a close friend and associate of Orage was in Paris for the show, wrote that on the basis of the Paris demonstrations "the prestige of the Institute rose to its highest level" (*Gurdjieff and Orage* 35).

On Saturday, 15 December, the day before the second and gala performance, Orage and Stjernvall boarded the boat train to Le Havre, and the next morning sailed on the *Savoie* for New York to prepare the stage for Gurdjieff's American venture. Ouspensky was dismayed with Gurdjieff's decision to cross the Atlantic. He complained to his London group a few weeks later that the "Saint Petersburg conditions were not kept"; that is, in Petersburg he had screened prospective pupils for Gurdjieff ("Ouspensky Memorial Collection", Box 17, Folder 821). This understanding between the two changed in the Caucasus, though it seemed to be revitalized in Constantinople. From London, Ouspensky sent pupils from his group to the Prieuré in 1922 and 1923. Now Orage would assume screening responsibility in the United States, a circumstance that broke the understanding that Ouspensky considered still viable concerning seniority; "People who did not belong to groups before, like Pinder and Orage, were given certain power over people who were much older in the work" (*ibid*). As Ouspensky recalled, "I was still very interested in his work, but this time I very firmly decided to stand apart. G. went to France. I helped him in many ways to organize his work there, and in 1922 and 1923 went many times to Paris and to Fontainebleau. At the end of 1923 I found I could not remain connected with G. because I ceased to understand him completely . . ." (*Remembering Pyotr* 13).

When Orage and Stjernvall arrived in New York on 23 December, they had hopes that the architect Claude Bragdon, editor of Ouspensky's *Tertium Organum*, would meet them at the pier, but he wasn't there. Orage, with a one-way ticket and only fifty dollars in his pocket, went to a hotel in mid-town, leaving Stjernvall, who had $500 in his wallet and a return ticket to France, to seek out contacts among Russian refugees downtown. The next morning, Orage went to the office of Margaret Anderson's and Jane Heap's *The Little Review* on 28th Street. He outlined to them Gurdjieff's plans, and from their office telephoned the editor of *The New Republic*, Herbert Croly, whom he had met in London years earlier. He agreed with Margaret Anderson's advice to post an announcement for a talk at the *Sunwise Turn*, a bookshop on the corner of Vanderbilt Avenue and 44th Street in the Yale Club building across from Grand Central Station. He called the shop and made an appointment to talk with the proprietors on 2 January 1924, then relaxed for the holidays.

Meanwhile, Gurdjieff remained in Paris in his apartment with one or two pupils who took turns guarding the materials at the theater. Others found temporary housing in Paris to avoid looking for late-night transportation back to Fontainebleau. Two or three automobiles besides Gurdjieff's were available to transport the remaining performers to and from Paris on performance days. The Tuesday Christmas Day show was a matinee, so the entire group was able to return to the Prieuré for a late celebration. There were one hundred persons at the long table for a celebratory feast. Into one serving of the pudding dessert, Gurdjieff said he had placed a gold coin. Whoever found it would be marked for goodness. Olgivanna was the lucky finder, and Gurdjieff looked sternly at her and said: "Olga, you don't know what you got" (Friedlander and Zellman, *Fellowship* 71).

With the successful demonstration behind him, Gurdjieff was ready to book their passage for the United States in early January. It is obvious he had been ready to do so before Orage and Stjernvall left, but sufficient funds were not yet assured. The Paris demonstrations had lost rather than made money. Besides the anticipated result, the six-month payment on the Prieuré was due in February, a debt he would ignore for the moment (*Meetings* 292–93). On the plus side of the ledger, a check "finally . . . arrived from the United States," and Olga was sent to Paris to make arrangements (*Our Life* 111). Who sent the check that was awaited is a mystery, but may have come from friends of Jessmin Howarth in America. Olga's brother in the United States did not yet know of his sister's plans. Gurdjieff later said that he borrowed $2000 against the value of a brooch he had confided to the care of his mother in Essentuki and then forgot about it. She still had it in her possession when she arrived in France in May. With that money and the cash from the check, Olga bought twenty-three tickets for the *CGT Paris* due to sail on 6 January. She booked first-class passage for Gurdjieff and second class for the others.

On 31 December, the day before Gurdjieff sometimes observed his birthday (at other times it was 13 January, or even on both dates), he received an early gift in the form of a son born to Jeanne de Salzmann. The name Mikhail ("like unto God") was chosen, though he would be known by the French as "Michel" but not by Gurdjieff who spoke Russian to him as he grew up. Nikolai de Stjernvall told me that his half-brother was named after the two Mikhail Romanoffs, the first Tsar (1613) and the one-day last Tsar Mikhail Alexandrovich, brother of Nikolai II. The Tsar's patronymic echoes the name of the child's legal father across the water and linked the two half-brothers to an entire dynasty if not to a destiny.

7

2 January–15 June 1924: America

Early Wednesday morning, 2 January 1924, Orage entered the *Sunwise Turn* to negotiate with its director, Mary Mowbray-Clarke. Jessie Dwight, a direct descendant of the Connecticut Wit, Timothy Dwight, member of a wealthy Albany, New York, family, and a twenty-two year old part-owner since the summer, saw the handsome Englishman and asked an associate who he was. Her associate did not know the visitor's name, but Jessie listened in on the conversation, during which Orage was given permission to use the shop for a talk in a week's time. Another shop employee, the Englishman [Charles] Stanley Nott, recognized Orage and added his recommendation to Mowbray-Clarke. After Orage left, a notice of the talk was posted, and throughout the rest of the week and the first two days of the next, the two full-time and two part-time employees urged customers to attend.

On 9 January at the *Sunwise Turn*, Orage gave a talk to a full house summarizing the description of the work in the Institute brochure, then exposed Gurdjieff's ideas about man's mechanical being, self-remembering and self-observation. He concluded: "The work of the Institute is to make such a change in oneself that nothing can occur that does not agree with one's qualities" (*Invention* 60). Jane Heap was in the audience, electrified by what she heard about Gurdjieff. The experience was "super-real." "I am in the front row of the show, I don't rave about this, I have been waiting for it" (Friedland, *Fellowship* 74). Others, equally impressed, asked for another talk before the arrival of Orage's master. To a larger audience at the Neighborhood Playhouse in the days that followed, Orage gave two more talks. Claude Bragdon attended them and looked upon Orage as Gurdjieff's "Saint Paul." Another listener, the critic Gorham Munson, called Orage a kind of Peter, a "fisher of men" (Taylor, *Invention* 61). No better description of the impact of Orage's talks to his very knowledgeable and critical audience was that of the cultural historian and novelist Waldo Frank: "What it [the method] does—or claims to do—is nothing less than the whole and utter turning over of everything you live by" (*Invention* 70).

Meanwhile, Gurdjieff had said his goodbyes at the Prieuré to his mother, his sister Sophia, his brother Dmitri and family, his nephew Valia, Elizaveta de Stjernvall and Nikolai, Jeanne de Salzmann and the newborn Mikhail ("Michel"), the Merkurov family and another dozen or so "permanent" residents. He left Frank Pinder in charge of the direction of the property and went to Paris on 5 January to settle his affairs there. On the morning of departure, Gurdjieff and his party were increased by one when Antoine Finch, who had been delayed at the Prieuré because of family problems, found Gurdjieff at the Café de la Paix and asked if he could go with him. Gurdjieff told Olga to go and buy another ticket at the CGT office across the street on the Place d'Opéra. Finch, an excellent pianist, was an important addition, since his playing at the demonstrations would free Hartmann to conduct whatever orchestra could be assembled. So, twenty-four persons comprised the group on board, and two awaited them in New York. Gurdjieff later told his New York audience that he sailed with forty-six persons (*Meetings* 292), and James Moore counts thirty-five (*Anatomy* 328).

It was a rough passage of the *Paris*, as winter crossings often are. Many of the group suffered from sea-sickness, but all recovered for the ship gala evening on 12 January, for which Gurdjieff led a demonstration of the movements, concluding with the "stop" exercise, whose execution even the rolling of the ship could not disturb (*Our Life* 113).

First Visit to America

On the morning of 13 January, as the ship was being tugged into its berth, immigration authorities collected information on all the passengers, including gender, age, civil status, nationality, last permanent address, occupation, native language, race, nearest relative, length of stay, height, hair and eye color, birthplace, destination, and birth place. The names of the twenty-four—twelve men and twelve women—were listed as George and Julie Gurdjieff, Thomas and Olga de Hartmann, Leonid Ivanoff, Alexis Merslioukin, Helene Gorb, Tcheslaw Tchechovitch, Alexandre de Salzmann, Nina Zavroff, Adel Kopcinte, Olga Hinzenberg, the three Polish brothers Eugenieusz, Wladyslaw and Adam Kozlonski, Elizabeth Galoumian, Edith Gladys Alexander, Barbara Marion Craster, Antoine Finch, Constant Elizabeth Gordon, Jessmin Howarth, Dulcie Marion Leggatt, Bernard Metz, and Boris Ferapontoff. Gurdjieff listed his occupation as Professor, the Hartmanns as teachers, and most of the rest as students. Gurdjieff declared the languages he could read and write as Russian, English and Greek. Almost everyone else listed English as one language. Gurdjieff's race was noted as "Greek," and besides the seven passengers who identified their race as English, eleven, including Julia, the Hartmanns and Salzmann declared them selves Hebrew. Jessmin Howarth noted a New York City address, and all the others named as a local contact Leon Schoumatoff, Olga's brother in Napanoch, a small town in Ulster County, west of Poughkeepsie on the eastern fringe of the Catskills, about 125 miles from the city.

Orage was able to go aboard to help the troupe through customs. Stjernvall and Muriel Draper were at the dock waiting. Draper (1886–1952) was a powerful convert to Gurdjieff's ideas, one whom he would, years later, call his "first American friend" (*Anatomy* 198). She had lived in Vienna, Florence and London before settling in New York in 1915 as an interior decorator and music critic. She was on close terms with Gertrude Stein, Pablo Casals, Feodor Chaliapin and Arthur Rubinstein, and she was willing and eager to use her influence on Gurdjieff's behalf. Three days after his arrival, she gave an order to Burrelle's Press-Clipping service.

By the time Gurdjieff walked down the gangplank of the Hudson River pier, Orage had enlisted a large group to welcome him. Olgivanna's daughter Svetlana, now six years old, was there among many of them waiting to see her mother (*Fellowship* 77). Orage brought Gurdjieff and the Hartmanns to the Ansonia Hotel on Broadway, while others in the group were lodged in hotels nearby and, within a few days, friends of Muriel Draper offered accommodations in their residences. An acquaintance of Muriel's, Nunnally Johnson—who was to make his reputation later in Hollywood as a screen writer—interviewed Gurdjieff on the afternoon of 15 January at the Ansonia for the *Brooklyn New York Eagle* and wrote a humorous but respectful article about the "Harmonious Greek who would put man in tune with his nature." Many of journalists flocked to Gurdjieff and most of the New York City newspapers displayed announcements of Gurdjieff's arrival and descriptions of the Institute work (*Invention* 63–65).

On 16 January, the work began. Orage brought Gurdjieff to a select audience at the *Sunwise Turn*. After an introduction, Gurdjieff made a few remarks translated by Boris Ferapontoff. In the days that followed, Orage and Hartmann looked around for halls big enough for rehearsals and performances of the demonstrations, or "meditations in motion" as they were often called. On 23 January, a private rehearsal demonstration was performed not far from the Ansonia at Leslie Hall, on West 83rd Street, for specially invited guests, including artists and members of the press. Hartmann assembled and rehearsed a five-piece orchestra, a stage was constructed, and the full Paris program was repeated. The length of the program wearied many who got up from their seats and left as soon as it was over. When Hartmann tried to talk with some, Gurdjieff ordered him to remain at the piano and play "The Fall of the Priestess" while the dancers continued (*Our Life* 115). The dancing so impressed two daughters of the philanthropist Adolph Lewisohn that he offered his Neighborhood Playhouse on Grand Street for future performances.

Ever the trickster and gadfly, Gurdjieff did something of the same tactic at one of his first talks to the members of Orage's group. His talk of man's three-brained being and the disharmony of his centers, with Ferapontoff and Orage struggling to translate the discourse simultaneously into understandable English, moved many in his audience to get up and move toward the exit. Gurdjieff stopped and told his listeners that for the first time in their lives they were hearing "serious," and their response only displayed their emptiness. He invited those who wanted to leave to do so immediately, and after they did, he told two of his party to go and hold the door closed. That done, he smiled and invited those left in the hall to sit on the floor before him, and the rest of the evening passed well (*Tu l'aimerais* 162–64).

Coincidentally, the pastor of Saint Mark's in The Bowery, Dr. William Norman Guthrie, had been staging a series of performances of sacred dances throughout the autumn, and Orage accepted an invitation to speak there of Gurdjieff's dances. The New York Times of 21 January announced Orage's talk which he delivered on 27 January. On 2 February, the first public demonstration took place at the Neighborhood Playhouse before an extraordinary audience. The names of eminent spectators make a long list (*Invention* 65–66), but among the few of those who would be crucial to Gurdjieff's future work in the United States were the literary critic Gorham Munson, novelists Nathan Jean Toomer and Zona Gale, editors Jane Heap and Margaret Anderson, and music critic Muriel Draper. The majority of literati and artists had been drawn to the demonstration by Orage's talks.

That evening it was Orage who introduced the program, and he was noticeably moved by the occasion, struggling, he said later, to exercise Gurdjieff's habitual admonition "remember yourself" (Welch, *Orage with Gurdjieff* 8).

Besides the extraordinary energy and bodily control exhibited by the performers the most spectacular spectacle for many was the "Stop" exercise. The journalist and specialist on paranormal phenomena William Seabrook, reported an extraordinary occurrence which has become a staple of Gurdjieffian lore: "The troupe was deployed extreme back stage, facing the audience. At his command, they came racing full tilt towards the footlights. We expected to see a wonderful exhibition of arrested motion. But instead, Gurdjieff calmly turned his back and was lighting a cigarette. In the next split second, an aerial human avalanche was flying through the air, across the orchestra, down among empty chairs, on the floor bodies pell-mell, piled on top of each other, arms and legs sticking out in weird postures—frozen there, fallen, in complete immobility and silence." When Gurdjieff released their frozen stances, no one was the least hurt (*Invention* 67–68). Other witness repeated the same story, but some who were not there assumed that it must have only "seemed so."

Overall, the demonstration was a great success. Newspaper reports the next day particularly praised the dances. With free use of the Neighborhood Playhouse, demonstrations followed every other evening for several days, but audience numbers tapered off quickly. A few minutes before each performance began Gurdjieff went outside to invite anyone passing to come in gratis. Hartmann recalled that after a while "we had no further prospects" (*Our Life* 113), and Gurdjieff ordered his pupils to go out and find jobs in the city.

By chance, after looking for a job and giving his name to musical agencies, Hartmann received a telephone call from Adolph Bohm whom he had known associated with the Imperial Ballet in Petersburg. After listening to Hartmann's description of the Gurdjieff tour, Bohm offered to help arrange a demonstration in Chicago where he directed a ballet school (*Our Life* 114). Needing money for tickets, Gurdjieff consulted with Orage about other cities nearby to visit before going west. After considering Philadelphia and Washington, Gurdjieff decided on Boston and dispatched Orage there on Tuesday 19 February to make arrangements. Orage went about Boston and Cambridge busily, granting interviews, speaking to professors at Harvard, arranging to rent Judson Hall, and ordering tickets to be printed for a demonstration. Not able to provide a down payment for Judson Hall, he turned successfully to the Fine Arts Theatre on Massachusetts Avenue for a scheduled performance on Wednesday 5 March.

Meanwhile, on 28 February, the *New York Times* announced a forthcoming performance at 8:30 on 3 March at Carnegie Hall, with seats at $1.10 and $5.50, boxes at $55 and $99. It is doubtful that many paid the high prices, but as usual, Gurdjieff opened the doors to one and all once tickets had been sold and the performance about to begin. Moore says that the Carnegie Hall performance on 3 March "was the first, last and only occasion when he charged for tickets" (*Anatomy* 202), though Gurdjieff sold tickets for every demonstration after the first New York exhibition for an invited audience in Leslie Hall.

Although the Carnegie Hall performance followed upon ones given at the Neighborhood Playhouse, the review in the New York Herald the next morning said, "Twenty-one pupils of the Institute for the Harmonious Development of Man, a school founded by G. I. Gurdjieff . . . gave the *first* (my emphasis) public demonstration of their work last evening in Carnegie Hall" (*Invention* 76). Apparently, the demonstration was not a success (*Gurdjieff and Orage* 53).

On Wednesday afternoon, 5 March, Gurdjieff left for Boston by train, having sent the others off by boat the night before.

Orage met the 4:20 afternoon train and brought Gurdjieff to his hotel before escorting him to a meeting with Harvard Faculty members whom he asked for certain materials for his exhibition of tricks and half-tricks. The Professors agreed to attend the demonstration but could not supply the requested accessories to the dances (*Gurdjieff and Orage*, 53–54). The show went on that evening at 8:30 before a full house, thanks to the earlier appearance in the *Boston Post* on 29 February of a long interview with Orage. Among illustrious spectators the most noteworthy convert to the Gurdjieff work at the Boston performance was the concert pianist Carol Robinson who had performed on the same stage the night before. A full and complimentary review of the demonstration appeared the next morning in the *Boston Post*.

Though Gurdjieff had planned to return to New York City on Thursday, he decided to give one more demonstration that night. Perhaps because of the newspaper reports, there were over three hundred paying customers in the audience, and the Post reported over four hundred in attendance (*Invention* 80–82). One of the attractions on both nights was the tricks of memory that he had had pupils study at the Prieuré. In his exposition of them, Hartmann called them "transmission of thought" (*Our Life* 116). The *Post* review described them as follows:

> One of the catching tricks was to have a spectator write a word upon a slip of paper. An attendant would then take it in her hand and walk with it to the piano, where another pupil [in this instance Antoine Finch] was stationed. Without looking at the word written on the paper the latter would improvise a tune on the piano to transfer the name to the group of pupils on the stage. At the conclusion of a few bars of music the entire group on the stage would then yell out the word in English. They did not miss once, despite the fact that many of them are not experts in such American words as Teapot Dome and Mississippi (*Invention* 80–81).

129

Between scenes, the *Post* reported, Gurdjieff, who spoke "150 languages and dialects," explained to the reporter "the elemental principles of his unique theory" about three-brained man and the lack of harmony between his centers.

After the performance, resting over coffee and brandy, Gurdjieff and Orage considered their move to Chicago. Gurdjieff suggested for the first time that Orage might stay on in the United States for a longer period of time than originally planned. Orage wrote that same night to Jessie Dwight in New York: "Someone will be necessary in America, if only to advise intending emigrants to Fontainebleau, and who else knows them?" (*Invention* 83). That last comment contains the core of Gurdjieff's realization that Orage had assembled in New York and Boston a formidable intellectual and financial support for the Institute. Orage's listeners and the demonstrations had raised enough to pay off most of the New York City debts, but Gurdjieff would need to find more funds to take his troupe to Chicago.

Orage, exultant over the success of the Boston demonstrations, saw Gurdjieff and the others off on the boat Friday morning and boarded the late Friday night train for Chicago. He spent Saturday night at the invitation of a professor in Evanston, Illinois, the home of Northwestern University, and on Sunday moved into the Southern Hotel in Chicago for $1.50 daily, ready to start out the next day with his list of local contacts, some of whom he had met in New York. On Tuesday 11 March he gave a talk to members of the faculties of Northwestern University and the University of Chicago. With Juliet Rublee, he gathered together a committee to find a hall, print tickets, and spread the word informally. Zona Gale arrived near the end of the week to lend her support. Within a few days a committee was formed headed by the French Consul, Antonin Barthélemy, that included Mrs. Will Slanton Monroe, Mr. and Mrs. John Alden Carpenter, Mrs. Chauncey Blair, Professor and Mrs. James Field, Mr. and Mrs.

Adolph Bolm, Miss Helen Dupee, Russell Tyson, Mr. and Mrs. Arthur Bissell, Herman Waldecki and Juliet Rublee. The committee succeeded in persuading eight subscribers to hire boxes at fifty dollars a piece for the first performance.

Meanwhile, Hartmann found cheap train tickets for Chicago in Hoboken, across the Hudson in New Jersey. Jessie Dwight wrote Orage on Friday 15 March that she had handed enough money to Olga for the tickets on the condition that Gurdjieff would allow her to accompany the group (*Gurdjieff and Orage* 57). Gurdjieff agreed and sent Olga to Chicago right away to find lodgings near Bohm's Dancing School which would serve for rehearsals. Hartmann wrote in his memoir that Gurdjieff, Olga and Orage went directly to Chicago, and that he led the others by an indirect route via Niagara Falls (*Our Life* 116). This statement contradicts Orage's letter information and the route of the New York Central Line from New York to Chicago which went by way of Albany, Utica, Rochester, Buffalo, Erie, and Toledo, Ohio (it was only in 1935 that an alternate rail line was opened through Niagara and Canada to Chicago). The trip took some 17 hours to Chicago, while any of the southern routes through Philadelphia, Washington or Baltimore took well over a day.

Orage, Rublee and Gale were able to set up a demonstration for Friday, 21 March in Orchestra Hall seating 3000. To fill the hall, Orage wrote Jessie, the committee set ticket prices low "from 50¢ to 3 dollars, with boxes of $50 and of the latter we have sold 13 out of the 23" (*Gurdjieff and Orage* 57–58). Orage had an interview published in the Wednesday 19 March edition of the *Chicago Daily News* with a description of the scheduled demonstration. He was pleased enough with the arrangements to think that the demonstrations would raise the money needed to pay for the troupe's passage back to France.

Jessie Dwight, Olga and Thomas de Hartmann arrived on Wednesday. Gurdjieff and the others arrived a day later, and the performance took place as scheduled at 8:15 on Friday 21 March. The next morning, the *Chicago Daily News* featured a photograph of the dancers, naming the front three as Miss Hinsenberg [sic], Miss Howarth and Miss Paleologue. The identity of Miss Paleologue is not clear. Maurice Paléologue was a renowned French ambassador to Russia from 1914 to 1917, and the "Miss" may identify one of his relatives who had studied the movements somewhere. Perhaps Paléologue had visited Armenia when he had a post in Sofia earlier in his career. A certain Helena Paleologue had settled in Canada at the time. Perhaps it was simply a Gurdjieff joke: the name of the wife of the autocrat Ivan the Great was Sophia Paléologue.

Moore writes that this was the last public demonstration Gurdjieff directed in his life (*Anatomy* 204), but this is clearly not the case, for the performance was such a success that a second one took place on Monday at the Blackstone Theater. Jessmin Howarth, however, was no longer among the performers. She had suffered food poisoning over the weekend and took a train back to New York where she met Rosemary Lillard, who had arrived in early March, then went to Maine to rest with her friend, Esther Whiteside. Jessmin was pregnant. In 1924, Rosemary Lillard and Stanley Nott became romantically attached and married three years later.

On Wednesday, 26 March, the Hartmanns and Jessie took the train back to New York City. The other performers stayed on with Gurdjieff who proposed another demonstration in a week's time. Orage and Gurdjieff granted interviews, and Orage gave his first radio talk on the 28th. He left on the 30 March night train for New York where he was to re-assemble the troupe for a last performance. Gurdjieff was set to present another demonstration in Chicago on Tuesday 1 April (*Gurdjieff and Orage* 59), but there are no newspapers reports of it. Apparently Gurdjieff left Chicago on 3 or 4 April, but many members of his troupe did not have the money to pay for their own their own return tickets to New York. Zona Gale settled Orage's hotel bill but did not contribute to the others (*Fellowship* 85). Metz approached Travellers Aid Society for funds and others were aided by the Community Chest charity. At any rate, Gurdjieff and the remainder of his troupe were finally reunited in New York to offer one last demonstration in Carnegie Hall at the beginning of April (*Our Life* 117).

Preparing to leave the United States, Gurdjieff made plans to attract, or lure, American pupils who could afford to pay an Institute fee. He had Orage pass out to interested parties the Institute brochure and compose and print "certificates of membership" to be sold in New York for $120. They certified that the holder had certain lodging privileges and access to talks, conferences, and classes. Orage was the official issuer, and others authorized to sign under Gurdjieff's name were Rublee in New York, Professor Comstock in Boston, Edgar Hamilton in Chicago, and Frank Reed Whiteside in Philadelphia. Whiteside and his wife, Esther, were friends of Jessmin Howarth from days before the war when Jessmin worked there.

The mention of Whiteside in Philadelphia coupled with Hartmann's statement that Gurdjieff had "arranged" for a demonstration in Philadelphia has led to a general assumption that Gurdjieff had staged a demonstration there. No other member of his troupe who spoke or wrote of the trip to America—among them Orage, Olgivanna Hinzenberg, Jessmin Howarth, Tchesslav Tchechovitch, Bernard Metz, Olga Hartmann, Carol Robinson to name a few, as well as Gurdjieff himself—make mention of a Philadelphia demonstration. No notice of one has been found in Philadelphia newspapers. The correspondence between Jessie Dwight and Orage at the time does not mention Philadelphia. Nonetheless, on the basis of Hartmann's remark, James Moore, Louise Welch, James Webb, and John Bennett (drawing from information he claims he saw in the diary of Gladys Alexander) state unequivocally that Gurdjieff gave a demonstration in Philadelphia before the demonstration in Boston's Judson Hall. Moore cites evidence in Gurdjieff's talk given to the New York group on 29 February 1924 in which he said that "all must get to Philadelphia—this is the basic aim of all religions." Gurdjieff's "Philadelphia," however, is not in eastern Pennsylvania, but east of Ephesus in Asia Minor, the site of one of the seven churches of Asia (Rev. 1:11 and 3:6). In that talk, Gurdjieff cited Philadelphia as the locus of the achieved human soul to be strived for, a point made quite clear in the rest of his talk.

Money was lacking for to tickets for the return to France. Gurdjieff needed Olga de Hartmann to return in order to assume direction of the Prieuré (*Our Life* 117), and so he urged her to go right away. She pawned her wedding ring to pay her passage and pleaded with Gurdjieff to contact her brother Leon Schoumatoff to redeem it. When Gurdjieff told Jessmin Howarth that he could not pay her return trip, she decided to stay in the United States with Rosemary Lillard and Rosemary's mother. On 26 September of that year she gave birth to Cynthia Ann Howarth, whom, she called affectionately "Dushka" ("darling" in Russian). Every one who boarded the *SS George Washington* had a story to tell about their difficulties to obtain their boat tickets, perhaps buoyed by Gurdjieff's frequent admonition: "Do not look for results, but concentrate on efforts."

Gurdjieff and Lily Galumnian remained in New York until they could raise money for their return. On 8 April 1924 in Juliet Rublee's apartment at 242 East 49th Street in Midtown Manhattan, Gurdjieff, obviously exhilarated by the welcome Orage's group offered him, formally established a New York Branch of the Institute for the Harmonious Development of Man. After midnight refreshments, Dr. Louis Berman questioned how the Institute was financed. Orage transcribed Gurdjieff's reply, filtered through two translators, and collated it with the transcription made by Boris Ferapontoff. Years later, Gurdjieff entitled his reply "The Material Question" the concluding chapter of the published *Meetings with Remarkable Men.*

The "Material Question," adds to the story of an early search for remote and storied remarkable men who transmitted esoteric lore, an account of a punctual search for remarkable men and women who would transmit funds necessary to carry that lore and its pedagogical psychology to others. So impressed was his audience with his story that Samuel Hoffenstein handed over a check on the spot, and pledged more for the future. Lady Lewis promised Gurdjieff half of her pin money.

To add to those sums, Lily Galumnian raised money giving movement lessons, and Orage lectured, wrote articles and gave talks in a room above the antique shop of Jean and Annette Herter. Annette, née Ponce, was from Geneva and had known Jessmin at the Dalcroze School in Paris. Gurdjieff contemplated going into business with Jean importing antiques (*Meetings* 299), but at the time, besides talking occasionally to Orage's group, he occupied himself dictating stories of his youth that would later appear as chapters of *Meetings.*

On or about 15 June, Gurdjieff took passage for himself, Lily, and Carol Robinson. As was his wont, he went first class. Olgivanna Hinzenberg, who had been spending time in New York with Jane Heap, sailed in the week that followed, as did Lucy Calhoun, Jessie Dwight, Heap, her fellow-editor Margaret Anderson and Georgette Leblanc. Stanley Nott had already sailed sometime in April for England, and crossed the channel two weeks later to go to the Prieuré (*Teachings* 43–44). Orage stayed behind to settle Gurdjieff's outstanding American debts, screen applicants for the Institute and draw new pupils into the work, tasks he accomplished with brio. He had another compelling reason for staying behind. He had fallen in love with Jessie Dwight.

What Gurdjieff did not know either before or after he left

the United States was that the American Immigration Service and the American Bureau of Investigation, renamed the Federal Bureau of Investigation when J. Edgar Hoover became director on 10 May 1924, had carefully scrutinized Gurdjieff and the members of his troupe since his arrival. They were all subject to deportation for exceeding alien quotas according to the Johnson-Reed Immigration Act.

Their status and their activities were reported to the authorities by the Landing Agent for the United States Line who was none other than Olga Hinzenberg's brother Vladimir Lazovich, who gave a Bureau agent a false picture of Gurdjieff. The English Home Office sent to Washington their own file on Gurdjieff, including information given them by Bennett. London described Gurdjieff as a follower of Uspensky [sic], both of whom were under suspicion of being Communist agents (see Taylor, *Real Worlds of G. I. Gurdjieff* 40-54). Olga's brother's motives for slandering Gurdjieff must have been his feelings about Olga's daughter Svetlana with whom he had moved to the United States in May 1922. Gurdjieff and his group, however, seemed not ever to have been bothered in the least by the Bureau.

Alexandropol

Das Institut

für

harmonische Entwicklung des Menschen

Nach der Methode

von

G. J. Gürdschijew-Georgiadis

1921

Buchdruckerei Otto Hellwig, Berlin-Wilmersdorf, Uhlandstraße 61

Gurdjieff in Hellerau 1920's

Gurdjieff's Armenian passport (29 June 1920)

Gurdjieff's mother at the Prieuré

Dmitri's family:
Asta, Luba, Valia
in back;
Lida and Genia
in front.

Family Gurdjieff:
Valia, Lucia,
Kapanadze;
Julia Gurdjieff,
Evdokia, Sophia
in front.

Dmitri's family:
Asta, Luba, Valia
in back;
Lida and Genia
in front.

Dmitri

Lili Galumnian and Jane Heap,
summer 1928
(Sergei was just born then)

Bernard Metz and Stjernvall, probably 1923

Children at the grave of Gurdjieff's mother

A.R.Orage, San Francisco, August 1928 *Photo by Ansel Adams*

Jessie Orage with son Richard 1930

J. Toomer, Mill House 1936

G.I.Gurdjieff 1931

Gurdjieff and Russell Page, July 1949

X, Dushka, Petey, Vivian, Tania, and small girl, 1949

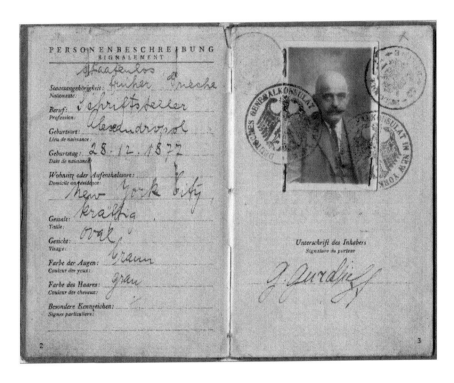

Fremdenpass : "Staatenlos" (Without country)
"Schriftsteller" (Writer)

Gurdjieff with Martin Benson and Rita Romilly
on their marriage day.

G.I.Gurdjieff, Spring 1949

G.I.Gurdjieff, Paris 1949

8

15 June 1924–6 January 1928: Prieuré

The several pupils who met Gurdjieff's boat train at the
Gare de St Lazare saw their master for the first time with a beard.
Together they all went by taxi to the Gare de Lyon where he saw
them off to Fontainebleau, except for Olga de Hartmann whom
Gurdjieff insisted go with him by car. On the way, he passed to
her the ring that her brother had redeemed and returned to him
and chided her for having pawned it (*Our Life* 117–18). The day
was bright and the two arrived in Avon in good spirits, but when
Gurdjieff rolled through the gates of the Prieuré he was greeted,
as he would say, by "Mrs. Serious Trouble."

The first problem was revealed to him when he discovered
an apparent theft of personal papers by Pinder whose motive
was to find documents that would unmask Gurdjieff's fraudu-
lent persona. Pinder found nothing, but left Gurdjieff's files in
disorder before he quit the premises in haste (Tchechovitch, *Tu
l'aimerais* 56). Another problem was the outstanding debt on the
Prieuré. He had not paid the full purchase price on the property
before he embarked for New York. He had, instead, taken out
a mortgage either with Madame Tabori—a common practice
when a purchase price could not be settled on time—or with one
of his other creditors, probably Thompson. Bennett wrote that
the money Gurdjieff returned from America with, was enough
to pay off his debt (*New World* 160), but this is clearly not the
case. Orage was left with a $2000 outstanding debt in the Uni-
ted States when Gurdjieff sailed back (*Gurdjieff and Orage* 80).
Hartmann recalled that Gurdjieff's funds on hand could hardly
cover the daily maintenance of the Prieuré (*Our Life* 120). So
Gurdjieff went back to work in Paris, staying in a new apartment
at 47 Boulevard Peréire, north of the Parc de Monceau. He spent

several days during the week away from the Prieuré at a variety of occupations.

Meanwhile, only a small number of Americans were awaiting him at the Institute. Orage had sold barely a handful of certificates. Those who sailed with Gurdjieff in mid-June and those who arrived shortly after were all women: Carol Robinson, Lucy Calhoun, Jane Heap, Margaret Anderson, and Georgette Leblanc. Olgivanna Hinzenberg arrived on the same boat as Jessie Orage a few days later, and was housed on Monk's Corridor with Carol Robinson, who became a good friend in short time. Several other women who had asked Orage for certificates to the Institute—Muriel Draper, Nessa Cohen, Betty Hare and Juliet Rublee—stayed home. Jane Heap and Margaret Anderson had sailed from New York on 25 June, arriving on 2 July with Margaret's two nephews, Arthur ("Fritz") and Tom Peters, whom they left at the Prieuré and took lodgings themselves nearby.

If American men were few, one reason was because they did not have the means to leave their occupations for an extended period, especially at a time when the American economy was accelerating at a record pace. Jean Toomer seems to have been the only adult male American who arrived that summer, though others, including Waldo Frank, who was in Europe at the time, had thought seriously of going. The only new Englishman at the Prieuré that summer was Stanley Nott, who writes, curiously, that in April 1924 he sailed for England and went to the Prieuré two weeks later, where Madame de Hartmann said everyone had been waiting three weeks for him. He goes on to describe the many talks and activities he engaged in with Gurdjieff throughout the spring and summer (*Teachings* 41 ff.), though Gurdjieff was not there with him more than a few days in late June and early July.

Another factor that explains the smaller than anticipated number of Americans in June and July was Gurdjieff's unanticipated long stay in New York. Pupils were loath to go to France before being assured of his presence and the anticipated expenses were not clear. After establishing the New York branch of the Institute in early April, Gurdjieff announced that those who wished to become disciples in France would have to attend Orage's "classes" in New York for three months. To comply, they would have to dispense $120. If they preferred to take classes in Fontainebleau, they were told that the cost would be proportional to their fortunes. Gorham Munson could not afford the price for both himself and his wife, Delza, so he paid only her tuition to Orage's classes and the movements, urged her to absorb all that she could, then teach it to Gorham and their friends (Taylor, *Invention* 97). Delza was an accomplished dancer, and she attended Lili's movement classes in New York and, following Lili's departure, practiced them assiduously with others.

Therefore, Orage raised very little money by his talks and sales of certificates. He had received only a handful of replies to over 600 circulars he sent out inviting subscriptions for the work, and had sold only a dozen or so certificates. Besides Jean Toomer, by the end of June, there were no other candidates for the Institute ready to embark, and Toomer, unaware that Gurdjieff by then was not disposed to welcome him or anyone else at the institute, did not sail until 17 July.

The Accident, July 1924
The next axial turn in Gurdjieff's fortunes propelled his vector of concerns in another direction. Driving back from Paris one afternoon, he swerved at a cross road near Chailly to avoid an automobile coming from another direction and ran his car into a tree. Moore speculates that he was going too fast for the road—ninety kilometres per hour—and that he had probably had too much to eat and drink at an Armenian restaurant in Paris (*Anatomy* 206–207). The 10CV Citroën model Gurdjieff was

driving had a top speed of only 65 km/h (42 mph), however, so speed could not have been a decisive factor.

Hartmann was waiting for him to work on some music, and "on July 5, 1924, Mr. Gurdjieff was expected back at the Prieurè at about five o'clock as always." Olga's version repeats the date 5 July, when she went to a garage with him to check the car, and then, at his insistence, returned to Fontainebleau by train. Gurdjieff had lunch at an Armenian restaurant before driving back in mid-afternoon (*Our Life* 120–21). 5 July at 5 p.m. is the day and hour Olgivanna Hinzenberg cites in her memoirs. Bennett records the date 6 July (*New World* 150). Fritz Peters, who had arrived only a few days earlier, recalls: "it was not until sometime on Monday afternoon—Mr. Gurdjieff had left Sunday evening—that the rumor that he had been in an automobile accident filtered down to the children at the school. We heard first that he had been killed." It was said that Gurdjieff was in the hospital and returned to the Prieuré a few days later (*Boyhood* 10–11). Though Peters' memory is not always accurate, his hearing of the accident on a Monday would fit with a Saturday, 5 July date for the accident. On a Saturday afternoon, Gurdjieff would have been driving back from Paris to be at the ritual baths that evening; Hartmann's "as always" suggests a regular schedule.

In a late revision of her memoir, Olga describes his recovery: "Finally, near the end of the sixth day, he opened his eyes. . . . But then again two days, sleep and sleep. Wednesday for the first time he began to eat." In all, this adds up to eight days, and eight days back from a Wednesday would be a Tuesday. Clearer is Jane Heap's statement in a letter to Florence Reynolds that "Tuesday, July 8th at seven o'clock in the evening a gendarme came to the Institute to say that Gurdjieff had been found unconscious and smashed up in his car . . . He had a brain concussion and was in a coma until Sunday . . . Though revived, he remained in his room for another week or so" (Patterson, *Ladies of the Rope* 53).

Curiously, neither Georgette le Blanc nor Margaret Anderson who were on the scene at the time, mention the accident.

Gurdjieff himself, with obvious tongue in cheek, told Nott years later that the accident occurred because he lost control of the car when he reached out of the window to pluck an apple from a tree (*Teachings* 100). The story circulated among the pupils at the time that Gurdjieff, having been thrown out of the car by the impact, was found on the grass, his head on a car cushion (*Teachings* 80). Both Jane Heap and "Tcheko" Tchechovitch recall, however, that the man who found Gurdjieff at the accident scene and brought him to the hospital in Fontainebleau—a highway patrolman, according to Tcheko—had lifted him carefully from the driver's seat of the car (*Tu l'aimerais* 221).

The *Petit Parisien* reported the accident under the headline "On trouve inanimé, sur la route près de Fontainebleau le prince Gurgieff, près de son auto." The article read: "Le prince Gurgieff, habitant le château du Prieuré à Fontainebleau, revenait de Paris en automobile. Le prince était seul dans sa voiture, lorsqu'en arrivant au croisement de la route de Perthes-en-Gâlinais et celui de Pontheirry, l'auto fut préciptée contre un arbre. L'accident n'eut aucun temoin. Ce ne fut que quelque temps après que l'on découvrit le véhicule brisé et le prince gisant inanimé, une grave blessure à la tête. La victime a été transporté à l'hôpital de Fontainebleau" ("Prince Gurdjieff, resident of the Château de Prieuré, was returning from Paris by car. The prince was alone in his car when arriving at the crossroads of the roads from Perthes-en-Gâlinais and Ponthierry, the car ran into a tree. There was no witness to the accident. It was some time later that someone noticed the damaged car and the prince unconscious with a serious head wound. He was transported to the hospital in Fontainebleau"). The press clipping date is blurred and unreadable.

Gurdjieff's own account of the accident that Olga recounts does not mention either date and time, but details the circumstances. Olga says that when she visited the scene of the accident with Gurdjieff some time later, he revealed that he had swerved to the right to avoid a car coming out of a crossroad (probably today's D64 near Chailly-en-Biere), ran off the road into a field where he thought to stop on the grass. When the car hit a low stone embankment, the steering wheel snapped off and fell on the floor. He tried to steer with his hand in his hat on the steering column, but had to jump free of the uncontrollable vehicle. He was not in the car when it hit the tree; had he been, he might have been impaled on the steering column. Hurt and bleeding, he got to the car and removed a cushion before losing consciousness. When "they" found him, he was in a position suggesting he was reaching for his handkerchief (*Our Life* 1992, 231–32). Who "they" were is not clarified.

Some assumed that Gurdjieff had carefully orchestrated his accident. "Of course, he may have meant it, and we may all be finding excuses for him to save our own self-images," writes Webb, but nonetheless "the evidence points to the fact that Gurdjieff knew he was going to crash" (*Circle* 296). Ouspensky wondered "whether it's really an accident? . . . Has he not gone too far?" (*The Fellowship* 88). Ouspensky gave Boris Mouravieff the impression that the disaster was in some way a punishment for Gurdjieff's offence against heaven (*Circle* 295). Orage wrote Jessie from New York: "It is absurd to suppose it self-directed. What the devil next? Or that he uses any supernatural powers with which to direct Dr. S[tjernvall] etc. S[alzmann] and the rest are such 'diplomats' that they would say anything, but don't you believe anything you cannot verify with your own senses" (*Gurdjieff and Orage* 80).

There is also considerable confusion about the extent of Gurdjieff's injuries. Moore says he was hospitalized in Fontainebleau with severe head injuries and a major concussion that rendered his condition critical, possibly terminal (*Anatomy* 207).

Olga de Hartmann says that he was returned to the Prieuré early in the morning after the accident, with head injuries but without any broken bones. He remained unconscious for five days (*Our Life* 122). Peters says that for several weeks there was no change in his condition, and when he finally re-appeared on the grounds, he was almost blind; at least Gurdjieff told him so (*Boyhood* 16). In the "Second Talk" to the New York group in 1930, Gurdjieff said that he was without memory for three months and bedridden for six (*Life Is Real* 93).

This was not the case, however. In mid-August, Edith Taylor and Jane Heap visited him in the Study House, where he told them: "'I sick man, truth very weak, now institute die for everybody'. . . This was said with the broadest of smiles . . . we filed out of the Study House, he leading the way leaning heavily upon a stout walking stick" (*Shadows of Heaven* 68–70). A scant two weeks after the accident, Hartmann cabled Orage in New York to say that Gurdjieff was much better and would soon be back to work (*Gurdjieff and Orage* 81). Indeed, he was back some six weeks later at the Café de la Paix in Paris where he told Olgivanna Hinzenberg to return to Chicago and finish up her business with her estranged husband (*The Fellowship* 90–91). One gathers from all recorded testimony that Gurdjieff was bed-ridden no longer than a month.

There is also a contradiction of opinion concerning the effects of his injuries. On the one hand, Hartmann reported to Orage that, although Gurdjieff was unconscious for four days, he sustained no concussion or serious injuries. C. Daly King, who never concealed his antipathy toward Gurdjieff the man, assumed that a frontal lobe injury from his accident would have reduced his capacities considerably (*Oragean Version* 17). Ouspensky told his followers in London that he was never the same man again; his mind had deteriorated and left him in delusion.

Ignorant of what had happened to Gurdjieff three weeks

143

earlier, Jean Toomer arrived at the Prieuré with certificate number 619 in hand (Orage had started the series of certificates with the number 601 for psychological reasons, but he had sold only twelve, half of which had not yet been paid for). He was surprised to find the residents walking about like zombies: "These people, so it now struck me, simply were not aware of my existence. To them I wasn't present" (*Shadows* 75). Jessie Orage recalled: "When Gurdjieff was nearly killed . . . what went on at the Prieuré? Practically nothing. This I know—I was there. A form of madness went on . . . when there were fifty others all behaving so oddly . . . In spite of slammed doors, of animated Russian discussions about his bed, Gurdjieff recovered and that almost makes me believe him a superman. Then a great white and gold chair was carried out to the forest and Gurdjieff sat in it all day and watched while we felled trees and burned them" (*Gurdjieff and Orage* 87). Hartmann reported that he had us make "big bonfires in the park almost every day . . . we thought he drew a kind of force from it" (*Our Life* 123).

There were two immediate consequences of the accident. The first was Gurdjieff's cancellation of his plans to return to America in the autumn or winter. Before leaving New York, he and Orage had outlined a yearly schedule to spend summers at the Prieuré directing pupils, and autumn and winter months in the United States giving talks and assembling new groups. He had already considered Philadelphia, Chicago and Washington D. C. as possible sites for branches of the Institute. The second consequence of his forced physical inactivity was a decision to concentrate his attention and energy on the writing he had started in New York in April.

In early August, Gurdjieff called all the residents to assemble on the lawn in front of the terrace where he announced that he was closing the Institute. Nott remembers him calling everyone to the Study House to announce that he was going to liquidate the Prieuré, and that in two days everyone must be gone (*Teachings* 83). Others heard him say that he was closing the Institute, but a few Americans could stay on. Olgivanna Hinzenberg recalled that he posted a list every day or so with names of those whom he would allow to stay, but one day she noticed that her name was not on the list. When she met Gurdjieff in Paris to ask why, he was intransigent. Despairing, she spent the next few weeks as an attendant in a women's lavatory before leaving for New York with her daughter Svetlana on 21 October aboard the *Rochambeau* (*The Fellowship* 89–90). At a performance of a Bolm group of dancers on 30 November, she met Frank Lloyd Wright, and she found herself ineluctably enchanted to a new master.

Most of the Americans were still there. After his accident he "mingled" only with Americans (*Life Is Real* 50). The English Metz did not leave, Carol Robinson left the Prieuré on 4 October 1924, while Jane Heap and Tom and Fritz Peters left on 11 October. Stanley Nott crossed the Atlantic to establish a book business in New York on 16 October just before Gurdjieff left the Prieuré for a cure (*Teachings* 86). Orage, however, headed the other way across the Atlantic toward the Prieuré in August. After hearing of the closing of the Institute, Orage considered changing his commitment to the work, but on 15 August he received a cablegram from Gurdjieff reading: "May come September but necessary to return October with others" (*Gurdjieff and Orage* 88). On 20 August, Orage sailed from New York on the *Mauretania* and arrived in Cherbourg on the 27th. He arrived at the Prieuré the next day, not in October for a brief conference, as Moore has it (*Anatomy* 211), but for a six week stay during which he consulted with Gurdjieff daily. They reviewed plans for the maintenance and expansion of operations in America, as well as means for raising money for the Prieuré (*Invention* 105).

Gurdjieff had called Orage to him at this crucial moment for a number of reasons. First of all, he wanted someone with him whom he considered a close friend as well as colleague. Secondly, Gurdjieff had confidence in Orage's stewardship. He had seen its results during his months in the United States, not only by the number and quality of people Orage gathered about him, but by the understanding of the "Work" displayed by Orage's group members. Thirdly, Orage's presence in America promised to draw a good deal of money for the maintenance of the Prieuré and the Institute. After all, Orage had raised the money for Gurdjieff's return from New York in June. Finally, besides these considerations, there was no one else better qualified to represent Gurdjieff in America. If the "mandate," was pro tem, Orage was preparing the ground for an eventual return of Gurdjieff himself.

An Objectively Impartial Criticism of the Life of Man

Having begun in New York the previous spring an account of his early life, even before Orage's arrival Gurdjieff decided to become an author. As early as five or six weeks after his accident, he had told Edith Taylor: "necessary something, do you agree? So like ordinary man I to think how be, many years much do, but never before one thing I do, I wish write book. Surprised? No? Some time in life every man must write book, but such book already I begin, and if you very much wish we can even English read" (*Shadows* 71). Friedland and Zellman imply that Gurdjieff had embarked on *Beelzebub's Tales* before Olgivanna left France in October (*Fellowship* 93). Jessie Orage reported that Gurdjieff was writing when she left the Prieuré on 3 October (*Shadows* 76n).

Because Gurdjieff found it difficult to write in the early days of his recuperation, he dictated to "one of the people near me" four scenarios before deciding to compose "Three brothers," based on a film he had seen entitled "Two Brothers" (*Herald* 42). Some time later he may have seen a 1926 German film about two brothers entitled *Die Bruder Schellenberg* (known also as *The Two Brothers* in America). I would suppose that a story of three brothers that involves family killing reflects Dostoyevski's *The Brothers Karamazov*, whose three brothers, Ivan, Alyosha and Dmitri, reflect Gurdjieff's number three, two and one man, respectively: thought, emotion and body. I would venture that Gurdjieff knew Tolstoy's "Three Hermits," a story of magical powers.

Gurdjieff also dictated a number of small "episodes in the lives of different people" that was probably a trial draft for *Meetings*. When he could write with pencil, he began to put on paper the "legend he had heard in youth about the first human beings on Earth" (*Herald* 45); that is, the *Tales*. Olga de Hartmann's story is that Gurdjieff dictated to her before he could write. When she expressed dislike for the "melodrama about brothers killing one another," Gurdjieff said: "All right, let us try something else." Then, in the evening of 16 December, he dictated: "It was in the year 223 after the creation of the world" (*Our Life* 126). 16 December was the anniversary of the day in 1916 Olga and her husband had met Gurdjieff as well as the day in 1922 when a fire broke out in the Prieuré. Gurdjieff later said that he began the first series on 1 January 1925 (*Life Is Real* 32). No matter the date he thrust Beelzebub into the universe, one can assume that in the last days of August and throughout the autumn Gurdjieff was composing a number of scenarios before finally deciding to record the legend he had heard about our earliest ancestors.

What he dictated to Olga cannot be verified from other testimony. If he dictated, it would have been in Russian since Olga did not know more than a smattering of Armenian. Persons who were at the Prieuré during the composition of *Beelzebub's Tales* reported that Gurdjieff dictated the text to Lili Galumnian in Armenian which she translated subsequently into Russian. Then, Hartmann translated those words literally into English with the help of Bernard Metz. In the Café Henry IV in Fontainebleau and at the Café de la Paix in Paris, Gurdjieff scribbled notes in Russian which Lili later transcribed and passed on to Hartmann. Nott writes that Gurdjieff wrote his first draft in Armenian, and that Lili's Russian was turned "into English by English-speaking Russians, together with emendations by some not very literate English pupils" (*Teachings* 92), but there is no evidence that Gurdjieff composed in Armenian. Though his mother was illiterate (*Tu l'aimerais* 187), Gurdjieff would have learned the rudiments of reading and writing Armenian at the Alexandropol municipal school. He did not mention his Armenian instruction but says he had studied Greek and Russian assiduously in his early years. It is not unlikely that Gurdjieff wrote a draft in Russian, which Olga and Gurdjieff translated with Orage when he was with them (*Our Life* 128). Nott says that in New York Orage received a manuscript in March 1925 but found it unintelligible and sent it back (*Teachings* 92). It is surprising that a manuscript draft could have gotten into Orage's hands in New York that soon.

Orage and Jessie Dwight sailed back to New York on the *Rotterdam*, arriving on 17 October, followed by Toomer two weeks later on the *Rochambeau*. While Gurdjieff toiled on his first series with its double title, *An Objectively Impartial Criticism* and *Beelzebub's Tales*, Orage was organizing the "work," which he understood to mean "the totality of Gurdjieff's enterprises." Bennett preferred to call it the "invisible world which has to be perpetually created in order that it should *be*" (*Great Enigma* 65).

In the autumn of 1924, Orage appointed Toomer, Gorham Munson and Daly King as potential teaching assistants, Muriel Draper as his executive director and Jessie Dwight as his personal secretary. He sent out notices of his first talk at the Lenox Theater on 2 November. Back in France, Gurdjieff had resumed work in Paris, had re-opened the Institute to "Americans," and was writing his book. Olga de Hartmann wrote Orage that Gurdjieff had recovered enough to start driving a big car he had acquired.

Fritz Peters writes that Gurdjieff made a trip to the United States from autumn 1925 until spring 1926 with a number of pupils in order to raise money and describes activities at the Prieuré without Gurdjieff during that period. He notes that Gurdjieff gave demonstrations in the United States which netted him over $100,000. In fact, it was Fritz who left the Prieuré that autumn with Margaret Anderson and Jane Heap when French authorities who had visited the Prieuré in early September declared that the children there were obliged to attend school. Tom and Fritz Peters, as Americans, were not required to attend a French school, but being of school age they were not allowed to stay at the Prieuré. Gurdjieff himself had no reason to support them during his gradual recovery, so they left for Paris and Maria Jolas' bi-lingual school on the Rue d'Orléans.

1925

By mid-winter 1924–25, Orage's groups were in full operation in mid-town Manhattan, and Jean Toomer gathered a group in Harlem. Orage's groups numbered over a hundred paying members and occasional visitors, many whose names figured among the city's prominent scientists, philosophers, writers and artists (*Invention* 107). Toomer's group included many who were associated with the so-called Harlem Renaissance: poets, painters, novelists, and sculptors (*Invention* 138). Out of the fees Orage charged for attending his talks he was able to send the Institute $1000 every other month. Toomer struggled to raise money as well, but few if any in his Harlem group could afford to pay even a token amount to Toomer for his time. Orage, supported by Jessie's money, allocated a modest allowance for Toomer's personal needs. At the end of spring 1925, Orage authorized Daly King in the autumn of 1925 to direct a group in lower Manhattan and another in Orange, New Jersey, where he resided with his wife, Mildred.

In late June 1925 Gurdjieff's mother, called affectionately by the Russians "Baboushka" (Grandmother), died of a cancer of the liver. Gurdjieff and others at her bedside heard her last words from a traditional Armenian song: "The flower is snipped, its life departed, the wind carries its seed to the soil and the bird, silenced in song, took flight to find life in another land" (*Tu l'aimerais* 188). Her death certificate named her Eudoxie Kalerof, daughter of Elepter Kalerof and widow of Yvan Georgivich Gurdjieff. Her eldest son bought a plot in the cemetery in Avon, among the tombs of French soldiers fallen during World War I, and he placed over her grave a dolmen inscribed with a French phrase: "Ici Repose La Mère de Celui Qui se Vit par Cette Mort Forcé D'Ecrire Le Livre Intitulé Les Opiumistes" ("Here lies the mother of him who by this death finds himself forced to write the book entitled "The Opiumists"). What he was signalling by this curious epitaph remains a mystery. It disappeared from the stone some time later.

Work went on as usual at the Prieuré. Gurdjieff worked with Hartmann scoring new music. The movement exercises continued in the Study House, but under the direction of others, for Gurdjieff was spending the greater part of his time writing. He preferred to write at the Henri IV in Fontainebleau and the Café de la Paix in Paris close to his room at the Grand Hotel, rather than at the Prieuré, though he occasionally wrote notes while sitting on a bench between the Prieuré and the Paradou. When asked later why he chose crowded and noisy places to work, he answered: "I always work in cafés, dance halls, places where I see people, how they are; where I see those most drunk, most abnormal. Seeing them I can produce impulse of love in me. From that I write my books" (*March* 25).

He asked Orage to come to the Prieuré in the summer, both to report on the work of the New York groups and to look over the English version of *Tales* prepared by Hartmann and Metz. Orage and Jessie Dwight sailed on 22 August aboard the *Mauretania* and arrived at Boulogne on the last day of the month.

When they got to the Prieuré the next day, they were told that Gurdjieff was waiting for them in Paris. He came down to meet them. Jane Heap, Margaret Anderson and Stanley Nott were at the Prieuré then, but Gurdjieff trusted Orage alone to oversee the editing of the book which was almost completed in draft form. On 5 September, Orage went to work with Gurdjieff reading chapters during breaks in writing. When Gurdjieff drove with Orage to Geneva, Jessie was behind him in the back seat typing.

On 23 September, Orage and Jessie went to London to visit with old friends and to consult with lawyers about the status of Orage's divorce petition to his wife, Jean Walker. The two left England on the *Mauretania* on 3 October for New York with a complete draft of the book to edit. Gurdjieff had also charged Orage with the task of contacting possible publishers and raising money for publication. Orage felt he could do both things. He relied upon Muriel Draper to assemble groups and Jessie Dwight to collect fees at the door of his talks. Among Orage's followers were many persons of means. One was Blanche Grant, heiress to the Grant Five-and-Dime chain of stores. Another was Robert Schwarzenbach, the Swiss consul in New York City who had made a fortune in the silk business in Zurich (Schwarzenbach's wife, Marguerite, was a survivor of the *Titanic* disaster in 1912). To handle incoming money, Orage organized a group committee with Gorham Munson as treasurer of group funds.

1926

It was Jean Toomer, now promoted to "colleague" in Orage's salutations, who mined the richest lode in the person of Mabel Dodge Luhan (1879–1962), a wealthy patron of the arts who had presided over salons in Florence and New York, before moving in 1922 to Taos, New Mexico, where she married her fourth husband, the Tiwa Tony Luhan. Mabel had met Orage and Toomer at Jane Heap's apartment in the winter of 1924 and had become interested in Gurdjieff's work. In the second half of November, 1925 she had lunch in New York several times with Toomer and Orage, and on 1 December she invited both to visit her at her ranch in Taos over the coming holidays. Orage urged Toomer to go after checking for a possible group location in Chicago, a city Jean knew well from his university studies.

When tall olive-skinned Jean with his seductive voice and manner arrived at the Luhan ranch, he encountered a Mabel infatuated with him. Moore writes that Mabel gave Toomer $15,000 for Gurdjieff and "offered to throw in her ranch" (*Anatomy* 215). The truth is far more complicated. In effect, she offered $14,000 to Gurdjieff for a study center on her property, and $1000 to Jean to cement her affection for him (*Shadows* 81). Toomer sent Luhan's check to Orage and followed it to New York a few days later to discuss accounts. Orage was pleased with the contribution, because Gurdjieff had asked him to raise $20,000 over the course of the winter. He had already raised and sent $500 of fee money before the end of 1925, and pledged another $950. Orage estimated that in the first six months of 1926, he could raise another $6000 toward the $20,000 that Gurdjieff had asked for in the autumn. Toomer had raised $50 in Harlem. Mabel's money would put them "over the top."

Orage accepted her money as an investment in the Institute. When he and Toomer met in New York in mid-January, Orage decided to send Gurdjieff $2000 right away. Toomer had already sent Gurdjieff a check for $1000 with an unpromising description of the ranch—too remote, without a railway link—and of Mabel—her "ego outweighs the virtue of her energy" (*Shadows* 82). Lili Galumnian wrote Mabel thanking her for her gift, but saying that Gurdjieff found the ranch offer unsuitable, since he would have to liquidate the Prieuré.

Obviously, misunderstandings were being compounded concerning the exact nature of Mabel's offer. Olga de Hartmann wrote "Tummer" saying that $14,000 should be reserved entirely for Gurdjieff's use, since he was in the process of liquidating the Prieuré. Toomer was disappointed that Gurdjieff had not written himself, and Orage was furious that Toomer had written a negative opinion of the property and misrepresented the amount of money involved. Orage had Munson put $2000 into the group publication fund, and to hold in reserve $1000 for Toomer's use. Munson forwarded $11,000 directly to Gurdjieff. For several years both Gurdjieff and Mabel Luhan accused Toomer of withholding money. Mabel reminded Toomer that her condition was that Gurdjieff would only take the money if he accepted the use of the ranch for a work center.

On 4 January 1926 Orage received "The Holy Planet Purgatory" chapter from Gurdjieff and plunged into it, telling his groups that he had read a thousand books of philosophy but none rivalled this text. Beginning with his 17 January meeting, he read and explicated each newly edited chapter. Toomer soon assumed a role as his assistant editor in order to speed along the revision. The readings encouraged many of the New York groups to apply for "inscriptions" for the Prieuré over the summer, and Gurdjieff sent word that he would be pleased to welcome "dollar Americans." Edith Taylor sailed for France in early May with the gallery owner Betty Parsons, and Toomer followed on the 14th with a letter of recommendation to Gurdjieff in his hands and a stern warning from Orage on his conscience not to make any monetary offers. Israel Solon, another of Orage's group members, warned Toomer that Gurdjieff was liable to "steal" money, to which Toomer replied laconically: "He asks and takes" (*Shadows* 88). Jessie Dwight sailed on 29 May, arriving at the Prieuré late on 8 June, and Orage himself, who had arrived in England on 9 June, went down to the Institute on 17 June. Among the many other Americans who arrived that summer were Gorham and Delza Munson, and Waldo Frank and his wife, Margaret Naumburg, the founder of the Walden Schools. Nott writes that he was there that summer (*Teachings* 106–17) but I find no record of his presence. Sometime that summer Daly King and his wife arrived at the front gates, rang and announced themselves to the gate keeper, who did not admit them. In a huff, they took a train to Paris and then sailed back to New York.

Meanwhile, Julia Osipovna was agonizing in the terminal phase of a cancer that was misdiagnosed until it was too late to treat. Gurdjieff regretted that the long recovery from his accident had prevented him from helping her himself. Her death certificate records her death at 3:30 A.M. on Saturday 26 June, at thirty seven years of age. Gurdjieff was sitting by her bedside (*Our Life* 127). That evening Gurdjieff had the Study House decorated and, after the baths, he held a vodka party in his wife's honor (*Gurdjieff and Orage* 112). Hearing of Julia's death, Madame Ouspensky and Jane Heap came down from Paris the next day for the funeral and burial next to Gurdjieff's mother and a few meters from the grave of Katherine Mansfield. Earlier on 5 March, due to continued surveillance of the Institute by the authorities, Gurdjieff had made a formal request for French nationality. It was turned down.

In July Gurdjieff renewed his motorcar trips. The first one to Orleans and Vichy was complicated by a collision with a fiacre when Jessie Dwight was at the wheel, and by Orage's apparent food poisoning from old caviar, eaten during a roadside picnic. Jessie blamed Gurdjieff for purposely poisoning Orage and back at the Prieuré near the end of the month, with too much drink clouding her judgment, found Edith Taylor's pearl-handled Browning revolver and went down the corridor of the "Ritz" toward Gurdjieff's room. When Edith intercepted her, she admitted in tears that she intended to shoot him. Neither Gurdjieff nor Orage ever mentioned the incident that Jessie recorded in her diary.

On 1 August Gurdjieff took another trip, this time to Geneva, and on 15 August to Contreville, a week later to Nevers, and on the last day of the month to Rouen. Each of these trips with Orage and Jessie were occasions to discuss the progress of the work on the book. They also discussed the logistics involved for another trip to the United States. Gurdjieff wanted to give more demonstrations, but there was not enough money on hand to pay for the transportation of a large group. He would go with a small group, visit Washington and Chicago besides New York where he would observe the workings of Orage and Toomer's groups. Orage wrote letters to his followers in New York to ask of possibilities for raising money, but there were too few positive responses. Leaving Toomer to edit the text of the "third descent," Orage and Jessie crossed the channel to England, and when they returned a month later to the Institute they learned that Gurdjieff had cancelled his plans to go to America.

In Orage's absence in England, two incidents occurred that raised eyebrows. The first was the arrival at the Prieuré of Edward Alexander ("Aleister") Crowley (1875–1947), prominent member of the cult organizations The Hermetic Order of the Golden Dawn, Argenteum Astrum and Ordo Templi Orientis. Crowley, reputedly "the wickedest man in the world," had known Orage in England. Who invited him to the Prieuré is not known, and records of his brief encounter with Gurdjieff are contradictory. He had met and talked with Nott in Paris before moving into a Fontainebleau hotel. From there, he may have simply wandered to the Prieuré out of curiosity. Nott said that Crowley had a brief conversation with Gurdjieff before he parted, and that was all. Webb reports a different scenario, without citing his source, writing that Crowley arrived for a weekend, attended the Saturday evening activities, and was treated like any other pupil. On Sunday evening, however, as Crowley turned to bid goodbye to his host, Gurdjieff cried out to him: "You filthy, you dirty in-side! Never again you set foot in my house" (*Circle* 315, see Hall, *Beelzebub and the Beast* xxiii-iv).

The second incident occurred after a Saturday supper during which Waldo Frank introduced to Gurdjieff his new wife, Alma Magoon. Gurdjieff handed her a sheep's eye to eat, addressing her as "Blondine," then berated Frank for not marrying a Jewish woman. On Monday morning Gurdjieff was at the Café de la Paix with Edith Taylor when Frank came in, shook his fist at Gurdjieff and yelled: "Go back to Hell you devil, and leave us alone." Gurdjieff pretended not to understand (*Shadows* 91). Waldo stormed out in rage. Curiously, when he returned to New York, he asked Orage for permission to lead a group. Orage refused.

Another incident of some note that summer was the pregnancy of Lili Galumnian. Peters recalled that some time after the death of Julia Osipovna, Gurdjieff was living with a married woman whom he made pregnant (*Boyhood* 116). Lili gave birth to a boy, Sergei, in the spring of 1927. During World War II, she and her son were back in Armenia, and Sergei, it was reported, died serving in the Soviet army.

Throughout the summer, Gurdjieff proposed plans with Toomer that would have Orage stay at the Prieuré until the editing work was completed, while Toomer, whom Gurdjieff had come to enjoy and trust would return to America and establish a group in either Chicago or Washington, Toomer's hometown. Toomer argued that Chicago was a much better possibility, and both Gurdjieff and Orage, who had turned their thoughts away from Boston, agreed. Toomer would also work with Jane Heap checking Orage's editing. On 16 October, Toomer sailed on the *De Grasse* for New York and arrived on the 26th. Jessie, Ethel Gordon and Jane Heap sailed on the *Majestic* on 20 October and arrived in New York the same day. Jane felt she had a mandate from Orage to take over the editing, but Jessie protested that she alone was Orage's proper agent in New York.

Toomer mediated the dispute satisfactorily and left for Chicago at the end of November to organize a group. Orage, who assumed Toomer was there weeks earlier, wrote to say that Gurdjieff expected money from the Chicago group. What neither Orage nor Gurdjieff knew was that Toomer was talking again with Mabel Luhan, not only to explain what had become of her money, but to encourage her to renew her offer of her ranch for a Gurdjieff center. An informal Gurdjieff group was already operating in Santa Fe under the auspices of Betty and Meredith Hare, New York friends of Orage who had moved to New Mexico. In New York, Sherman Manchester inherited the office of treasurer of the combined groups from Munson, who cleared Toomer of debt (*Shadows* 116). Before Orage returned from France, Manchester had raised money ranging from five to one hundred dollars per group member for the maintenance of the Institute, added to the $1400 Munson had collected during the summer (*Invention* 134–35). Meanwhile, the French "Sureté générale" filed a report that Gurdjieff had bad credit.

Before Orage left the Prieuré in the late autumn of 1926, he had reviewed the second series, *Meetings with Remarkable Men*. Orage agreed to "translate" (i.e. edit) that text and Gurdjieff told Orage that he proposed to publish the three series at the same time. Orage did not yet know the contents of the third series. He sailed on 14 December with Margaret Naumburg aboard the *Leviathan* and arrived in New York on 20 December. After the Christmas holidays, he initiated a new set of talks on the *Tales*.

1927

Throughout the winter and spring of 1927, Orage's New York group and Toomer's Chicago group were flourishing. With the Schwarzenbachs, Orage organized a German-speaking group in Manhattan (*Invention* 154–55). Before summertime, he succeeded in raising three thousand dollars per month for the Institute, and Toomer smaller monthly amounts. Orage, Toomer and Jane Heap finished editing a full draft of *Beelzebub's Tales* and Orage exposed his commentary on it to his pupils, several of whom recorded his readings carefully. At the Prieuré, meanwhile, Gurdjieff's problems with French authorities were reduced temporarily when on 29 January, he received from the Ministre de l'intèrieur, official permission to reside in France.

Many pupils from both New York and Chicago sought inscriptions for the Prieuré in the coming summer. Ethel Merston had sent to the United States the new fee-schedule: $10 per week for shared rooms and $15 for single rooms, all on Monks' Corridor, third floor. A number of visitors who were to become important to Gurdjieff's work arrived that summer. Payson Loomis, a polyglot who was a Russian specialist, invited his Harvard friend Lincoln Kirstein and collegiate acquaintances Nicholas Putnam and Philip Lasell to join Orage and himself at the Prieuré. In May Putnam had suffered, in Texas, the crash of a plane he was flying from Santa Barbara to New York, and he was glad to take a vacation to rest and recuperate, but that rest would change the course of his life.

The Munsons and Schuyler Jackson (later husband of Laura Riding) were among the New York contingent, Toomer and the poet Melville Cane arrived from Chicago, Jane Heap, Margaret Anderson and Georgette Leblanc came down from Paris, and newly married Rosemary Lillard and Stanley Nott came from England. Gurdjieff had the finished draft before him, brought over by Toomer. The one person Gurdjieff was eager to see was Orage, who remained inexplicably in the United States. So, Gurdjieff worked with Toomer on the text of *Tales* and flattered him with the suggestion that Toomer might replace Orage as editor and promoter of *Tales* as well as *Meetings* for eventual publication. It was imperative, however, to discuss the work with Orage.

The Prieuré was very much a school that summer with Gurdjieff as principal and other members of his inner circle teaching different skills to the numbers of American "guests." Summers from 1925 until 1930 were similar in intensive work, but there were more Americans there that summer who in the future became influential teachers of the Gurdjieff work. Edith Taylor brought a sixteen millimeter motion picture camera with her to the Prieuré and filmed Jeanne de Salzmann and Lili Galumnian directing a dozen or so children on the front lawn in the stop exercise and movements, while Gurdjieff watched from the terrace. Gurdjieff gave special attention to the intellect as well as the physical development of children, and they responded with obvious pleasure and interest. Gurdjieff called the children "candidates for initiation."

Adults followed strict regimes at the Prieuré. They were assigned specific tasks in the main building, the kitchen, gardens, and grounds. Some resented Gurdjieff's rules. Nikolai de Stjernvall recalls that "No one was permitted to leave the grounds of the Prieuré without a valid reason. . . Close to the main gate there was a sort of guard house where someone was usually stationed to maintain order and to carry out orders from the main house," but no one was aware that Daly and Mildred King had been refused entry the summer before. When Jessie was there in 1924, she saw a notice posted in the Prieuré that declared: "All outgoing letters must be put in a special box—all incoming letters must be signed for and names of correspondents given" (*Gurdjieff and Orage* 67-68.) Gurdjieff insisted upon unquestioned obedience to his directives, but in practice he was tolerant.

When Donald Whitcomb came down to breakfast at 9 a.m. in a bathrobe, other residents were furious and said that Gurdjieff should throw Whitcomb out of the Institute. He smiled a refusal. There is no record of Gurdjieff expelling any of his followers from the Institute. He had asked Doris Tyndall to leave for unruly comportment and he excluded some from the Paris Demonstrations if he thought them not ready. The Saturday baths were special occasions. Women bathed first in the bath house and men later. The men profited from the informal atmosphere in the baths to tell stories, often competing in salacious wit. In *Gurdjieff Reconsidered* Roger Lipsey recounts Gurdjieff's pleasure in the stories of Salzmann, the best joker of all (Lipsey, *Gurdjieff Reconsidered* 134)

The animals on the property were taken care of with great care. Gurdjieff had his dog, Philos, by his side most of the time outdoors. A mule Dralfit pulled a plough. There were cats and peacocks running free on the property, and there were ducks and chickens in a large coop. The kitchen garden, tended by residents, supplied the vegetables for meals. Gurdjieff told gardeners that plants responded well to music and speech (*Shadows of Heaven* 112). Everyone was up before six in the morning most days, and preparation and serving of breakfast rotated. Gurdjieff supervised preparations for other meals with residents following his directions. I was told that it was at Saturday evening feasts that Gurdjieff continued his ritual of having toasts made to idiots—aspects of being—among his followers. He himself was the unique idiot and Orage was super idiot.

As the summer waned in 1927, Orage was the most important "adept" absent from the Prieuré. Ethel Merston had sent letter after letter to Orage to say that he was expected right away, but Orage was off in Quebec with Jessie Dwight, Sherman Manchester and Daly King, ostensibly to scout the possibilities for a group in Montreal. Finally, Orage responded to Gurdjieff that he would arrive in the middle of August. He sailed for England on 16 August, arriving in London on the 23rd in time to take part in the final divorce decree from Jean Walker, which was granted on 2 September. On the day his divorce was decreed he sent Jessie a single-word coded wire. He was back in New York on the 16 September, and next day he and Jessie were married in Stamford,

Connecticut, with Robert and Marguerite Schwarzenbach standing as witnesses.

This chronology hides a mystery, for Munson, Nott and Louise Welch all locate him at the Prieuré that summer: Munson said June, Nott and Welch the entire summer (*Invention* 159). Nott was in England most of summer and sailed from Southampton aboard the *Leviathan* on 2 November. Though Orage wrote Jessie daily, sometimes twice in the course of a day, he posted no letters to her from France in either August or in September after the divorce. In the few days between the divorce and his sailing, it is remotely possible that he paid a quick visit to the Prieuré. The fact that he sailed on the *Volendam* to New York from Boulogne-sur-Mer gives some credence to the supposition, but if he did visit there, Jessie never knew it and Gurdjieff never mentioned it.

In fact, Gurdjieff continued to have Ethel Merston send messages to Orage to come to the Prieuré right away. Orage was reluctant. He was not only concerned with his new marital status, but was in the midst of his autumn program, teaching "psychological essays" and writing-classes as well as giving his talks and overseeing Delza Munson's movement classes. When she was in the city, Jessmin Howarth coached New York movements as well as Toomer's movement classes when she stopped in Chicago. In October, Olga de Hartmann wrote a stern letter to Orage telling him to return as soon as possible. On 19 November, Ethel Merston sailed from Southampton on the *Mauretania* for New York with new material to be edited and a message from Gurdjieff. Orage decided to go to the Institute after Christmas.

Gurdjieff indicated the reason behind the call to Orage was that on 6 November 1927 he saw that "the form of the exposition of my thoughts in these writings could be understood exclusively by those readers who, in one way or another, were already acquainted with the peculiar form of my mentation. But every other reader . . . would understand nearly nothing. . . . it would be necessary to write in order that it might be accessible to the understanding of everyone" (*Life Is Real* 5). In short, after looking over his work, he realized that the style of the existing draft was inadequate on two grounds. First, it failed to incorporate his self and sound his voice to reflect the orality that, as he had learned throughout his youth, conveys essential lore. Secondly, *Tales* appeared as a translation, when he would have it be an English language text in all its stylistic particulars, a text that could serve as the base for translations into other languages: French, German and Russian; thus, the urgent need to have Orage at his side.

9

7 January 1928–11 November 1930:
Depression

1928

Orage and his bride, Jessie, sailed from New York on New Year's Eve 1927 and arrived at the Prieuré on 7 January 1928. Gurdjieff received them well and the supper served that night after midnight was capped with Gurdjieff's favorite dessert, melon. The next morning, he met with Orage, Jessie and Edith Taylor at the Café Henri IV in Fontainebleau to set a work schedule for rewriting the entire first series. From that day until the 29 February, the four worked as a team up to eighteen hours per day, in Paris, Fontainebleau, on the road, in restaurants, with a break only on 13 January to celebrate Gurdjieff's birthday and the Orthodox New Year. Gurdjieff implies that from the first day of 1928, he worked half of his waking hours on ideas which he would develop in the third series, and half of his waking hours until his name day on 23 April on a variety of writing activities (*Life Is Real* 42–43). Full-time work on the revision of the first series was the task at hand.

Though Gurdjieff and Orage worked speedily and efficiently together on the basic shift of style Gurdjieff sought, there was tension between Gurdjieff and Jessie who was not happy with the little time Orage spared her during road trips and hotel stopovers. She wrote in her diary one evening that at lunch in Paris earlier that day, Gurdjieff called her a squirming idiot and candidate for a harmful one, adding that she should not try to keep Orage, his "super idiot" from him (*Gurdjieff and Orage* 148). Jessie sulked for the rest of the stay, but that did not in the least discourage Orage from the task at hand. When he sailed from Cherbourg with Jessie on the last day of the leap year February with page corrections, he assured Gurdjieff that a new typed draft of the *Tales* would be sent back to him in a short time. Gurdjieff, for the rest of his "will-task" period before his name day, worked on the third series. He was already satisfied with Orage's editing of *Meetings*, though he would eventually add some lines later to "The Material Question."

It is easy to lose sight of the person of Gurdjieff behind a banal chronology of the dates, events, and movements that fill a biography. One can presume that he possessed certain virtues: mechanical inventiveness, artistic creativity, powers of persuasion, medical and psychological skills, but these fail to characterize the humanity of the man. One can wonder how he attracted so many people of diverse bloods and backgrounds. That he possessed hypnotic powers is obvious, that he used them for the good of others is apparent. One aspect of Gurdjieff's character that is not recorded sufficiently, however, was his paternal comportment. Gurdjieff was father to all those children who "knew him in the skin." There were always at least a dozen about him at the Prieuré, and he enjoyed their company, just as they felt comfortable in his. There was a "purity" of communication between him and the children. There were no social, psychological, emotional, or intellectual impediments in the way. The essence of the young ones who lived with him was not yet laminated irrevocably with "personality," the stereotypical influences of social convention, school and church, for example.

Gurdjieff gave talks to children and convinced them that life must be played as a game without fixed rules. One must make one's own rules rather than be ruled by those of others. Gurdjieff told children not to be passive to adult instruction. They must "do" rather than "be done to." The children at the Prieuré thrived under his care, and the effects of that care permeated their being. His methods of engaging his energy with children were not, perhaps, noticeably distinct from the way he dealt with adults, but his relations with children were intransitive—reciprocal, if you will—while much of his dealing with adults was transitive—one way.

There were many young children at the Prieuré in 1928. Among them, Fritz and Tom Peters, Valia Anastasieff and Luba, Dmitri's eldest daughter, were in their teens, and Luba's sisters Genia and Lida, Nikolai de Stjernvall, Mikhail de Salzmann, Toly Merkurov, Iréne and André Lapina and others were under ten. He considered all of them "his" children. They all played games about the property. The most popular "stop" was recorded by Edith Taylor on her movie camera in 1927. They all did movement exercises freely without adult direction under the eyes of Gurdjieff sitting on the terrace or in the conservatory.

Gurdjieff was never known to use force in correcting, upbraiding or chastising a child. He expressed disfavor with his look. One advantage young children had over adults was that they did not bear grudges or stamp impressions in their memories. When Dmitri's daughter Lida was serving Gurdjieff his afternoon coffee once, she showed him proudly the play watch someone had given her. With a stern look, he took it off her wrist, threw it on the terrace and stepped on it. Lida ran crying to her father. The next day, when Lida brought the coffee, Gurdjieff reached into his pocket and handed her a real watch. She was only seven or eight at the time, and perhaps the smile that accompanied the watch was more meaningful than the time it registered. The distinction between what is real and what is illusory was a forceful lesson. Another was applying the individual will to overcome distaste. He taught children to accept and appreciate what they had learned earlier to disdain and dislike.

Gurdjieff's smile and sparkle of eyes had a magical effect on all. His was a limitless generosity of spirit. Often, older children would push a younger one to approach Gurdjieff while he was having his coffee to beg for a morsel of the sweets Gurdjieff had before him. Gurdjieff would throw buns and chocolates at the fleeing child, but it was not really "at" the child, but "for" him or her and the others who would scramble for a share. Gurdjieff talked often to children and addressed them as if he deemed well their capacity to understand. Though they would not always understand immediately what he meant, the sense of his words would in time often permeate their consciousness.

Because they were not yet "spoiled," young children came to consider the conditions and values under which they lived at the Prieuré as "normal." They accepted without any qualms the concept that they possessed a plurality of being, what Gurdjieff called "I" s. They knew without having to learn from parents or schools that "I" and "it" are conflicting aspects of being. Every child who lived for any length of time under Gurdjieff's care grew up observing himself or herself automatically. If Gurdjieff and those children who had known him "in the skin" met later in life, they responded automatically to the language of their Prieuré contact. Children also felt that Gurdjieff could see into their inner being. If parents punished children's acts, Gurdjieff did not because he seemed to see a deeper and innocent core of being.

It was not so with adults, and demands made upon him by his pupils seemed to him informed often by an essential misunderstanding of who he was and what he taught. As late as 1928, Orage petitioned Gurdjieff constantly to give him the key to *Tales*, certain that the "key" to the text was a key to a hidden primordial secret of life. Toomer was less insistent, if only because he believed, as Gurdjieff had told him, that the "secret" is hidden within him (*Shadows* 131 note). Curiously, Gurdjieff got along very well with the young Nick Putnam who moved into the Prieuré in 1928, because Putnam expressed no demands of Gurdjieff except to enjoy his company.

In May 1928 Edith Taylor found herself pregnant, and she expressed to Gurdjieff expectations of his paternal care. Perhaps because of her solicitations, Gurdjieff decided, "because of a certain action toward me on the part of one of the people near me, I decided . . . to remove from my eyesight all those who by this or that make my life too comfortable" (*Life Is Real* 45). It is more likely that Gurdjieff meant that it was time to send people away whom he no longer needed for demonstrations and other "work" activities. He had said repeatedly that pupils were not there to follow him, but to follow the directions he pointed; that he was a helper for others to achieve their life aims. Once pupils had obtained what they needed for their self-development, it was time to leave. The one thing he did not want was for pupils to become attached to him as a person.

In the case of Edith Taylor, he did not send her away, but kept her close at the Prieurè. To "regularize" her social position, he arranged her marriage with Caesar Zwaska (former assistant to Margaret Anderson in Chicago at *The Little Review*) at the Town Hall of Fontainebleau on 31 August 1928. When Taylor gave birth to a daughter in Rouen on 13 November, he gave the girl his mother's name, Evdokia.

Meanwhile, across the Atlantic in June 1928, the Orages had left on a belated honeymoon that served as well as an informal reconnaissance for possible group sites in the Southwest and West. They motored through the South to Santa Fe where they visited Mabel Luhan and other former members of Orage's New York groups. They met New Mexico Senator Bronson Cutting and Governor H. W. Hockenhull, both of whom showed interest in Orage's outline of Social Credit as a political and economic panacea for social class injustice. They went from there to California, where Orage gave talks at Big Sur and in San Francisco. His lectures on the West Coast drew interested crowds, and the press reports were favorable; Ansel Adams took portrait photos of Orage, and Charlie Chaplin received him in Los Angeles. In November they boarded a train for Chicago to visit Toomer, and then returned to New York to re-organize the groups there before the end of the year.

After the departure of the Orages from France, the finances of the Institute seemed to be in good shape. Orage had sent $3000 to Gurdjieff soon after his return to the United States, though Olga de Hartmann wrote back to Orage asking for a further $10,000. Though it would appear that Gurdjieff was in a position to rest from his labors, his economy of energy did not allow for unproductive interludes, and his economy of money in the hands of both Ethel Merston and Olga de Hartmann was a constant confusion to Orage and Toomer. While Orage's New York group had a treasury and a committee to audit its accounts, the Institute had no formal treasurer and money was deposited haphazardly in at least three Paris banks: Lloyds, Morgan, and Barclays. In the summer of 1928 Metz and Loomis wrote Orage and Toomer from the Prieuré vaunting plans for a swimming pool and other new amenities, though Loomis's reports were less sanguine than Metz's.

While Orage and Jessie were visiting Santa Fe in the summer of 1928, Gurdjieff's affairs took a turn for the worse. Orage and Toomer received word that Gurdjieff's creditors were calling in his debt on the Prieuré. It was said he was still in debt for 350,000 francs (*March* 52). Earlier in the spring Gurdjieff had sent Edith Taylor to Paris to solicit funds from her friends there, including Gertrude Stein. When she came back empty handed, he sent her to Lady Rothermere in Fribourg, Switzerland. After a tiring motorcar voyage, she received a cordial reception from her friend Bea, who told Edith that she had terminated contributing to the Institute. Instead she was supporting Krishnamurti and T. S. Eliot's *Criterion*.

On 9 June, Orage sent a letter to Toomer saying: "I have a feeling something will happen to the Prieuré this summer. Supplies are short. I should have liked one of us—and not me—

to be there to witness it." He had no plans, of course, to be there. "I suppose you can't contribute immediately substantially toward the sum of $10,000 which G has called for? No? Well, anyhow, I send in the S.O.S." (*Invention* 185). Orage had told Toomer a year earlier that it was clear to him that Americans would be the Institute's sole support, and while the summers of 1926 and 1927 had brought a good deal of money to the Prieuré, Orage had reason to suspect that fewer Americans would visit the Institute in the summer of 1928.

Olga de Hartmann says Gurdjieff decided to revisit America at Orage's insistence (*Our Life* 129), but Orage had no reason to invite Gurdjieff. Gurdjieff might well have wanted to take stock of the condition of the New York and Chicago groups. When he made his travel plans, Olga reported that he invited only her and Thomas de Hartmann to accompany him. His purpose was to make *Beelzebub's Tales* known to a broad readership. By this time, however, both the first and second series were known to Orage's and Toomer's American pupils. Though Olga does not mention it, Gurdjieff had sent Metz ahead to New York on the White Star Line *SS Majestic* Tourist third class from Cherbourg on 9 January1929. He arrived in New York on the 16th, a day or two before Gurdjieff and the Hartmanns sailed from France. Metz, thirty one years of age at the time, was in effect Gurdjieff's regular American secretary.

Gurdjieff's Second Visit to America

On board the *Paris* en route to New York, Olga wrote, Gurdjieff told Hartmann that it was time to organize his life independently in Paris (*Our Life* 129). He had already told him in Tbilisi and Constantinople to give up his music. This time, Gurdjieff's insistence was to continue for the entire time they were in the United States. It is not out of place to remark that Olga had become less and less esteemed by other pupils since their arrival in France. She displayed openly a proprietary attitude in her relations with Gurdjieff, seemingly guarding him from others. She let it be known, unwittingly perhaps, that she and Gurdjieff shared information and ideas that others did not have. Orage once wrote Jessie at the Prieuré to advise her that, if she wished to get an idea to Gurdjieff, she should tell it to Olga as a secret, since Olga held no "secrets" from Gurdjieff. A scan of her memoirs gives the reader a sense of her "exclusive relationship with her master." One can assume that Gurdjieff's repeated demands to Hartmann to leave his music were steps toward an eventual distancing of the two from him.

The three docked in the Hudson River on 23 January 1929 where they found Orage awaiting at the pier. Muriel Draper hosted a party for Gurdjieff that evening at her apartment at 312 E. 53rd Street, and in the course of conversation, Gurdjieff mentioned to the group his urgent need of a considerable amount of money, at least $10,000, for the Institute.

One paper had noticed his arrival and under the headline "Harmonizer of Mankind arrives Here for Visit" and a photo of Gurdjieff in a fedora, reported:

Wearing an Astrakhan fez, Georges Gurdjieff, leader of the Institute for the Harmonious Development of Man, arrived yesterday aboard the French Line Paris. He explained painfully in difficult English that his program for the harmonious development of man was somewhat arrested by his close escape from a complete demolition in an automobile accident. Since then, he said, he is lessening the work in his program.

Before the war Gurdjieff, who is a Greek, founded a group in Constantinople, later in London and Paris and more recently in America. His devotees gathered around their leader in a bare barracks outside Paris and listened to his discourses on the beliefs of the world. The barren building was furnished within with a luxury that was Oriental, despite the bleak exterior. During the day the members of his cult, weaving rude and coarse clothes, would do manual work or cultivate them selves with rhythmic exercises.

In the week that followed, Gurdjieff and Orage met with Mabel Luhan to ask her if she would renew her offer of her ranch as a work center. She refused flatly on the grounds that the $15,000 she had offered three years earlier was not accounted for. Besides, she had decided to lease her property to a Dude Ranch operator. In February, Gurdjieff gave a demonstration at Carnegie Hall, using the New York group movement pupils. In the course of the evening, Gurdjieff told the audience that Orage had been a faithful steward during his five-year absence. The next day, Orage wrote Toomer to say Gurdjieff intended to go to Chicago where he expected $1000 from the group there. Gurdjieff made a brief visit to Chicago a few days later to observe the group activities there. He flattered Toomer with his observations.

It may have been during this trip that Muriel Draper's young son Paul was struck by a bus in New York City, and was hospitalized in a serious condition. Muriel went to Child's to find Gurdjieff, but he was not there, so she left a message at his apartment. A short while later, he called her and told her not to worry. She told him, however, that the attending doctor said only an operation would save Paul, but Gurdjieff insisted that it was not necessary. Without the operation, Paul recovered quickly (*Invention* 211).

On 8 March Orage met with Mabel and Tony Luhan to explain Gurdjieff's monetary needs. Mabel was favorable to further discussions if they included Toomer (*Gurdjieff and Orage* 154–55). On 25 March, Toomer arrived in New York to speak with Gurdjieff about the Chicago group and to give him checks totaling $1050 and a pledge for more. Gurdjieff was justifiably anxious about his American operations. While he expressed satisfaction with Toomer's work, he was not altogether pleased with what he saw in

New York. First of all, Orage was now a family man with a wife in her last months of pregnancy. Secondly, Orage had been teaching his "psychological exercises" and giving writing classes. Gurdjieff had reason to feel that Orage's stewardship was coming to an end. Though several members of the New York groups indicated that they would go to the Institute in the summer of 1929, Orage would not. Toomer agreed to go but told Orage that he was planning at the same time to resume his literary career.

On the morning of 5 April, Gurdjieff and the Hartmanns sailed homeward on the *Paris*. Within two hours the ship ran aground off Jones Beach and did not float free until three in the afternoon. It was an inauspicious omen, perhaps, for throughout the voyage Gurdjieff put more pressure on Hartmann to leave the Prieuré and set up a household in Paris. Olga's parents would have to move out of the Paradou as well (*Our Life* 130). In June, after Gurdjieff told Olga her husband was a pederast, the Hartmanns moved to Paris, though Olga continued to go to the Prieuré for the next few months to do tasks for Gurdjieff.

After his return from the United States, Gurdjieff started new projects at the Prieuré. He had Metz write Toomer to say: "G said very nice things about your group. He was impressed by their earnestness and general attitude. I'll tell you details when you arrive." A week later, Metz wrote that the Prieuré was being renovated, and in June he wrote that construction of a swimming pool had begun and added: "Monks' corridor would now be called millionaires' corridor." Metz's letters suggest that Gurdjieff was flattering Toomer in view of turning over more responsibility to him in America. Toomer replied in May with a check for $200.

Gurdjieff had expected more Americans than actually arrived that June and July. Payson Loomis and Nick Putnam were there, and a Swiss-German art student Louise Goepfert (born 1900 in Frankfurt), whom Gurdjieff had met in New York the previous winter, arrived to take up duties as translator and typist for the German-language version of *Tales*. Armed with letters of introduction by Orage, Louise Welch, Allan Brown and his wife, and the actor Edwin Wolfe with his future wife Helen Hunt all made brief forays to the Prieuré. Edith Taylor was there with her daughter Eve ("Petey").

Toomer arrived but seemed more intent on finishing a novel, *Transatlantic*, based on his sea voyage. He had begun it on board and tried to have the *Compagnie Générale Transatlantique* pay him a stipend for the publicity. One of the characters in the novel was based on Gurdjieff. Perhaps Toomer's apparent lack of enthusiasm for the real work incited Jeanne de Salzmann's remark to him after he arrived at the Prieuré: "Once you were an eagle. Now you are a sheep" (*Shadows* 138).

It appears that Mildred Gillars was also there that summer. After the end of World War II, Gillars, known as "Axis Sally" for making radio broadcasts in favor of the Axis, testified at her trial for treason that she and Bernard Metz "had both been more or less students with the philosopher." She was in France for several months in 1929 as well as 1933, when the Institute was no longer functioning. On 10 October 1929, Tom and Fritz Peters sailed from France on the *Leviathan* with Margaret Anderson, and were never to be at the Prieuré again.

Louise Goepfert recalls that after she completed the German translation of the first book of *Tales* that fall, she and Gurdjieff went to Frankfurt to read some chapters to Alfons Paquet, and afterwards to Berlin for two weeks of readings. Gurdjieff also announced that readings in various languages would be given in various places: in French by Jeanne de Salzmann, English by Orage, German by Goepfert, and Russian by Lili Galumnian Chaverdian. The same persons would oversee translations from the base English version (Galumnian's 1933 Russian version was published in Toronto in 2000).

In the fall of 1929, with debts accumulating in inverse proportion to the numbers of Americans contributing to the Institute, Gurdjieff planned to return in the winter to the United States. He took a brief trip to Berlin with Olga de Hartmann, perhaps to have passages from the completed German translation read there to remnants of his 1922 group.

To gather information for Gurdjieff about the New York group, Loomis sailed on the *Mauretania* from Cherbourg 17 December 1929 and arrived in New York on 23 December 1929. Six weeks later Gurdjieff dispatched Metz to New York to make arrangements with both Orage and Toomer that would guarantee enough money to cover his own costs of the trip. Metz left aboard the White Star Line *SS Majestic* from Cherbourg on 12 February 1930 arriving in New York on 18 February 1930. Then, while Gurdjieff was making his own plans, the New York Stock Exchange accelerated its long descent after the market's initial "crash" on Black Tuesday, 29 October 1929. On the day appointed for his embarkation aboard the *Bremen*, Gurdjieff went with Olga de Hartmann to the boat train at the Gare Saint Lazare. Waiting to board the train, they were drinking coffee in a café when Gurdjieff suddenly demanded that Olga and Thomas accompany him. When she demurred, he demanded that she come in a week, and when she said she could not, he said that he would never see her again (*Our Life* 132). Five years earlier it was Ouspensky who left, now the Hartmanns. Next would be Orage.

Third Visit to America

Though he had sailed on 18 February, a day later than Metz, the two arrived on the same day. When Gurdjieff walked down the gangway from the *Bremen*, accompanied by Jeanne de Salzmann and Louise Goepfert, he was greeted by Louise Welch and Dorothy Wolfe who conveyed him straight away to the Great Northern Hotel. That evening, Orage and Gurdjieff walked together to Muriel Draper's apartment where she and some sixty-five group members greeted them (*Orage with Gurdjieff in America* 81–86). The topic of discussion that evening was the scheduling of reading from *Tales* during weekdays for a scale of fees. Curiously, Welch says that on Fridays Hartmann would play music (*Orage with Gurdjieff* 87), but he was in Paris.

Orage made it clear in conversations in the days that followed that he intended to re-assume his editorial career in England. He assured Gurdjieff that the New York groups would be directed by pupils that had been well-trained over the past five years. Toomer came from Chicago and took up residence in the Hotel Brevoort on lower Fifth Avenue and had several conversations with Gurdjieff. Daly King joined some discussions, though he continued to distrust Gurdjieff (as his exposition of Orage's teaching in *The Oragean Version* makes clear). He considered Orage the better man and better teacher.

In a last private interview with Orage that winter, according to Jessie Orage's diary, Gurdjieff congratulated his "super idiot" for having such faithful pupils and urged him to dispatch as many pupils to the Institute as possible for the summer of 1930. Orage cautioned against false expectations, considering the state of the economy and the caution of most group members. What Orage meant by "caution" was the reluctance of many of Orage's pupils to shift their allegiance from Orage to Gurdjieff. They knew Gurdjieff's ideas well, but they knew them principally through the agency of a man with whom they had become close socially as well as intellectually.

On 14 March 1930, four weeks before Gurdjieff's departure, Carol Robinson wrote to Jane Heap news of the situation in New York. After telling Heap about the contents of Orage's recently published *Psychological Exercises*, she writes:

> Caesar [Zwaska] says "G" and party sail back to France April 12. No trip to Chicago —but that plan may be changed

several times. Absolute quiet—the family like Lillian, Loomis, Gertrude works at the apt with O[rage] on book 4 languages. "G" has been writing day & night. Orage's group met on Tuesday night—he didn't seem to know what to do—finally someone went out & phoned G—was he coming—he had not planned to—it was 10 oclock by that time—but they all fit in taxis & came to Muriels—read a chapter, had music, then he announced a plan—break up such groups forever. None of us in N.Y. of any use to him now—all candidates for the madhouse but he felt a great responsibility & an obligation. So stop everything and start afresh. Those which come & read book—he will give the right chap. To the right person—from 2-8 Sat & Sun. which entitles one to privilege of coming Mon. eve to discuss the ideas with him—questions & music. So I'll have that for 2 or 3 times. Monday he said is esoteric, and Tues. even, closed to us, for brand new pupils—exoteric, Thursday night is German reading.

Took Mme Salzmann out for tea yesterday. They have been so pushed into work that they could not come down to 28 St. though I've suggested it. She wants me to take her to Wall St & downtown & for some shopping. [Blanche] Grant talks with her? Goepfert is too busy and tired to talk to anyone. I like her too. Mme. S. says all the Orage-Gurd counter manifestations of no importance at all—very good for the group at the moment etc. Jessie is quite impossible. Lives extravagantly—keeps 3 servants & a $285 apartment!

Do please write soon how you are & your letters will be forwarded. I will see Florence [Cane?]—not surprised at her letter to you. After 4 years of hearing about the ideas from you and living at Fontainebleau & hasn't made a dent, you can't ever expect anything. My dear mother is in the hospital with a broken leg—or the hip—may be many months—too sad. I have the feeling if I can live through the next 4 or 5 weeks, all will be well? Love and kisses. Carol (unpublished papers of Carol Robinson in possession of Barbara Walker Todd Smyth)

It is clear from Robinson's remarks that Gurdjieff was already restructuring the New York group. He approved of the German group that met at Marguerite Schwarzenbach's apartment at 9 East 62nd Street for a fee of $2.50. Orage was concerned about the morale of his groups as well as the state of mind of his wife who feared that Gurdjieff would succeed in wresting her "man" away from her. It also appears that Orage's pupils were in a mood of rebellion against the master of their master. At a meeting on April Fools Day, Muriel suddenly interrupted a reading and asked Gurdjieff: "Is this group so conscious that nothing else but hearing this book read is necessary?" Gurdjieff feigned great anger and uttered insults at Muriel, but she replied to his tirade by saying that she, too, was angry, but his anger did not answer her question. Gurdjieff looked sternly at her, and then gave an explanation why reading the book was important (*Gurdjieff and Orage* 163).

It is clear that Gurdjieff foresaw problems with the future control of the teaching in New York. He intended this visit as an occasion to test the work atmosphere in New York. The full effects of the Depression were not yet felt, but people were reluctant to commit their money to the Institute. A few months later, reflecting on the consequences for the Institute of the "Depression," Gurdjieff wrote: "When I first had the idea of developing my antique business in America [with Jean Herter] on a large scale, I estimated and was fully convinced that this project of mine would yield a profit that would suffice not only to pay off all my accumulated debts, but would also enable me, without depending on anyone, to publish the first series of my writings—which I counted on having finished by then—and after that to give all my time to the second series. But unfortunately this unforeseen American crisis has plunged me, as Mullah Nassr Eddin would

177

say, into such a 'deep galosh' that today I can scarcely see a single streak of daylight out of it" (*Meetings* 300).

Gurdjieff sailed from New York on 12 April and three days later Muriel gave a going-away party for the Orages who sailed for England on the 22nd. For the remainder of the spring Schuyler Jackson directed the principal group. Marguerite Schwarzenbach continued the German-language group she had initiated in 1927 with her husband Robert, who had died the previous August.

The Prieuré in the summer of 1930 received few guests. Madame Ouspensky made an occasional visit from Paris. Her daughter Helene Gorb Savitsky ("Lenochka") had given birth there to a daughter, Tatiana Mikhailovna Savitskaya ("Tania") in May 1929. In a Paris café about this time Alexander de Salzmann met the French writer René Daumal, whose attraction to Gurdjieff's ideas saved him from a number of serious psychological problems. In later years Daumal was to say that Gurdjieff was his "life buoy." The association of Daumal with Gurdjieff is the topic of an article on 1 March 1954 in the *Les Cahiers du Sud*.

At the Prieuré, Payson Loomis had settled in as Gurdjieff's translator and editor. He reviewed the manuscript of *Meetings* and worked with Gurdjieff on the third series, *Life Is Real*. Fred Leighton, a close friend of Toomer who had moved his Indian Trading Post from Chicago to New York City, spent most of the summer at the Institute and sent regular letters back to Toomer with news, most of which concerned financial problems. Gurdjieff needed $18,000 immediately to finish his writing. Orage had arranged before his departure to have $15,000 available for Gurdjieff, and Leighton told Toomer that the rest was expected from him. When it did not come right away, Leighton reported to Toomer that Gurdjieff called Chicago "a ball of shit" and Toomer "already-sitting-in-an-old-American-galosh." Leighton warned that Gurdjieff was planning to return to the U.S. in November.

10

11 November 1930–13 March 1931:
Losing America

Gurdjieff's Fourth Visit to America

Gurdjieff sailed from Cherbourg on the *Bremen* and arrived
in New York on 11 November, accompanied by Louise Goepfert,
Payson Loomis, Lucia Kapanadze, Jeanne de Salzmann and her
son "Michel" (Alexander de Salzmann remained in Paris, either
uninvited or unwilling to accompany his wife). That evening, according to Gurdjieff in his Introduction to *Life Is Real*, he listened
to a reading at Carnegie Hall given to the New York groups assembled by "Mr. S" (either Israel Solon or Stanley Spiegelberg). He
interrupted the reading to explain briefly that he was in New York
to verify certain suspicions he had about the nature and operations
of the group, and concluded with his opinion that those in the audience were candidates for a "lunatic asylum" (*Life Is Real* 70).

Metz and Leonid de Stjernvall arrived a day later on the
France. On the next crossing of the *Paris* on 3 December, Elizaveta
de Stjernvall arrived with her son Nikolai for her first and only
visit to the United States. Nikolai recalls that they were met at
the boat by Payson Loomis in his Rolls-Royce and put up at his
home on West 59th Street (*My Dear Father* 26). The 204 West
59th Street building consisted of twelve apartments, one of which
Gurdjieff was occupying. His was in the $450 per month catego-
ry. Others went for as low as $75 per month. There was a Child's
restaurant only a few steps away on Columbus Circle. Loomis was
staying at the time in the Hotel Woodward on 55th St, since he
had let others occupy his own home at 755 Park Avenue.

Gurdjieff decided to have professional photo portraits made
and ordered Goepfert to find the best photographer in town for
the next day, but one day's notice was not enough for the best.

Instead, Louise contacted a German friend who worked for Condé Nast who agreed to do the job (*March* 50–51). So, the next day Stjernvall, Jeanne de Salzmann, Louise Goepfert and the two boys sat for Antonie (Toni) Von Horn in her studio (why Nikolai's mother Elizaveta's place was occupied by Goepfert is a mystery). Pleased with what he saw of Toni Von Horn's work, Gurdjieff had her take several individual portraits of him. The next day, Stjernvall and Gurdjieff shaved their beards. Gurdjieff had let his grow for the past year, and it was already full. The act was an emblematic signal of the fresh start he intended to make in New York financially and ideologically. He explained later that he had come to America at the end of 1930 to review "the financial question" and to "uproot . . . this evil occasioned by the misunderstanding of my ideas" (*Life Is Real* 66).

His financial situation was complicated further immediately after his arrival. In the classified section of the *New York Times* of 12 November appeared: "Lost. Portfolio Brown marked G. Gurdjieff containing typewritten manuscript left in taxi Tuesday midnight. Reward offered for return to 204 West 59th Street." Did he lose his portfolio on his way to the hotel after his arrival, and if he lost it at midnight, how did he get an advertisement into the *Times* the next day? One can assume that the manuscript was a draft of the third series.

A day or so later he had Loomis write a letter to Toomer in the name of him who is "neither a half-baked American nor a possessor of the organ Kundabuffer, but a descendant of "possessors of the spiritualized presences of three-centred beings." The letter explained that the reason he was in America was Toomer's financial debt to him. The Prieuré was liable to be seized for debt, and he required a monthly allocation of $1500 until October 1931 to secure it. He reminded Toomer that he had borrowed money in France on the basis of Chicago's prior promise to send him $5000 (*Shadows* 147–49). Toomer was justifiably upset by the tone and tenor of the letter, especially when it came at a moment when his own group was prospering in the work but adding nothing to his own pocketbook. Before going to Chicago to visit Toomer and his group at the end of the year, Gurdjieff re-grouped the New York pupils into exoteric, mesoteric and esoteric categories. After giving the talks recorded in *Life Is Real*, whose contents none of the people who attended could recall to me, Gurdjieff took a train to Chicago after Christmas.

Then, when Orage, his wife Jessie and son Richard arrived on the *George Washington* on 8 January 1931 with a young nurse, Denise Fairall, the stage was set for a succession of confrontations that would have Gurdjieff and Orage go separate ways, well almost. To grasp what happened between Gurdjieff's arrival in New York City on 11 November 1930 and his departure on 13 March 1931 would appear both a fascinating episode in the lives of two close friends and a puzzle why they parted ways. I say "would appear" because exactly what happened in the complex play between the two during those months, particularly during the first two weeks of January, could not be understood by those who did not know both men personally, and was enigmatic to even those who were close to both.

What happened between Orage and Gurdjieff constituted an axial turn in both their fortunes. One is tempted to say an epiphany. What is difficult for the historian is to reconcile the pieces of testimony of Jessie Orage in her daily diary entries, Louise Goepfert in her memoirs, and by Gurdjieff himself in *Life Is Real*. Orage left no record, as was his wont throughout his life, but his part in the drama is scripted, ironically, by Gurdjieff, and Gurdjieff's words about the split of two who considered themselves brothers are painfully difficult to plumb for sense. It is difficult from this distance to comprehend the extraordinary "power" Gurdjieff exercised over those who were in contact with him personally. That he was held in awe by persons of various artistic and scientific persuasions is well documented. It is easy enough for current spectators to assume he was a charlatan with malefic hypnotic powers. As such he is described by the psychologist Anthony Storr who judges Gurdjieff among the most dangerous of teachers. "Gurdjieff was a dictator," he writes. "He had the capacity to completely humiliate his disciples so that grown men would burst into tears . . . Those less infatuated are likely to think that, like other gurus, Gurdjieff enjoyed the exercise of power for its own sake" (*Feet of Clay* 28). Sir Frank Kermode, eminent critic and student of the Bible, has recently pronounced that "some gurus are wrong and others are dangerous: Gurdjieff is both wrong and dangerous" (*Shadows* 5). Neither presents evidence to back up their ill-considered judgments, and scores of books by sober critics who know something about the Gurdjieff work say otherwise.

The one certain fact is that Orage, after Ouspensky and Hartmann, left Gurdjieff. To those who feel that Orage had deserted his master, it should be recalled that Gurdjieff did not insist that his pupils should devote their lives to following him. On the contrary, as Hartmann recalls, Gurdjieff made it a practice to send those people who have reached a certain stage in the work back into the world (*Our Life*, revised 1992 edition vii, 253–55). The basic premise of Fourth Way work was its stipulation that pupils need not abrogate worldly occupations. All three men had careers to pursue outside of the circle of Gurdjieff's power.

Other participants in the drama—Welch, King, Romilly, Benson, Manchester, Metz, Robinson and March —commented on the events, and others not present but aware of the happenings—Nott, Heap, Toomer, Howarth—recorded their impressions of them. None were privy to Gurdjieff's own account written shortly after and circulated some years later before the third series was published a quarter of a century after his death. Both Webb and Moore accept Gurdjieff's version of events in *Life Is Real* as the "truth," even though much of it is carefully crafted fiction.

Perhaps the most enigmatic feature of Gurdjieff's Third Series is the place and importance he assigns to Orage in his narrative account of happenings in late 1930 and early 1931. Rarely is a pupil or associate more than simply mentioned by name in his writings, but he writes the character of Orage into the lesson embedded in his "esoteric" series. To appreciate the reason why Gurdjieff has Orage play a crucial role in Gurdjieff's Third Series, one need recall the personal relationship between the two that developed over the years since October 1922.

During the fourteen months Orage worked at the Prieuré before departing in December 1923, the two men developed a close friendship and efficient work rapport despite different cultural and language backgrounds. They came to laugh together, exchange jokes and anecdotes, although Gurdjieff was known to keep a certain emotional distance from his associates. The two seemed to understand each other well, though Orage's native English and school French would not seem to be compatible with Gurdjieff's rudimentary French and slight passive understanding of English at the time. Not even the early pupil and loyal associate Leonid de Stjernvall was a close friend; nor was Ouspensky, though Gurdjieff honored him as being a good fellow with whom to drink vodka. Putting aside the associations with other Gurdjieff exposés in *Meetings*, he never had another friend he cherished as much as Orage.

From January 1924 until the end of the decade, Orage alone was Gurdjieff's voice and spirit in America. When Gurdjieff turned to writing *All and Everything*, he chose Orage to supervise and edit the translation for publication. When on 7 November 1927, while looking over a complete draft, Gurdjieff decided to revise *Beelzebub's Tales to His Grandson*, he summoned Orage to the Prieuré. Because Orage had married Jessie Dwight two months earlier and was loath to leave his nuptial quarters and abandon his New York group in midst of his new series of talks, Orage felt, perhaps for the first time, some reluctance to follow his master's directive.

On his third visit to New York in early 1930, Gurdjieff planned to consolidate the New York City groups and to control the raising of funds for the Institute. The market Crash of 29 October 1929 had already prompted a diminution of contributions from American pupils, and the birth of Orage and Jessie's son Richard six months earlier had turned Orage's commitment to his new family as well as to his professional interests, including writing and teaching psychological studies. Gurdjieff had taken measure of the strong bonds Orage had forged with members of his groups. More than an instructor, Orage had become a friend of his group members, and Gurdjieff deemed such close emotional as well as intellectual ties impediments to an "objective" stance toward the teaching.

Behind Orage's decision to return to his editing career that he communicated to Gurdjieff in February 1930 was a desire to raise his son in his native land. Another influential factor was his wife Jessie's desire to lead a "normal" married life. It seems that before Gurdjieff sailed back to France in April 1930, he and Orage had outlined together a strategy that would allow Orage to leave honorably while keeping the Gurdjieff groups intact. Gurdjieff was already exploring the possibility of emigrating to the United States where he would have the New York City branch of the Institute in profitable operation. Regardless of how much members of the American groups knew of Gurdjieff's intentions they were anxious about relations between the two. Orage had notified them of his family and career intentions, but they had no idea what Gurdjieff's plans for them were after Orage's departure. Earlier in 1930, Gurdjieff felt no need to modify Toomer's work in Chicago. In fact, having Toomer assume control of the American groups was an option for him, though Toomer at the Prieuré during the summer of 1929 had indicated an intention to return to his writing.

Before Orage left for England in the late spring of 1930 to establish a new journal, *The New English Weekly*, he had promised his New York friends that he would return to America at the end of the year to settle his affairs. During the summer and fall of 1930 he was petitioned by members of his New York groups for advice on how to negotiate with Gurdjieff who they understood was returning to America to completely re-organize the work. On 11 June, Orage answered a letter from Allan Brown asking if Orage had renounced the work. Orage replied that he had not, but reiterated his decision to leave Gurdjieff, saying that Gurdjieff has "ceased to teach me" (*Orage with Gurdjieff* 86). Whether this was the truth or a pretense to justify a withdrawal from his role as Gurdjieff's agent is impossible to confirm, but, obviously, Orage had not told his group members of any strategy he and Gurdjieff might have worked out.

In the fall he replied to an inquiry by Israel Solon, acting secretary of the New York groups, about Gurdjieff's intention to break the New York group dependence on him: "If after these years G. himself comes along and, declaring that I have failed him as a good servant, proposes to take over the group himself, or to nominate a new agent in my place, I certainly have no complaint to make . . . I've not been, in relation to the New York group, just an agent of G. Perhaps that has been my failure from his point of view. . . I, if you like to say so, fell in love with the group personally . . . and in the end, I was more disposed to side with the group than with my master" (*Orage with Gurdjieff* 114). Orage went on to say that he never had "absolute faith" in Gurdjieff. Unlike Abraham, he would not slay his own son on command.

In October, Sherman Manchester wrote Orage on behalf of the New York group to apologize for not having asked earlier for advice in on how to receive Gurdjieff, considering that the New York groups still considered Orage their leader. Orage wrote back on All Hallows' Day:

About Gurdjieff—who really appears to be en route at last—I haven't wished to prescribe an attitude for the Group or for any individual, but only to acquaint them with certain facts and to recommend them to get from Gurdjieff something useful, if they can. Certainly and naturally, I shall be exceedingly interested in the outcome of G's visit. Equally, things cannot be unchanged by it. But my relations with G on the one side and the Group on the other side is such that I shall not blame either party if things do not turn out happy for me. What "personally happy for me" means concretely I'm not sure. I cannot be, for the simple reason that it assumes that G would be starting something new, in which the NY group and I can be enthusiastically interested. As I can hope, but not forecast what that something may be, I can't exactly say what I wish from G's visit. You can be sure, however and anyhow, that anything you do, collectively or individually, I shall understand and sympathise with. Approval or disapproval is a matter of objective judgment which, in any case, involves no personal attitude. (Orage Papers, Special Collections Library, Leeds University)

It is clear from this letter that Orage knew already of Gurdjieff's intentions for re-organizing the work in America, but whether Gurdjieff knew or cared of Orage's own ideas concerning the groups is not known.

Orage Agonistes

So, the stage was set for the strange conflict of wills that Gurdjieff describes at length in *Life Is Real*. The story Gurdjieff writes there resembles a medieval morality play in which he and Orage play allegorical roles in conflict and after in reconciliation. Gurdjieff says that he arrived in New York on 13 November 1930 to look over the handling of both money and ideas. In effect, the situation in New York was topsy-turvy, as if the effects of kundabuffer had infected the Orage groups. In the evening on that first day, he attended a general meeting of the New York group directed by Mr. S (Israel Solon? Stanley Spiegelberg?).

Three days later, according to Gurdjieff, he met with Solon and five others, including Sherman Manchester and Muriel Draper, and proposed the formation of a committee to organize general meetings in his apartment 10H in the Parc Vendôme at 333 West 56th Street to ascertain whether the group, in Gurdjieff's words, should either "become completely disappointed in my ideas or there should disappear the faith crystallized in their individuality during these years in regard to Mr. Orage and his authority" (*Life is Real* 72). In establishing these levels of pupils in his first talk, he complained that Orage had not advanced his pupils beyond the exoteric stage of self-observation (*Life Is Real* 85). Gurdjieff must have known that in the Oragean version of the work, self-observation—an acquired virtue—required prior self-remembering—an action.

Bennett observed that in 1924, Orage "was far too much of an individual to be able to play the role of second-in-command," and that Gurdjieff "could not accept Orage's undertaking as the natural development of what he himself had launched a few months earlier" (*Making a New World* 164). New York group members who had listened to Orage before laying eyes on Gurdjieff, however, had reason to feel that the "launching" had been Orage's.

Now Gurdjieff proposed a "purification of undesirable elements from your group" (*Life Is Real* 99). For the reformed group there would be thirteen obligatory conditions for membership, seven of objective character for everyone, and six of subjective character for members of Orage's old group (*Life Is Real* 99–100). He called his secretary (Bernard Metz and Louise Goepfert both served in that capacity in America) in front of the audience to dictate a "special oath for a newly formed exoteric group" to the

187

effect that no one was to have any relations with Orage without the special permission of Gurdjieff or his substitute (*Life Is Real* 100). In her memoirs, Louise Goepfert March says that she was the one to whom Gurdjieff dictated the oath that was to be taken (*March* 49).

Curiously Gurdjieff remarks that Orage was present at his "Fourth Talk" to the new group on 12 Dec. 1930 and then spins out an extraordinary tale. "Two days before the fourth general meeting reorganized by me on new principles, Mr. Orage himself finally arrived in New York, already informed about everything that had taken place here in his absence" (*Life Is Real* 120), he said, indicating that Orage was in New York on 10 December, a month before his actual arrival.

It is interesting to note that Orage, who knew well from the many friends who met him on the dock on 8 January, what Gurdjieff had been saying in his group talks, ignored the blame put upon him and his wife. The letter he sent on 9 January 1931 from the Irving Hotel to Gurdjieff was carefully composed. Orage's offer to complete his principal task on Gurdjieff's behalf to publish and sell one thousand copies of the first series within the calendar year is important if only because it produced an ur-text of the book published twenty-nine years later. He ended his letter in a tone of restrained humor with hopes of seeing Gurdjieff in person soon.

Gurdjieff's version is slightly different, saying that upon arrival in New York in December, Orage requested an interview (*Life Is Real* 120). "Remembering the alarming news received by me one hour ago [earlier?] of the bad turn of my material affairs," writes Gurdjieff, "I decided to delay the answer" (*Life Is Real* 121). He had his pro tem secretary (Goepfert? Metz?) write a formal letter to Orage asking him to sign the "obligation I proposed to all the members of the group you have directed." Orage arrived promptly at Gurdjieff's apartment and signed while Gurdjieff was in the kitchen. In explaining to the assembled people that he understood at once what was hidden beneath the proposal, he confessed "the maleficence of my verbal influence on people whom I guided so to say in accordance with his ideas" (*Life Is Real* 122). Recognizing that there were deep thoughts beneath the superficial terms of the renunciation, continues Gurdjieff, he "decided therefore to begin by signing the obligation required by Mr. Gurdjieff" (*Life Is Real* 123). He resolved as well not to have anything to do with his former self and asked to join the new group as an "ordinary member."

During Orage's putative confession, Gurdjieff was in the kitchen, cooking a "gravity-center dish." What he heard through the wall or door so distracted him that, in chaplinesque fashion, instead of ginger, he dumped a large amount of cayenne pepper into the casserole, then swung his right arm into the back of whomever was washing dishes, and flung himself into his room where he buried his head in half moth-eaten cushions and sobbed, to be consoled and relieved only by Dr. Stjernvall's prescription of an ample portion of Scotch whisky. He then returned to the main room to host a dinner consisting of "the dish I had so immoderately peppered" (*Life Is Real* 124–25).

The next day, stirred by Orage's fictive example, pupils besieged Gurdjieff with requests for membership, to which he replied positively on the condition that they all pay fines of either $3,648, $1,824, $912, $456, $228, $114, or $57, depending on their slowness and reluctance to sign. He charged them for copies of his talks at rates of $10 for those who signed without hesitation, $40 for those who doubted him, and $20 for those who waited for Orage before deciding. The total gained from fines and sales, he wrote, amounted to $113,000, of which one half he decided to keep for himself and the other half to go into a fund for the operation of the exoteric group (*Life Is Real* 127). There is no further mention of Orage in the talk which breaks off in midsentence (*Life Is Real* 130).

Gurdjieff's version of Orage's behavior is a "fable" that eschews "fact." The Orages arrived in New York City at 9:30 in the morning of 8 January (*Gurdjieff and Orage* 172). The next day, from the Irving Hotel, Orage posted a letter to Gurdjieff with an offer to print one thousand copies of *Tales* to be sold for ten dollars each. Gurdjieff replied with an invitation to his birthday party on 13 January. Orage attended but was absent from the general meeting on 15 January during which Gurdjieff told group members why Orage should be repudiated. He added that those who wished to join his new group, now to be called the "New York New Esoteric Group," must sign a paper renouncing all communication with Orage (*Gurdjieff and Orage* 174). Whether Orage signed the paper is not clear, but 16 January 1931 is some time from 10 December 1930. I suspect that Gurdjieff had reason to date and fashion his account as he did, but what that reason was I have not yet determined.

On the one hand, it is extraordinary that Gurdjieff would devote so much of the third series to the story of the dismantling and re-assembling of Orage's New York groups and the disavowing of Orage's teaching, all of this in the context of his personal confrontation with Orage. On the other hand, it is curious that Gurdjieff dates his confrontation with Orage in December 1930 instead of January 1931. Gurdjieff's accounting of the fines collected from Orage's pupils was not recalled by any of the pupils who were there and wrote of the events, such as Louise Goepfert March, Muriel Draper, Daly King and Louise Welch.

Gurdjieff's morality play, or parable, baffles interpretation. Gurdjieff, in recalling important events in the history of the work, quite purposely altered the chronology of events as well as the décor in his luxurious Central Park West apartment furnished with "half moth-eaten" cushions. It seems to me that his breaking off his recollection at the instant an essential secret is to be revealed is not a manuscript lapse on his part, but a strategy for concealment. No one who was there at the talks, including Louise Welch, Daly King, and Sherman Manchester, recalled to others the divulging of a secret particularity of initiates, let alone the general gist of his talks. The scene in which Orage signed the paper of renunciation of self and Gurdjieff reacted by peppering his banquet is more slapstick comedy than esoteric code. Gurdjieff's account reads like post-modernist fiction; and yet, what reason have we to believe that it is not a carefully woven design whose message is truncated and whose image is blurred only by our lack of insight? I have not read any satisfactory analysis of it.

Carol Robinson wrote letters to Jane Heap in Europe about the events in New York. The first is undated, but internal references indicate that it was written in late January or early February 1931.

Dearest Jane,

I haven't written because the only news would have been Gurdjieff and there was nothing but disappointing tale there. Very bad situation. No one sees him—he works at book [*Life?*] all day & night with Salzmann, Miss Goepfert, Loomis, Gertrude [?] typing, Lillian [Whitcomb] cooking, Ilse Manchester typing German. Will see no one—no meetings, all because the group has acted outrageously—Orage and Jessie impossible and insulting. He says he didn't come here for groups—New York, very bad, groups here finished—There are no groups—only come to write about America in America. Hate New York, abnormal disgusting place etc etc. But he began a German group last night for only new people who have never heard of Orage—by written invitation. I wrote first, didn't I, that he came direct from book to meeting the first week—read from book & some music – was very charming to every one, but it seems that quite a few began [   ] him about money and that the 3 or 4 maintainers in a large way—like Mrs. Grant and Mrs. Schwarzenbach etc told him immediately that he need not expect a penny from them—rude and unnecessary. Almost all of them—those chosen monied ones of last winter—refused all his invitations to suppers. I went up to his apt one of the first evenings. Mme. Salzmann played some lovely music. But they have stopped that too. Orage has been left out completely—he all but ignores him & O. didn't know at all whether G. would take the meeting the 2nd Tues—nervously phoning everyone to find out for him. Then it seems G. sent a message to O. to dine with him that evening 7:30. Orage just didn't show up (Jessie) & Gurdjieff got to Muriel's first. When Jessie & O. came in Gurdjieff walked over to O., began to say what an idiot their maid was over the phone & Jessie who he hadn't noticed & who had not seen him since his arrival a week before [from Chicago?] shouted "Idiot yourself" & threw something at him. He came over to her (audience of 30 people) & held out his hand—she looked such hate as I've never seen—silence for a long time, at last she gave him her hand. He began a long explanation about how he didn't understand the phones in America, how it was all his fault that he missed Orage at dinner etc. I could have wept.

I don't know why Orage is acting this role. He has a large group on his side—but which side I don't know—groups divided because of his actions for O, for Gurdjieff.

. . . I know that they are working at something all this time. And we have been told in group & separately that we are all bad—not one person that he wants to see, that he can carry out the work he had planned for us. But I have decided—anyway to call Mme. S. tomorrow. Dr. Stjernvall arrived & they have 3 apartments now. Staying 2 months before going to Chicago. I can't think what other news there is—nothing important. Someone said to G. 'Carol Robinson is a very good person, makes effort.'—he shrieks—'no good person, no good, no method, I hate everything, everyone, New York etc etc. &

then 'who knows her being good effort to just her own form of madness'! Did you dream it would be like this. . . . .All my love, Carol

(Robinson-Heap Letters, Smyth collection)

Robinson's citing the "role" Orage plays supports the general impression of his group members that he was responding to Gurdjieff as if he knew very well what part he should play in a pre-designed drama that would serve both himself and Gurdjieff.

A month later, on her way westward from New York City, Robinson wrote Heap again:

. . . Gurdjieff staying on another 10 days. There is music—only a few minutes —twice a week—the rest of the time he sits reading chaps of the book—and occasionally it is read aloud. There is one German evening by special invitation. I have read a good many chapters—was never able to get to me about the old Dervish and music. Seems to be in a gayer mood since coming back from Chicago, but has very little to say to anyone—engaged in 'his own affair'—asked me to come Prieuré this summer. I said I couldn't. He said last chance—book finish—everything finish. Well I didn't get a good deal out of the visit except unrest & discontent with my life etc. Nothing really to go on. . . . All my love. Carol

(Robinson Letters, Smyth collection)

On 13 March, Gurdjieff sailed back to France. Curiously, however, as he was writing the conclusion to "The Material Question" that closes the second series, Gurdjieff located himself in Childs (sic) at the corner of Fifth Avenue and 56th Street. He remarks on the "pure coincidence or even the effect of supernatural providence" that he finished the revision "today in this same city, exactly seven years to the very day since the evening which has just been described" (*Meetings* 297). The evening described—the night of 8–9 April 1924— was the one during which the New York City branch of the Institute was founded; so, Gurdjieff's revision on 8 April 1931 was almost a month after his departure from New York. This apparent discrepancy raises two linked questions. First, why should Gurdjieff go to such care to situate time and place at the end of a work that completely eschews dating events by standard means? Second, considering his careful dating and placing of events, why should he *mistake*—or, if you will, *reshape*—the chronology of events?

He does not stop there at reshaping time. As he closes his addition to Orage's account of the proceedings of 8-9 April 1924, Gurdjieff says the date is 10 January, and that he is planning to leave the United States in mid-March (*Meetings* 302). Mid-March 1931 is indeed the time of Gurdjieff's departure from the United States. One might assume, then, that 10 January 1931, and not 8 April 1931, is the actual date of his writing, and that he had simply forgotten the actual date, but this leaves us with another anachronism. Seven years to the day before 10 January Gurdjieff was in mid-ocean aboard the *CGT Paris*. What Gurdjieff's purpose is in befuddling his reader's sense of time and place might well be a topic of investigation into the form and function of the third series.

The first reference I have found to a text of the third series that is based on his break with Orage is in Gurdjieff's letter sent from 204 West 59th Street to Orage, and dated 3 December 1931. Orage received it in London on 12 December (one year to the day after Gurdjieff's public denunciation of Orage), in which he says: "Am again in New York employing for carrying out my aim. I am rewriting the third series. Rereading it I saw your name . . ." (*Gurdjieff and Orage* 183).

Why Gurdjieff devoted so much of his "esoteric" culmination of his three-step instruction on how to obtain a real "I" and its attendant higher consciousness and prolongation of life on his relations with Orage is difficult to discern. It seems obvious, however, that Gurdjieff dramatized the 1930–1931 crisis of group

194

organization as a major "shock," or turn in his own affairs, similar to, but more significant than the "three incomprehensible fateful events" that he describes in the opening pages of his "Prologue" (7–11). Those were the three "accidental" gunshot wounds, recovering from the third of which Gurdjieff had an epiphanic realization that while there is a God of his outer world, he himself is God of his inner world (23). In brief, accidents from outside pertain to events of the outer world God rules, but man controls the inner reaction to them. This collaborative rule over outer and inner worlds is the starting point for the formation of a third world that mediates between them. This is the core subject that informs the structure of the third series, rather than the *ad hoc* occasion Jeanne de Salzmann identifies in her "Foreword" as the "shock given to Orage by the master in order to make him conscious of a state of affairs which Orage himself did not recognize."

Gurdjieff, for his own purposes, transformed Orage in his series of talks into a life storm, a condition against which it is necessary to struggle in order to accomplish anything. He makes of Orage an incarnation of cosmic friction, a form of *heropass*, the eroding force of time. To make the point that there is a "lawful" condition to which he responds, Gurdjieff divides the flow of time forward from 1923, when he sent Orage to New York, into seven and three year periods, representing the Laws of Seven and Three that are the creative and maintaining forces of the cosmos. Just as Beelzebub's Endlessness distanced *heropass* from him into his created universe, Gurdjieff distanced Orage from him into the realm of "ordinary" men. That done, conflict, or erosion, was rectified; that is, Orage rejoined Gurdjieff's circle of Being as a new and innocuous force. In renewing Orage, Gurdjieff was renewing time, energy and his teaching world. This is the object lesson he presented to his pupils, though few understood the lesson.

Gurdjieff and the Public

Besides his talks to the New York assembled group and his histrionic wrestle with Orage, Gurdjieff was in New York to advertise himself and his ideas. On 29 January Gurdjieff asked Muriel Draper to edit a letter he intended to send to the newspapers explaining his actions:

Owing to the fact that both the information given during the last few days in many New York newspapers about me personally and my activities and also about the reasons for my being at the present time here in America do not at all correspond to reality and in the objective sense even sully the significance of all that sincere, well-wishing and grateful attitude to Americans which has been formed in my common presence during the last seven years and of which everybody without exception will very soon be indubitably aware, I have decided to offer a brief account though the medium of your columns of the real reason for my stay in America, and at the same time to announce by the way to all who are seriously interested in my activities and my writings, that without waiting for the final completion of all the three books of the first series of my writings entitled "An-Objective-Impartial-Criticism-of-the-Life-of-Man," or "Beelzebub's-Tales-to-His-Grandson," which are the first I intend to publish, I have found it possible and have already given instruction to print one of the 3rd chapters of the 3rd book entitled "Beelzebub in America," which will not only help to put an end to the various fantastic rumours compromising my name, but may also, in my opinion hasten the actualization of those results concerning which every sane-reasoning man will on sincere reflection, indubitably understand for which good aims this chapter was intentionally written in an original form.

I am here now in America because since I became a writer, it has been my practice to travel from country to country in order to form on the spot an opinion about the ordinary life and the psyche of the people who constitute the group of which at the given time I write an objective criticism according to my own observation.

Owing to the above-mentioned practice which has already become thoroughly fixed in my character, my present visit to America has been necessary chiefly because I am just now writing that chapter of the second series of my writings which necessitates my recalling the history related by me seven years ago here in New York, of the arising and existence of the Institute founded by me under the name of the Institute-for-the-Harmonious-Development of Man—a history which although then taken down in a shorthand, yet for its better detailed revisions, according to the mentioned inherency already fixed in me, demands my presence for refreshing my memory by association at the place where this history was first related (Taylor, *Invention* 198–99).

The chapter referred to is the last of *Meetings*. I find no record of the letter in any newspaper, but the "Religion" page of the 14 March 1931 issue of *Time* magazine featured a long article entitled "Harmonious Developer" which opened: "Not many people in the U.S. have ever heard of Georges Gurdjieff":

Not many who have heard of him could repeat more than garbled rumors. Not many of those who know him know what to make of him. He is the strange head of a strange practical religion. Until two years ago his Institute for the Harmonious Development of Man was established in Fontainebleau, France. Then, an atrocious automobilist, he had an accident, closed the Institute. His subsequent movements have been obscure; always he has shunned publicity. Last week the few Manhattanites who knew he was in town gathered in Author Muriel Draper's studio to get another look at him.

An Armenian Greek in his 60's, he has a domed shaven

head, piercing dark eyes in an oval face, a walrus mustache, bull neck, a paunch, huge muscles. He is unaccountable, unpredictable. A clever man, he acts sometimes like a lunatic, sometimes like a genius, sometimes like a child. He loves to laugh, apparently enjoys being angry.

A laconic survey of Gurdjieff's beliefs follows, mentioning that "Gurdjieff defined a normal person as one 'capable of actualizing his own potentialities.' . . . The normal person, he declared, was developed for his biological limit. He believes, for instance, continual self-conscious attention to olfactory sensations would finally render a man's nose as keen as a dog's; that similar results could be obtained with other mental, physical, emotional potentials."

Sometime in February, the journalist William Seabrook organized a meeting in Gurdjieff's Central Park West apartment with John Watson, psychologist William Pepperwell Montague, Lincoln Steffens, Gilbert Seldes, Virginia Hirsch, Blair Niles, and others during which Gurdjieff entertained his guests with a reading from his chapter on America. Seabrook recalled the evening:

Late in the evening, Mr. Steffens and John Watson began whispering. Presently, Mr. Watson said: "Either this is an elaborate and subtle joke whose point is completely over our heads, or it's piffle. In either event, I can't see that much can be gained by hearing more of it. I propose, if Mr. Gurdjieff is agreeable, that we now converse for a while."

So we all relaxed and conversed and presently supped, with equal amiability on the part of both hosts and guests. Mr. Gurdjieff was more brilliant and more witty than the manuscript had been. He was so agreeable, so keen, so affable, that Steffens, Watson, Montague and all the rest of them took him into their complete confidence, and explained unanimously their conviction that—unless he was trying to put over a cosmic joke of some sort whose point had not been manifest—his future did not lie in the field of authorship. Gurdjieff suggested that his purpose might be too deep for our limited comprehension" (Seabrook, *Witchcraft* 214–15).

Gurdjieff laughed, and then pacified them with a number of stories and a considerable amount of alcoholic beverages. Both Welch and Wolfe, who identified himself as the reader, have versions of this meeting.

After the Break

Throughout the rest of Gurdjieff's stay in early 1931, he and Orage met almost daily. Group members observed them getting along together as well as ever. Private and public meetings took place in Draper's apartment, attended by Leonid de Stjernvall, Jeanne de Salzmann and Louise Goepfert. Welch recalled: "It was as though neither Gurdjieff nor Orage ever forgot his part" (*Orage with Gurdjieff* 90). At Gurdjieff's request, he contacted potential publishers for *Tales*, but without success, so Gurdjieff took Orage up on his offer to produce a private printing in mimeograph form.

Orage continued giving talks on Gurdjieff's ideas, as well as on his own Social Credit scheme. A notable listener that spring was Henry Asgard Wallace, soon to be Franklin Delano Roosevelt's choice for Secretary of Agriculture (1933–1940) and Vice-President of the United States (1940–1945). Another was Nikolai Roerich, a member of Gurdjieff's 1909 lodge, who was living in New York. Roerich was associated with Claude Bragdon at the time, and both attended Orage's talks occasionally.

On 2 May 1931 Fred Leighton wrote to Toomer in Chicago to sum up the situation: "There has been a great fight here over the question of Orage. Now I understand that Orage has returned to the fold" (*Shadows* 179). Five days later Toomer received a letter from Jessmin Howarth in Hollywood: "News from New York is quite amusing, as ever, when Gurdjieff has been tickling the initiates, but with a very correspondent undercurrent. I wish I could pay you all and Orage a flying visit" (*Invention* 201). Not exactly back in the fold was Orage, but he was continuing to serve Gurdjieff's interests in New York until 13 March when Gurdjieff sailed home, after extracting "loans" from Toomer to cover his passage and costs.

When he sailed for England to resume his literary career on 3 July, Orage left the New York group well-organized under the leadership of Jackson, Solon, Draper, Manchester and Munson. Gurdjieff had told Ouspensky in Petersburg that if one has to leave the work, "there is nothing that shows up a man better than his attitude towards the work and the teacher after he has left it," for he is liable to hold a grudge against both (*Search*, 228). Orage held no grudge. He said that he and Gurdjieff were like brothers who eventually went different ways and quipped that Gurdjieff had cut him loose just as Beelzebub had been cut loose. Perhaps a term of exile would do him good.

During Gurdjieff's wanderings he met an Armenian cousin who recognizes him as "Black Devil" (*Life Is Real* 14), an epithet whose significance is obvious in this context, when Gurdjieff considers, "why should he [God] send away from Himself one of His nearest, by Him animated, beloved sons, only for the 'way of pride' proper to any young and still incompletely formed individual, and bestow upon him a force equal to His own? . . . I refer to the Devil" (24). In effect, decades later in New York, Gurdjieff plays that demonic role in the course of displaying to Orage a force of his own before sending him away. The reader can consider Orage as Gurdjieff's model of an initiate under the direction of a master.

11

20 March 1931–4 June 1935:
End of the Institute

After Orage's "defection," it was Toomer's turn, and as Toomer withdrew little by little from active participation in the work, the Institute seemed doomed. Gurdjieff did not plan with Toomer a strategy for displacement. Toomer's decision to move out on his own began to take conscious prominence in his mind in the spring of 1931, a few weeks after Gurdjieff's departure from the United States. It was incited by the expressed dissatisfaction of his Chicago group with the repetition of material in his talks. In response to their appeal for some sort of "laboratory, rather than theory" (*The Lives* 192) he set up in the summer of 1931 an experiment in communal living in rough imitation of the Institute at Witt Cottage near the Big Slough outside Portage, Wisconsin, some 180 miles northwest of Chicago.

In the description of his "experiment," *Portage Potential*, written in 1932, Toomer explained that his purpose was "to explore the individual's ability to break away from behavioral patterns that by cultural expectations or by personal habit had constrained human potential" (*The Lives* 195). The *Madison, Wisconsin Capital Times* of 6 September 1931 gave a very positive and detailed coverage under the headline "Intellectual Portage Group delves into Intricate study of self direction," with a photograph of participants Margaret Cushing, Daniel Grady, Mrs Elizabeth Cushing, Zone Gale Breese, Mrs Daniel Grady, Katherine Klenert (sister of Georgia O'Keeffe), John Taras, and Mrs George Murison. The *Madison Wisconsin State Journal* had a similar positive report on the same date. During the exercises he directed in Portage, Toomer and one of the participants, Margery Latimer, fell in love, married in the fall and drove west to California on their honeymoon.

In September 1931, one thousand copies of the 638 page mimeographed copies of *Beelzebub's Tales* that Orage had produced for Gurdjieff went on sale to group members for $10 a copy. J. G. Bennett spins an unlikely story of the production of this version:

> Paul Anderson, who was then the treasurer, worked out a proposal for producing a mimeographed edition of Beelzebub from the chapters Gurdjieff had left with them [. . .]. Two were reserved for Paul and Naomi Anderson who had done all the work [. . .]. No authorized text was left either by Orage or by Gurdjieff himself. In some cases passages were missing and had to be reconstructed from memory. This was possible because the New York group had heard the chapters read many times from the time when Gurdjieff first brought them to New York in 1929 [. . .]. Copies were sent to Gurdjieff who smiled happily and seemed to be pleased. Copies were also sent to Orage for himself and Ouspensky (*Making a New World* 175–76).

The notion that missing passages were assembled out of a collective group-member memory is as far-fetched as the rest of his statement. Of course, Orage had a full revised text in 1928, but in the process of mimeographing, the short chapter XXXV in Book III was overlooked, and some passages were left out of chapter XL.

In the summer of 1931, Schuyler Jackson went to the Prieuré and reported his view back to New York that conditions at the Institute were deteriorating. The Study House, for example, was no longer fit for movements. In response, Israel Solon called for $5000 from members to refurbish the Institute. To help raise money, Liza Delza Munson conducted movements at the Noyes School of Rhythm at 215 W. 11th St. for $15 a lesson, and readings of *Tales* were offered to the public in Studio 61 of Carnegie Hall on Mondays and Fridays at $2.00. The group was still in contact with Orage and, to advance Orage's Social Credit scheme, Gorham Munson formed an Economics group and published a journal, *New Democracy*, to advocate it.

A short time later, Gurdjieff sent word to the United States that he was intending to visit in December 1931 and expected to hold general meetings. At the end of November, the New York and Chicago groups received a letter signed by Jeanne de Salzmann, translated and transmitted by Loomis, who had arrived in New York aboard the *Minnetonka* from Boulogne-sur-mer on 5 October. It read: "Every former member of the Orage group desiring to attend these general meetings must forgo five of his dollars, and moreover, the obligatory task is given to him, of handing these dollars to the translator-secretary on duty in such a way that no one else should see" (*Invention* 203–204). Louise Goepfert March recalls that she arrived in Paris in November, just two days before Gurdjieff was set to leave, and managed to find passage on a ship leaving a few days later.

Fifth Visit

In the company of Jeanne de Salzmann, Gurdjieff arrived in New York on the *Europa* on 16 November 1931. Few pupils there seemed to have taken enough notice of his presence to follow his activities. Louise Welch does not mention him being there at the time, and Louise Goepfert, who joined Gurdjieff on 27 November with Bernard Metz, both having sailed on the *Hamburg* from Cherbourg, says nothing more than the visit lasted two months (*March* 57). Nonna Pietovska arrived on 9 December aboard the *Ile de France*, but was delayed two days at Ellis Island for special inquiry before being allowed to enter the city and move into the same apartment house on Central Park West where Gurdjieff and others had stayed a year earlier.

Reports of Gurdjieff's doings during this visit are so unreliable that the biographer can only cite them with a warning that none can be authenticated. One is the story the journalist Rom

Landau mentioned in his book *God is My Adventure*, describing a party John O'Hara Cosgrave hosted, at which Nadir Khan recognized Gurdjieff as Dordjieff, saying later that "I wish I knew the things which Gurdjieff has forgotten" (*Anatomy* 243).

Another story is Fritz Peters' description of Gurdjieff's trip to Chicago to take stock of Toomer's group. Peters said Gurdjieff was probably on his way to Wright's Taliesin East (*Gurdjieff Remembered* 22–26). Nott contradicts Fritz's story of the Chicago trip (*Journey* 152), knowing that Gurdjieff did not go to Taliesin until 1934. Webb cites Munson's recalling Gurdjieff's affability and openness to Toomer in Chicago (*Circle* 419), though Munson was not in Chicago with Toomer. Moore adds the detail that Gurdjieff, despite the grim and humourless atmosphere, came away from Chicago with "the money he wanted . . .his wallet temporarily re-stocked" (*Anatomy* 244). This would all sound plausible if Gurdjieff had met Toomer there, but Toomer was not in Chicago at any time during this period (*The Lives* 200–207). After his marriage to Margery Latimer on 30 October, he cancelled his Chicago classes to go on his honeymoon. He returned to Wisconsin the following summer with his pregnant wife.

One sure piece of evidence of Gurdjieff's stay in New York is the letter he sent to Orage on 3 December, saying that he was "working on the third and last version of the third series of the books I had decided to write." He continues:

> Just now, while deciding to write you this letter myself, as I am sitting in my usual place, known to you, in Child's, looking at the first chapter of the third series, which is lying on the table in front of me, and with only half of which you are acquainted, and occasionally at the bi-ped Americans moving like automatons in Columbus Circle, and am thinking how to dispose the fundamental ideas, already outlined in this chapter, so that in its last version it should correspond to the sum total

of all my expositions and to my mental, i.e. theoretical, and organic, i.e. practical principles.

As I was thinking of this, in the aforesaid conditions, there gradually began completely to form in my thoughts two independent and, to me, satisfactory forms.

One of these forms which I have thought out in almost the final form, and which moreover corresponds more to my aims, may for you and of course for your family—for you, namely, a man towards whom, owing to the life-circumstances, there has gradually been formed in my nature a "something" engendering in certain instances the sensation as towards my own brother—be almost in the literal sense of the word "death"; and the other, although "life," yet only a little better than, as is said, "vegetation" (*Gurdjieff and Orage*, 183).

When Jessie Orage read the letter she detected a death threat in it. When the contents of the letter became known to Orage's friends in New York they expressed mixed concern. Most recognized a Gurdjieffian ploy, but no one could decipher its purpose, unless it was a strategy to persuade Orage to return to him. Whatever its intent, it inspired Jessie to compose a vitriolic end of the year poem:

> He calls himself, deluded man,
> The Tiger of the Turkestan,
> And greater he than God or Devil
> Eschewing good and preaching evil.
> His followers whom he does glut on
> Are for him naught but wool and mutton,
> And still they come and sit agape
> With Tiger's rage and Tiger's rape.
> Why not, they say, The man's a god;
> We have it on the sacred word.
> His book will set the world on fire.
> He says so—can God be a liar?

1932

On 16 January 1932, according to Moore, Gurdjieff returned to France on the *Bremen* with Jeanne de Salzmann, Payson Loomis, Nonna Pietovska and Nick Putnam (*Anatomy* 244),
though Gurdjieff's immigration form on his next entry to the
United States cited 17 April 1932 as his last departure date. Metz
and Goepfert had already returned to France before the end of
1931. Back in France, throughout the remainder of the first half
of the year, Gurdjieff made efforts, perhaps half-hearted, to save
the Prieuré. He had accumulated little money in New York or in
Chicago, if he went there at all.

Edith Taylor had been at the Prieuré with her two children
during Gurdjieff's absence in early 1932 and noted sadly the di-
lapidated state of the Study House: "tears came to my eyes seeing such magnificence in a state of decay, the prayer rugs sho-
wing huge rat-chewed holes and dog and cat remains, smelling
of damp rotting wool. The roof supports had given way under
the weight of winter snows, windows were broken, and the light
cast shadows like wounds on the stained patterns of the rugs"
(*Shadows* 70).

In April, having failed to settle his debts, Gurdjieff announced the closing of the Prieuré, saying that he lacked the
100,000 francs necessary to keep it going. On the first of May
the kitchen was closed, and Valia was told to tell all the residents
that the buildings would be boarded up in one week (*March* 59).
Gurdjieff took up living quarters in Paris, first in the Grand Hôtel and then in a dingy apartment on the Rue Tocqueville in the
17th arrondissement. Bennett writes that in 1934 Gurdjieff hin-
ted that he had traveled to Central Asia in 1932 (*Making a New
World* 181), but there is no evidence of this trip. Other reports
have him continuing to work diligently trying to reclaim his hold
on the Prieuré.

If the Prieuré was run down in the spring of 1932 never to

be renovated by Gurdjieff, it did not perhaps really matter much to him, since there had been few American pupils arriving from the United States since the summer of 1929. Certain old hands had appeared during summers after; but, the teaching routine of old—construction tasks, movements, readings, music—was no longer maintained. Instead Gurdjieff spent the greater part of his time putting finishing touches on the third series of his work. The old entourage that arrived with him from Russia had left. Dmitri and his family had moved to a small house in Fontainebleau, the Salzmanns moved to Paris and the Stjernvalls to Sotteville-sous-le-Val in Normandy where Gurdjieff would visit often in the next five years. Lili Galumnian Chaverdian returned to Armenia with her young son Sergei, and did not return to France. Most of the Russian contingent drifted to various jobs in Paris.

After the Prieuré was lost, and most of its former inhabitants scattered, Martin Benson, Caesar Zwaska and a few others hung on until evicted almost a year later. According to the business cards Gurdjieff handed out, the Prieuré and the Paradou (his business office) continued to serve as permanent addresses until the late thirties, even after he had moved to Rue des Colonels Renard in Paris. Loomis, who was serving as translator-editor through the summer, returned to the United States on 29 August 1932.

Although I find no evidence in any shipping records for another Gurdjieff voyage to America at this time, Moore mentions a "disastrous sixth visit" to America and cites Webb to the effect that Gurdjieff arrived in the United States at the end of 1932 and went straight to Chicago where "Jean Toomer watched with dismay the impact . . . on his following" (Moore 247; Webb 420). This could not have been so, since Toomer was not there and his handful of followers had dispersed. To those who questioned Toomer's plans, he said that he no longer exercised leadership in the Gurdjieff work (*The Lives* 206). His wife Margery died in childbirth on 15 August 1932 in Portage. Though he went down to Chicago to deliver a lecture in January 1933, he did not stay, and he cancelled plans for a projected lecture series.

1933

Webb writes that when Toomer met Gurdjieff in New York in the spring of 1933, he noted Gurdjieff's deteriorated state of health (*Circle* 420). Again, there is no evidence of Gurdjieff's presence in New York or a meeting with Toomer at that time. Moore says Gurdjieff sailed back to France in February 1933 (*Anatomy* 248), but in *The Herald of Coming Good* Gurdjieff locates himself in Fontainebleau in March preparing to rebuild the Study House on Saint George's day in April. Edith Taylor was with him earlier in January 1933, when Webb and Moore locate him in New York.

Despite closing the Prieuré, Gurdjieff announced that he would open a new Institute with the Paradou as its center. His "supplementary announcement" to the *Herald of Coming Good*, dated 7 March 1933, contained a detailed description of the new Institute in refurbished quarters which would house the same three separate groups of students he had formed in New York and Chicago. He announced that on his Saint's Day 23, April 1933 the cornerstone of the new Institute would be placed. Meanwhile, he maintained the Prieuré as his permanent address.

When he completed the draft of *The Herald of Coming Good* that he had begun the previous September, he sent it to Orage in London for editing. Orage refused politely on 15 February (*Gurdjieff and Orage* 2001, 191–92). Payson Loomis completed the job in March and in August 1933, Gurdjieff's only work to appear in print during his lifetime was printed in Paris. He sent one hundred and thirty-eight copies to New York to be sold at $5.50 a copy. The book, really a pamphlet, was not a success and at the end of November the New York group found itself with dozens of copies still unsold. Rita Romilly, who was acting as Gurdjieff's secretary in Paris at the time, had a number of copies sent to Toomer with a request to sell them throughout America. In the spring of 1934 a postcard with Metz's name on it arrived from France asking Toomer and the New York group to send all the subscription slips from the pamphlet as well as unsold copies back to France. In 1951 under the name Bernard Mayne, Metz published a novel, *The Great Atomic Disaster: Blueprint for Survival*, based on *The Herald*.

Meanwhile, Alexander de Salzmann, critically ill of tuberculosis, met Gurdjieff for the last time in Paris in April 1933, and died less than a year later in the Swiss Alps (Moore, 258). Jeanne de Salzmann remained there for a good part of each year until the end of World War II. The Stjernvall family ran a pension in Normandy (*My Dear Father* 60–61), and Leonid was beginning to suffer the pains of a cancer of the prostate. Metz left in 1933 to work for the British consulate service in Algiers.

In early May 1933, Jane Heap wrote a letter from the Prieuré to Israel Solon for the New York group and to Toomer in Chicago, recalling that Orage held $3000 and Toomer $2000 for the "Beelzebub" publication fund, and demanded that the money should be sent to her, "that it is to be used only for publication costs and that the money should be placed in escrow." After advising that an identical letter had been sent to Orage, Heap posed two questions: "does money exist, is it in Orage's name?" (*Shadows* 155) Neither Orage nor Toomer responded.

Despite Gurdjieff's efforts, the holders of Gurdjieff's mortgages on the Prieuré foreclosed in May on a debt that Goepfert says was 350,000 French francs, the equivalent of about $17,000 (*March* 52). Gurdjieff gave the appearance to Americans that he was still in control of the situation, but was obviously desperate for financial aid. On 31 August Israel Solon received a cable from Gurdjieff asking for money "to save Prieuré, already seized for debt and to be put up for sale." On 7 September Solon wrote Draper: "You might be able to find an opening of speaking about this emergency to Gertrude Stein Luhan [sic]. I know from Jean Toomer's own recent letter that two thousand dollars which Gertrude Stein had given to Toomer for G 'no longer exists,' and that G. had recently said that this was the second time Toomer had robbed him … Orage is not among us, and he might not be willing to help even if he were here" (*Invention* 209).

When Toomer arrived in New York from Chicago and Portage in October, he found awaiting him a copy of a wire sent by Rita Romilly from Fontainebleau, saying: "Gurdjieff absolutely destitute, Prieuré being sold. If you can arrange anything please cable funds writing Stanley [Spiegelberg]" (*Shadows* 156). Toomer had been out of the Gurdjieff work effectively since the previous spring when he announced to his group that he was finished with it. At the time, Gurdjieff was still considering him as a principal American representative. While the Gurdjieff groups were still functioning in New York, according to Orage and his committee's wishes, Toomer was in Portage, Wisconsin, collecting his late wife's papers. He had no intention to resume representing Gurdjieff.

Toomer's defection from Gurdjieff's American ventures marked a drastic falling off of Gurdjieff's hopes for a base in the United States. Ouspensky had drifted from Gurdjieff on the grounds that Gurdjieff had turned from teaching in the name of a brotherhood to teaching in his own name. The Hartmanns had been ejected from the work by Gurdjieff himself. With Gurdjieff's complicity, Orage had moved out of the work circle to resume a career that he was sure he was capable of pursuing with renewed vigor. Gurdjieff played an instrumental role in all their departures. Toomer, however, distanced himself despite Gurdjieff's desire to keep him in the fold. Though neither Ouspensky, Orage, nor Toomer turned from Gurdjieff's ideas, they all, in one way or another, renounced the man. Orage was torn between a personal debt to the man and a need to pursue a new life as a husband and father.

Toomer felt that he had absorbed enough of Gurdjieff's teaching to exercise his methods independently of their source.

In late autumn 1933, Gurdjieff left Paris for Berlin where he visited Louise Goepfert and Walter March who had married on 10 November. Moore, following Peters' stories, has Gurdjieff in New York at the time gathering several thousand dollars (*Anatomy* 249–50), though Gurdjieff remained in Berlin for most of the remainder of the year, planning his next major move. He still intended to re-establish the Institute in the United States, but he had passport problems to resolve. The United States had not ratified the 28 October 1933 League of Nations Convention for Nansen Identity Certificates and, consequently, the passports issued by the Nansen International Office for Refugees were no longer honored by the United States. Nonetheless, Gurdjieff was certain that he could obtain papers allowing him to return to America. On 21 December 1933, Fred Leighton wrote Toomer that Nick Putnam was bringing Gurdjieff to New York "to straighten things out." To avoid contending with Gurdjieff's insistent demands, Toomer wrote back that his group, though he had none at hand, would pay his boat fare (*Shadows*, 156).

1934

Putnam sailed from Cherbourg to New York in mid-January without Gurdjieff, but with his wife, the seventeen year old actress Jessie Wakeling whom he had married in Los Angeles in August 1933. Apparently he had brought her to France to meet Gurdjieff, rather than to Bermuda on a honeymoon as the two had announced to the press, but Gurdjieff was not to be found. He was in still in Berlin, and on 15 February he was in Paris where he obtained an American non-immigrant visa, perhaps attached to German documents. He had planned to return to Berlin to consult with Alfons Paquet at the behest of the Marchs, but sent a telegram to Paquet, saying "Kann leider nicht kommen, brief folgt, Gurdjieff" ("Regret I can not come. Letter follows"). On 7 March he wired Israel Solon in New York: "MUST GO AMERICA NECESSARY YOU SEND FARES." Three days later he sent another wire that Leighton forwarded to Toomer: "Cable three passages America immediately" (Taylor *Invention* 212). The New York group raised the money, but perhaps Gurdjieff did not need it for himself, since the Louise and Walter March bought a round-trip ticket for him. Who the others to travel with him were he did not identify. In early April, Leighton heard that Gurdjieff was booked on the next sailing from Bremen.

Sixth Visit

Gurdjieff sailed on the *Bremen* from Bremen on 20 April 1934 and arrived in New York on 25 April with a visa valid until 23 April 1935. This visit would be his longest consecutive stay in the United States. Muriel Draper's papers record a number of meetings with him in April and May, without mentioning the year, though their sequence indicates 1934. She mentions a meeting on 26 April that Gurdjieff held at her apartment at 32 East 53rd Street to organize spring activities. He took up residence in apartment 10H at 333 West 56th Street, and through much of May directed music and group readings at Carnegie Hall, for which he charged fees of one dollar for those pupils who had sold at least three copies of *The Herald*, and two dollars for all others. He was short of money as usual, and on 16 May, Leighton wired him fifty dollars. It is curious that several former Orage pupils in New York, like Bill and Louise Welch seemed not to know he was in New York.

That same April, Fred Leighton introduced Toomer to Marjorie Content, the daughter of Harry Content, a prominent Wall Street banker. They fell in love almost at once, and when she went to Reno in the summer to get a divorce from her present husband, Toomer went to New Mexico to write. He was back in

Chicago when Leighton wrote him on 12 June to report: "Last night, G. said to me: 'Toomer promised some money; write him right away and say I need three tickets to Chicago.' Is that all, Mr. G.? 'Idiot, of course need food, coffee drink, etc. . . .Sunday he lost his passport, $120, and other important papers and has been rather upset . . . PPS Rita [Romilly] married Martin Benson" (*Invention* 212). Goepfert reported rumors that Gurdjieff had thrown his papers in the Hudson (*March* 67), but Gurdjieff placed ads in *The New York Times* that read: "Lost. Wallet, pigskin containing passport, papers, money. George Gurdjieff 333 West 56th Apart. H Reward Columbus 5-4956."

Shortly after, Gurdjieff went to Washington to inquire about extending his visa. Apparently he was not successful, and Paul Anderson and Bayard Schindel lingered in the capital to petition French and German consular offices, according to Leighton's letters to Toomer 30 June 1934 and 5 August 1934. Nine months later Gurdjieff had success with the German Consulate in New York that issued him a *Fremdenpass*, a passport issued primarily to residents of German territories who exercised activities valuable to the Third Reich. Bennett heard from Paul Anderson that "nothing less than the intervention of very influential friends in Washington had saved him from deportation from America before the war (*Making a New World* 248). Dr. Hans Borchers, an ardent Nazi, was the Consul General in New York, and Gurdjieff's *Fremdenpass* was signed by his attaché Peter H. Schmidt, an Anglophone with German father and whose wife had an Australian mother.

Though Toomer was in New York in the fall spending time daily with Marjorie Content, Gurdjieff was able to charm him into a meeting at Child's to talk over the Chicago situation during which he demanded all the money Toomer had collected from his group, to return all the unsold copies of *The Herald*, and to re-enlist Mabel Luhan's aid for establishing the Institute

213

somewhere on American soil. A few days later, after Toomer went to Portage to finish his work on his wife's papers, Gurdjieff asked Leighton to drive him to Chicago to see the World's Fair. Before leaving on 17 July, Fred wrote to Toomer who was now in New Mexico: "Gurdjieff says he wishes to see the fair—to *smell* Chicago." Leighton and Donald Whitcomb drove Gurdjieff and Lillian Whitcomb to Chicago.

Back in New York a few days later, Gurdjieff hosted a "banquet to celebrate the end of a six or seven year vow period" that included giving up alcoholic drinks and rewriting portions of the third series. He told Leighton, whom he had taken to calling Fred Lighthouse, to inform Toomer that "he plans shortly a trip to the Pacific coast for establishing groups in various localities." He intended to go by way of Santa Fe and expected Toomer to raise the necessary money for his stay there.

On 14 August, Leighton wrote to Toomer to say that Gurdjieff decided that he would leave again for Chicago in a few days' time, stay there one week and then go to Santa Fe to see Mabel Luhan. He expected to see Toomer in Chicago, though he must have known from Fred that Toomer was in New Mexico with Marjorie and Georgia O'Keeffe who were together awaiting Marjorie's divorce from her third husband. During a conversation with Toomer in Taos, Mabel Luhan said that she would refuse to receive Gurdjieff in her house. When Toomer relayed the remark to Leighton, Gurdjieff struck Santa Fe off his itinerary (*The Lives* 219). Nonetheless, he went to Chicago, and from there north by northwest to visit Taliesin East in response to a long-standing invitation from Olgivanna Wright.

Fritz Peters, who had been employed at the Chicago Exposition in the summer of 1933, and may have been working there as well in the summer of 1934, writes that he went with Gurdjieff on the train to Chicago where they were greeted by Toomer's former pupils (*Gurdjieff Remembered* 41). Moore says that Toomer prevailed on Gurdjieff to make the trip in May (*Anatomy* 251), but this does not accord with either Peters' account or the records of Gurdjieff at the Wright's estate in Wisconsin. Gurdjieff paused only a day or two in Chicago before taking a train to Spring Green, some 160 miles from Chicago near the state capital, Madison, where both Wright and Toomer had studied. This trip through the dairy-lands of Wisconsin afforded Gurdjieff his first view of American heartland countryside, and his warm reception at Taliesin on 22 July 1934 pleased him (Gill, *Many Masks* 226–227; Friedland and Zellman, *Fellowship* 240).

In some respects, it must have seemed to Gurdjieff that he was treading on familiar ground. Olgivanna's and Frank's Taliesin Fellowship had been patterned very much along the lines of the Institute at the Prieuré. Gurdjieff's visit was not just social of course, since he probably hoped that with Mabel Luhan's Taos out of the question, he might prevail upon the Wrights to make space available at Taliesin for the American Institute. A second possibility was to ask Olgivanna, now the mother of daughters Svetlana, fifteen years old, and Iovanna, eight years old, to take over the role from which Toomer had defected, that is, raising money in the Chicago area. He may have "doubted Olgivanna's capacity to lead, but he needed someone to run things . . . and she seems to have led him to believe such a thing was possible; when Gurdjieff arrived, he acted almost as if he already had the deal" (*Fellowship* 240).

Gurdjieff joined in the schedule at Taliesin, cooking, playing his own music, discussing Gothic architecture with Wright and holding readings of *Beelzebub's Tales*. He paid particular attention to Svetlana who wrote Wes Peters that for her these days have been "horrible—most of the time spent with Gurdjieff: A strange, kindly at times, ferocious and violent at other times, man—O— I can't explain to you what it was like to see him treat us all like guinea pigs in his laboratory experimenting to see reactions set

215

in" (*Fellowship* 240–41). She went on to say that Gurdjieff was dominating Wright completely, treating her step-father as one of his followers. When Wright shot back at him after one of Gurdjieff's after-dinner teaching sessions, saying "Well, Mr. Gurdjieff, this is very interesting, I think I'll send some young people to you in Paris. Then they can come back to me and I'll finish them off." Gurdjieff replied in fury: "You finish! You are idiot . . . No, you begin, I finish!" To make peace, Olgivanna intervened to tell her husband that Gurdjieff was right, but several of Wright's apprentices took up the challenge before peace could be restored (*Fellowship* 241).

Gurdjieff left Taliesin to spend a few days in Chicago, but returned briefly before the end of August. Again, meetings with Frank and Olgivanna, this time without open verbal combat, came to nothing, and Gurdjieff went back to New York empty-handed. After Gurdjieff left, Wright announced in the *Madison Capitol Times* on 26 August 1934 that Gurdjieff was a man who made "the ancient wisdom of the East not only intelligible to the thought of the West but to make it a way of WORK."

In New York, Gurdjieff moved in with Fred Leighton, who wrote Toomer, now married and living with Marjorie and his daughter Margery ("Argie") at 39 West 10th Street in Manhattan, that Gurdjieff was again in town and "on the wagon," distributing his *Herald* to groups everywhere. He said Gurdjieff was disheartened by the petty sums of money he was able to raise in the Midwest. "Gurdjieff is living with me. He is cooking, etc. as usual, in my place, and to say life is hectic is putting it mildly" (*Invention* 216). The next day, Wright cabled Gurdjieff to say: "Olgivanna and I enjoyed our visit with you more than I can say."

It was probably about this time, according to a story Leighton told Putnam who repeated it to others, Gurdjieff was napping on Leighton's sofa when two burglars managed to enter the apartment. Gurdjieff awoke and grappled with them. He knocked them unconscious, dragged their bodies out into the hallway, and went back to nap. When policemen summoned by neighbors arrived, they asked Gurdjieff if he knew what had happened. Gurdjieff muttered something in Armenian and the police left with the two now-conscious intruders. It was not the first time that Gurdjieff had demonstrated prodigious physical strength.

For financial support that fall, Gurdjieff returned to the New York group for support. Soon after he started meeting members, in the early morning of 6 November 1934, Orage died. Gurdjieff was in Child's that morning with Sherman Manchester and Nick Putnam when he heard the news. It is curious that the news came to Gurdjieff during a discussion of the difference between "intentional suffering" and "voluntary suffering." Sherman Manchester told me that he had defended Orage's "voluntary" because Orage had told his group that voluntary suffering enhances spiritual consciousness by will power. I recalled that Dostoyevski said that the wives who voluntarily accompanied their husbands into exile in Siberia were examples of awakened consciousness.

That evening at a meeting on 57th Street, after a long silence, he wiped his eyes and said to the group: "This man . . . my brother" (*Orage with Gurdjieff* 137). Two years later, Gurdjieff said: "If two people have lived a common aim together, they will always have a feeling of brotherly love, whether they love or hate each other, and nothing in family love can equal this feeling" (*Solano* 25 July 1936), and "common aim is stronger than blood" (*Hulme* 156). It was likely that on that fateful November morning Gurdjieff felt he had lost the best friend he had ever had.

The immediate consequence for Gurdjieff of Orage's death was a general cooling of his relations with the New York group. Leighton, Putnam and Loomis were still loyal, but neither of them had been close to Orage or particularly active in his group activities. The death of Orage was particularly painful as well to

Toomer, who had entered the work through his influence and mediation. When rumors reached him that Gurdjieff was telling people in New York not to have anything more to do with Toomer, he felt his connections with Gurdjieff inexorably broken. Later that month, he wrote to his Chicago pupil and friend Yvonne Dupee: "I disavow any and all responsibility for those who enter [the Work] now [. . .] I believe G once had and perhaps still has a very great thing; I am skeptical he will ever use it [. . .] I simply withdraw—and hope against doubt for something constructive from the man G" (*The Lives* 220).

1935

Nonetheless, good friend Leighton persuaded Toomer to meet Gurdjieff in January 1935. When he, with Leighton and Israel Solon, spoke with Gurdjieff, "The Old Man's" charm prevailed once more, and he promised to contribute to the support of Gurdjieff for the coming month. His wife, Marjorie, had the wherewithal to add to Gurdjieff's coffers, but she was suspicious of his intentions. Gurdjieff and Toomer met again in February for dinner and the ritual baths. When, in the course of the evening Toomer asked Gurdjieff what he thought now of his psyche compared with what he deemed it to be in 1926 when they were getting along very well, "You not as I counted," grumbled Gurdjieff, "You manifest differently at different times, different from what I expected. You not as I counted, and I get angry" (*The Lives* 221). Gurdjieff announced to him that he was sailing for France on 2 March and needed money for his fare. Toomer gave it to him, but Gurdjieff continued to ask for more in the days that followed. Toomer felt swindled. He refused to give him any more money and never saw him again, uttering that "I have reached the limit of my possibilities" (*The Lives* 221).

Gurdjieff continued to revise *Life Is Real* through that winter and spring, adding to it the impact on him of Orage's death. In his privately circulated Introduction to *Life Is Real*, Bennett says that Gurdjieff began the third series in 1933, then destroyed the text and began to revise the text in November, 1934, though Gurdjieff had written Orage on 3 December 1931 that he was finishing the third and last draft of the book (*Gurdjieff and Orage* 183). Orage had seen or perhaps even worked on that that draft. Parts of it are still in circulation.

Gurdjieff did not sail for France in March as he had told Toomer. Instead, he played the tourist, going to museums in New York where the Egyptian Room at the Metropolitan Museum of Art was a favorite destination. He went often to the cinema as well. Peters writes that Gurdjieff observed that "the hopes, dreams and desires of Americans in general—were very accurately portrayed in films. In fact, he said that only in the movies was the prevalent attitude towards sex, for example, revealed for what it really was" (*Gurdjieff Remembered* 56).

Gurdjieff's visa was soon to expire, and he was running short of time to find some place to establish the Institute, as well as to raise money to support it. His thoughts turned again to New Mexico, not toward Mabel Luhan now, but toward other friends there of Leighton and Orage. Leighton believed that Orage's 1928 contacts with the Governor, a Senator and others might be useful. Senator Bronson M. Cutting, a close personal friend of Mabel Luhan, had met Orage in the summer of 1928 and had corresponded with him after. It is likely that Leighton got word to him through Meredith Hare, who had acted earlier as an intermediary between Orage and Cutting, to explain Gurdjieff's predicament. What exactly Leighton thought possible is hearsay, but Cutting had worked with immigration authorities during and after WWI, and had the political influence to arrange certain things in Washington. Perhaps Leighton thought Gurdjieff could be granted citizenship by an act of Congress, though that is a rare and seldom-used expediency (it was offered Einstein in the 1930s, but he preferred to become American by normal channels).

On 6 May 1935, six months to the day after Orage's death, Cutting set out by plane for Washington, carrying with him, some have assumed, an offer to Gurdjieff either for locating the Institute in New Mexico or pledging financial support. Bennett said that Paul Anderson "succeeded in arousing such keen interest on the part of Senator Bronson Cutting of New Mexico that he asked him to meet Gurdjieff with a view to buying back the Prieuré and leasing it to a resuscitated Institute" (*Making a New World* 182). Moore writes that Anderson called Gurdjieff in New York to say that "an eminent politician was expressing serious interest in backing Gurdjieff financially" and that Cutting telegraphed a firm date for his arrival in Washington, saying "he would be there on 6 May to vote on the veterans' bonus (*Anatomy* 255)." There is no record of this cablegram or any other evidence in the Cutting Papers at the manuscript division of the Library of Congress that Cutting ever mentioned Gurdjieff's name. Though he had the financial means to invest in the Institute, it was unlikely that he would commit funds to an enterprise of which he knew little or nothing.

In fact, Cutting was on his way to Washington to answer charges of electoral illegalities advanced by his democratic rival in the recent senatorial election. If he had any plans concerning Gurdjieff, he didn't mention them, though it is reasonable to assume that he had heard of Gurdjieff during and after Orage's visit to Santa Fe in 1928. Gurdjieff, whatever his hopes or expectations were, went with Nick Putnam, Philip Lasell and Paul Anderson down to Washington from New York City in late April and waited. Cutting never arrived. The plane on which he was traveling from Albuquerque crashed near Macon, Missouri, on the evening of 6 May.

Within days after Cutting's tragic disappearance—a last

"accident" in a woeful series— Gurdjieff made new plans. It is said that he had Paul Anderson enquire at the Soviet Embassy in Washington about the possibility of returning to Russia, but the conditions relayed back from the Soviet Union to Ambassador Alexander Troyanovsky were not acceptable, since they did not include freedom of movement or occupation. A week later, on 14 May, Gurdjieff was back in New York looking for travel documents. He managed to acquire a new *fremdenspass*, perhaps on the basis of either special skills valuable to Germany or long-term residence in Germany. Gurdjieff had been there from August 1921 until July 1922, and that might have qualified him. His "pass," identifying him as a stateless former Greek, whose profession was "writer," carried a visa for six months, and the consular stamp noted that a confirming telegram was sent to Germany. Two weeks later, Gurdjieff boarded the *Bremen*, and arrived in Germany on 4 June 1935.

12

4 June 1935–1 September 1939: Marking Time

Traveling

Gurdjieff walked down the gangway in Germany with a new *Fremdenpass*, and remained in Hamburg until the 15th when Hamburg authorities, following instructions in a New York Consular telegram, stamped his passport. The next official addition to his passport was a visa issued in Berlin by the Belgian Legation on 27 July opposing a Berlin police stamp. On 8 September 1935 his passport was stamped in Brussels, and on 4 October the French Consul in Brussels added a French visa, and his arrival in Paris the next day is confirmed by a French railway stamp on his papers.

The gaps of time and space between these dates and places indicate that Gurdjieff was on the move constantly between his departure from New York and his arrival in Paris. Louise March recalled that he visited her and her husband in Berlin: "All I know for sure is that he returned to Germany on a German passport which he hadn't had before" (*March* 67). She does not mention the date, but the German passport was probably the *Fremdenpass* he had acquired in New York.

It has been supposed by some that he had returned to the Soviet Union in July and August. Bennett writes that Gurdjieff went to Germany by train, and on to the Caucasus and Turkestan to consult with certain people: "From what Gurdjieff said once or twice in 1949, it seems that in 1935 he made a trip to Asia—he said 'Persia,' which might include Turkestan. . . . Presumably the purpose was to consult with persons he trusted about the next phase of his life" (*Making a New World* 182).

It is easy enough to dismiss some speculations by referring

to the dates in his passport. If Gurdjieff had traveled back to Central Asia in the summer of 1935, he could not have done so through Persia, simply because there were no railway services there in 1935. To travel through Persia to Central Asia, he would have had to take a trade route to the base of the Kopet mountains, pass over them to Ashkhabad in Turkmenistan—where Gurdjieff said he had set up his "American Traveling Workshop" a quarter of a century earlier—and board a train there for Tashkent in Uzbekistan.

Gurdjieff had enough time in the summer of 1935 to travel by train to Leningrad, though there is no current evidence he did so. Muriel Draper was in the Soviet Union at the time with a group of Americans to observe first hand the politics of collectivity. There is no reason to assume that either she or Gurdjieff knew that the other was in the Soviet Union. Another person who was in the Soviet Union at the time and who had been associated with Orage in the United States in the 1920s and Gurdjieff in 1909 was Nikolai Roerich, who, in the employ of the United States Department of Agriculture, had traveled to Central Asia in the summer of 1934 on a mission to find a drought-resistant grass. Coincidentally, Gurdjieff spoke of the possible utilization of vegetable materials in and under the sands of the Gobi (*Meetings* 168). Like Gurdjieff, who had been able to move between White and Red forces during the Revolution, Roerich was able to move freely in the West as well as in the Soviet Union. The staunch revolutionary Gorky proclaimed that Roerich was "one of the greatest intuitive minds of our age." Knowledge of Roerich's whereabouts and influence in the Soviet Union at the time would have been of great value to Gurdjieff, though one cannot be sure that he knew where Roerich and his family were that summer.

Besides Roerich and his wife, other members of the 1909 Petersburg group founded by Gurdjieff and identified by Bokii, were still active in important positions in the Soviet Union.

Gleb Ivanovich Bokii (1879–1941) was associated with Soviet State security agencies Cheka (Chrezvychaynaya Komissiya), OGPU (Obyedinyonnoye Gosudarstvennoye Politicheskoye Upravlenye) and the NKVD (Narodny Komissariat Vnutrennikh Del), where he headed a special department. Coincidentally, through Bokii's influence, the OGPU sponsored Roerich to return to Central Asia to continue his contacts. Bokii also sponsored an expedition of Alexander Barchenko (1881-1938), the named leader of Gurdjieff's group after he left Russia. The Bulgarian born Boris Spiridonovich Stomoniakov (1882–1941), Deputy Commissar of Foreign Affairs of the USSR, was Soviet Trade representative in Berlin from 1920 until 1935. When Gurdjieff contacted the Soviet Embassy in Washington, Stomoniakov was in contact with the Soviet Ambassador Troyanovsky, and Gurdjieff might have learned that Stomoniakov was in Berlin where he could manage to meet him. Ivan Mikhailovich Moskvin (1890–1939) was a member and chief of the personnel department of the Presidium of the Supreme Sovnarkhoz of the USSR. In 1937 both Bokii and Moskvin were executed, and Badmayev suffered the same fate in 1938.

Gurdjieff's cousin, the sculptor Sergei Dmitrivich Merkurov, was also in the Soviet Union in 1935. In connection with Gurdjieff's desire to return to Russia, the director of the Merkurov Museum in Gumri recently declared "When Gregori [sic] Ivanovich was on a lecture tour around the United States, he was offered the chance to visit the Soviet Union and to start work on studies of longevity in the All-Union Institute of Experimental Medicine. At the last moment Gurdjieff changed his mind. The visit was cancelled. The correspondence with his cousin suddenly ended." If the "offer" refers to the conditions transmitted to Gurdjieff in Washington by the Soviet Embassy, which is likely, then Gurdjieff was in correspondence with Merkurov until mid 1935.

Gurdjieff might well have managed to get into contact with any one or all of these former associates to inquire into his influence among former pupils, but he may not have needed to enter the Soviet Union to do so. It is probable that Gurdjieff did not go to there at all. Of course he might have been able to get information about pupils and conditions there, since he was in correspondence with his cousin. If he did not go to the Soviet Union during this time, where did he go? Gurdjieff might have wanted to visit places further east in the Soviet Union. Shortly before he quit the United States, he wrote that an Essene school still existed in Central Asia where pupils of his still functioned (*Life Is Real* 108). In *The Herald of Coming Good* he writes that he had confided his intentions for an Institute before 1911 to a "brotherhood" in the heart of Asia sometime prior to 1911, and had sent twenty seven persons of each sex to a particular monastery, some of whom are still there (59–61).

The Soviet psychiatrist Olga Kharitidi who worked in Novosibirsk in the 1980s heard that followers of Gurdjieff were still in the region of the Altai mountain range, but Gurdjieff would not have had the time to contact them in person. To do so, he would have had to travel by train from Berlin to Moscow and then by the Trans-Siberian line to Kazan, Sverdlovsk, Kourgan, Omsk and Novosibirsk. Webb speculates that he might have headed for Verkhnieudinsk, a bit further southeast in Buryat Mongolia, where Ushé Narzunoff and Agwan Dordjieff met together (*Circle* 56). Though one can speculate that Gurdjieff wished to check on the pupils he had sent to Central Asia before the Revolution, it is more likely that he traveled only as far as Leningrad to contact the pupils he had left behind there, but official records of his presence in the Soviet Union in 1935 have not yet been unearthed. Besides the vague possibility that Gurdjieff managed to get to Leningrad between 27 July and 8 September 1935, he might have visited other European groups. Near the end of his first talk to the New York group in 1930, Gurdjieff mentioned that, besides two existing groups in Russia, there was one in Bavaria (*Life Is Real* 86–87).

What he was doing in Belgium during the weeks between 8 September and 4 October is still unexplained. He may have visited former pupils there or perhaps he considered establishing his residence there. He was an alien now in France, but was back in Paris on 5 October 1935, though he had not sent word ahead to anyone there to say he was arriving. Even his brother Dmitri, living on the Rue des Colonels Renard, was not aware yet of his presence in Paris. Solita Solano wrote in her journal, that she went looking for Gurdjieff at the Café de la Paix: "In the autumn of 1934 in a crisis of misery, I suddenly knew I had long been waiting to go to him and that he was expecting me. I sought him out and sat before him, silent" (Patterson, *Ladies of the Rope*, 83). Of course, it could not have been the autumn of 1934 when Gurdjieff was in New York City, but 1935. Apparently, Solano learned of his presence in Paris from Elizabeth Gordon who had visited him at the Grand Hotel (Hulme, *Undiscovered Country* 75). As before, he was using the Café de la Paix next door as his "office."

New York group members had no idea of Gurdjieff's whereabouts since leaving New York. "Where is G?" asked Leighton of Toomer on 17 December 1935 (*Invention* 234). That fall, former Orage pupils divided themselves into different groups. Wim Nyland gathered a small group at Chardavogne Barn in Warwick, New York, with his wife Ilonka. Edwin Wolfe and Daly King instituted a regular Thursday evening group meeting in New York based on King's Orage notes (*Invention* 234).

The Rope

Jane Heap—"Miss Geep" to Gurdjieff—left Paris on 18 October for London with Gurdjieff's instructions to establish a group. One wonders what Ouspensky thought and how he reacted to an associate of Gurdjieff teaching in his territory. Few names are known of her pupils there, though Solano said later that Stanley Nott was one of them. Nott himself wrote that Heap took over a group he had founded himself in 1933 (*Journey* 80). She came back to Paris frequently to meet Gurdjieff throughout the late thirties and, after Ouspensky left for the United States in 1940, Heap "inherited" many of Ouspensky's followers.

On 19 October, the day after Heap's departure, Gurdjieff invited a number of women to his room at the Grand Hotel. They were all members of the group to whom Jane Heap had been talking in Paris since the late twenties consisting of Solita Solano ("Kanari"), Kathryn Hulme ("Crocodile") and Louise Davidson ("Sardine"). Elizabeth Gordon joined them in a group they called later "The Rope," after Gurdjieff's explanation that to mount the slopes of consciousness they must be tied together on a "cordée," or rope. Gurdjieff was the "premier de cordée:" that is, the guide and leader already at the top securing the rope for the others. All of these women, with the exception of Hulme, had been with Orage in New York. After a few days, they met at the Hôtel Napoléon Bonaparte near the Sorbonne, where Solano and Hulme were living. Later, in 1936, Margaret Anderson and Georgette Leblanc joined the group, though they were not in the eyes of the others proper members of The Rope. Gurdjieff called the late arrivals "Knackschmidt and Company," after the name given to poor peasants who come together at the end of the day to make something (*Undiscovered Country* 78). By then, Gurdjieff had moved into an apartment on Rue Labie, off the Avenue des Ternes, near the Arc de Triomphe.

It must appear odd that Gurdjieff, who made his disfavor of aberrant sexual practices and dysfunctional "sexual centers" quite clear on numerous occasions, would teach exclusively for the greater part of the next four years a select group of lesbian women. The titular protagonist of *Beelzebub's Tales* makes it quite clear that the future of Americans is being determined negatively by sexual habits. Gurdjieff's discussion of those sexual practices liable to have negative effects on one's being, castigated an onanist (which disqualifies one for a soul), prostitution, and homosexuality. He reminded them frequently of their abnormal personalities. In a June 1937 conversation, Gurdjieff told Solano: "Something wrong your sex. Sex very important thing is, like light, like air you breathe, food you eat. If you are in parts, two of your five parts depend from sex. You must more normal live." Solano replied that she had no wish to think about such things (*Invention* 237).

In his meetings with Solita Solano and others Gurdjieff's tone was quieter, more personal, and kind than it had been at the Prieuré. Rather than expose a "system" or a "method," he addressed topical and personal concerns. Occasionally he referred to *Tales* and *Meetings*, though he refused to divulge to the women the contents of the expunged chapter about Prince Nijeradze. He played his harmonium rarely, and there was never a question of movements. Instead, he assigned self-work tasks to the women. He occasionally applied injections of his own formulae and electric currents to them. As expected under these circumstances, his most enlightening talks took place at the table.

Though his brother Dmitri was suffering from a cancer at the time, Gurdjieff no longer felt responsible for his extended family, including the Russian entourage who had been with him in Fontainebleau. He needed money for himself and perhaps for future work projects he was formulating. The Rope brought in little. After a meeting that first autumn back in Paris, Solano noted: "He is in black moods and money difficulties" (3 December 1935). Gurdjieff earned enough for his daily expenses by treating alcoholics, drug addicts, arthritics, and sufferers of other ills with *piqures* "injections" of a home-made concoction, as well as with electrical impulses, probably with his Theremin machine.

Gurdjieff had always been reported capable of transferring

vital energy from himself to others. At the Prieuré he had cured the arm burn of Fritz Peters by thrusting the arm back into the offending fire (*Boyhood*, 124). Luba Gurdjieff told me of her uncle's thrusting her arms back into the hot water that scalded her. In the late 1930s Gurdjieff's medicinal practice involved such transfer by electrical impulses generated by machines he designed himself, at least he had others believe it was so.

Gurdjieff's conversations with the ladies of The Rope were just that: conversations. He talked about a wide range of Western attitudes and behavior, including eating habits, education, language, popular culture (newspapers and books), work, religion and, of course, money. These he contrasted invariably with the cultural habits and mores of the East. At the core of Western manners, he explained, was a love of money that thwarted moral aims. "The French can do nothing when hungry. The English a little better. American can forget and work on—especially if they get paid a little more money." Though *merde* cannot be transformed to diamonds, nonetheless "man can transform shit to honey, with knowledge," probably adding *sotto voce* that honey isn't money (*Invention* 239).

Gurdjieff took particular pleasure in reviling the English language. "Svoloch language your English" was a typical pronouncement (*svoloch*, a term of abuse applied often by Gurdjieff to people, means "dregs, dirt, refuse"). Early in his talks he told the women: "I can pronounce 400 consonants for your 36. Sound-producing organs in man are more important than his eyes. America worst nation for sound-producing" (*Invention* 240). More than the phonetic limitations of American speech, he railed against idle talk, "titillation," or verbal masturbation.

1936

On 24 January 1936 Gurdjieff finally obtained a driving licence, and motored to Normandy frequently during this period to visit the Stjernvalls. In the summer of 1936, he drove to Geneva to see Jeanne de Salzmann who was directing a group in Peyvoux, between Grenoble and Briançon in the Hautes Alpes. She was also earning money giving music lessons in Evian on Lake Geneva. In 1937 Madame Ouspensky told her that she should return to Paris to be close to Gurdjieff again. The 1938 group she collected there included the poet-novelist René Daumal, suffering from tuberculosis, his wife Vera Milanov (an American originally from Brooklyn), writer Henri Tracol and his wife Henriette, the Orientalist Philippe Lavastine (married to Salzmann's daughter Natalie or "Boussique"), journalist René Zuber, and writer Luc Dietrich.

In September 1936 Gurdjieff managed to acquire an apartment at 6, Rue des Colonels Renard, just down the slope of Avenue Carnot from the Arc de Triomphe, facing Rue d'Armaillé (the address on Gurdjieff's visiting card at the time, "6, rue du Colonel-Renard" misspells the street name). His ailing brother Dmitri left his family in Fontainebleau and moved there with Valia Anastasieff, who took care of him. After Dmitri died almost a year later in August 1937, Gurdjieff moved into the apartment, and maintained it as his permanent residence for the remainder of his life. To this day, Dmitri's survivors claim that the apartment had always been in Dmitri's name.

On 16 October 1936, Gurdjieff's French visa was extended and stamped the next day in his German passport. Eventually, his presence in Paris became known to Americans; and, those who had the money and leisure to spend time in Paris managed to join his dinner table. Putnam and Loomis were there often in 1936 and 1937. When Loomis was at the table, the topic of translation was apt to be brought into conversation. On one occasional Gurdjieff offered his guests the "dish of the day." Loomis complained that "It's not English." Gurdjieff then asked: "What would you call it, Loomis?" "In America we say," replied Loomis, and after an awkward pause, "well, we say plat du jour." Gurdjieff smiled: "That is not English either, Mr. Loomis" (*Invention* 242).

In early 1937, Putnam was courting Gurdjieff's niece Lida, Dmitri's youngest daughter, though she was not yet seventeen years of age. Apparently Gurdjieff approved of the relationship as long they refrained from doing "mama-papa business" (have sexual intercourse). Gurdjieff joked with Putnam, calling him a "fiancé chicken," "not yet play papa-mama." It would seem from the conversation that no one at the table knew that Putnam had been married earlier in 1933 and divorced a year later. On 4 March 1937, Nick and Lida went to Nice where they were married in the Russian Orthodox Church. Putnam told me that Lida's mother, Asta, approved of the union, but Dmitri knew nothing about it. For some reason, Nick had not taken the trouble to post bans and file the civil papers necessary to have the marriage officially registered. Curiously, when Putnam had arrived in New York from Cherbourg aboard the *Europa* several months earlier on 11 September 1936, he declared to immigration authorities that he was married, raising the possibility that he had married someone else a year earlier. No wife was with him on this crossing, and when he sailed with Loomis in December 1937 for New York, Lida was not with him.

Solano's journal entries in 1937 and 1938 mention several Americans who visited Gurdjieff. Her entry for 30 May 1937 records the arrival of Frank Lloyd Wright, Olgivanna and their eleven-year old daughter Iovanna for lunch during a stopover on the way to Moscow where Wright was to lecture. After a number of toasts to idiots, Wright remarked: "Very interesting, these idiots of yours. I've invented some also." Gurdjieff did not reply, and Wright went on: "Mr. G., you're certainly a good cook. You could earn a lot of money cooking somewhere." "Not as much as I can earn shearing," Gurdjieff replied coldly. After the meal, Gurdjieff brought out a typescript of a chapter from *Meetings with*

Remarkable Men and asked who would read. Wright said that he read quite well. When Gurdjieff absented himself from the room, the assembled guests overheard Wright mutter: "Damn, I'm sleepy. I can't take it. Still I don't want to hurt the old man's feelings." While he was reading, Gurdjieff re-entered the salon and sat down. Wright abruptly stopped reading, turned to Gurdjieff and said: "You know, Mr. G, this is interesting and it's a pity it's not well written. You know you talk English very well, too bad you can't dictate. Now if I had time you could dictate to me and I could write this for you in good English." Then he resumed his reading for a while, stopped, and excused himself, saying: "Now I must go and take my little daughter home. She's sleepy and so is her father." Gurdjieff said: "Yes, for her sake, stop. She is young. You, of course, you are old man now and life finish. But she only begin." Wright raged: "My life is NOT finished. I could right now make six more like her." Olgivanna broke into tears and took Iovanna by the hand to the door (*Invention* 247–48; *Fellowship* 350–51, have this meeting in 1939 after Wright's lectures in London).

The Rope had met throughout 1936 and 1937 and disintegrated as a group in early 1938. Other events in 1937 and 1938 changed the complexion of Gurdjieff's life. Alexander de Salzmann had died in April 1934, Dmitri Gurdjieff of a cancer in August 1937, Leonid de Stjernvall of prostate cancer in April 1938. Because of his brother's death Gurdjieff postponed the trip to the United States he had contemplated for the autumn of 1937, and after settling in 6, Rue des Colonels Renard, he curtailed his meetings with The Rope, but continued hosting visitors at dinners, with his nephew Valia and son Nikolai serving as assistants (*My Dear Father* 35-43).

Seventh Visit: Arrival on the Paris 8 March 1939

Almost a year later, in March 1939, most likely with German identity papers in hand, Gurdjieff sailed with Solano for New York on board the *CGT Paris*. He moved into a suite at the Hotel Wellington, not far from the Columbus Square Child's Restaurant, carrying boxes of eyelashes he had manufactured with the help of Luba, Valia and Nikolai in Paris. Fred Leighton, Donald Whitcomb, Martin and Rita Romilly Benson, Muriel Draper, Edwin and Dorothy Wolfe, Carol Robinson, Edith Taylor, Stanley Spiegelberg and Sherman Manchester met with him in the days after. Louise and Walter March, who had settled in the United States in 1936 (Walter was an American citizen) came to New York with their children from Nyack to see Gurdjieff in April. In the autumn of 1939, they decided to stay in America, and purchased Spring Farm in Bloomingburg, New York where they hosted innumerable Gurdjieff group members throughout the war.

Leighton telephoned the news of Gurdjieff's arrival to Toomer in Doylestown, where he and Marjorie had been living since April 1936. Though Toomer had gathered pupils each summer at the "Mill House" in Mechanicsville, Pennsylvania, to whom he expounded the Gurdjieff "system," he preferred not to face Gurdjieff. He left by himself for a vacation in Bermuda after telling Leighton that he suspected Gurdjieff had designs on the Mill House. Leighton tried to appease him with the news that Gurdjieff had put down a deposit on a château on the River Marne. Toomer returned to the United States on 12 May, a week before Gurdjieff left.

Later that month, Gurdjieff received a telegram from the Wrights in Scottsdale, Arizona, inviting him to visit Taliesin West. Gurdjieff accepted, but then cancelled the trip on 16 April when Nick Putnam, who had never been on good terms with Olgivanna, said he would not accompany him (several writers on

Wright, following Stanley Nott, say that the spat over who would finish off the other's pupils took place at this time, though there is no record of Gurdjieff being at Taliesin East or Taliesin West in April 1939).

Instead, Gurdjieff traveled with Nick and Fred Leighton to Atlantic Highlands, New Jersey, where Donald Whitcomb put his house at his disposition, and promised that he would help him find a residence nearby in the region should he want to settle there. Gurdjieff declined to stay for supper, let alone spend the night. After turning down Whitcomb's suggestion to settle in New Jersey and hearing nothing from Toomer, Gurdjieff looked elsewhere for ways of renewing his teaching in America. He talked at length with Putnam and Leighton, two persons in whom he trusted.

Since the defection of Orage and the deaths of Dmitri, Salzmann and Stjernvall, Gurdjieff had few close friends or associates remaining besides Loomis, Putnam and Leighton. Loomis had succeeded to Orage as a translator, but not as a close associate. With Putnam and Leighton, however, Gurdjieff could laugh and play as he had been able to do with Orage. Both had lively senses of humor and were committed to Gurdjieff's teaching, though they had neither money nor property to dedicate to the establishment of the Institute in America (Putnam had inherited a fortune in 1929, but his brother Carleton and the courts had frozen it in a trust from which he could touch annually only a portion of the income). Further, neither Leighton nor Putnam had the confidence of Orage's New York successors who had shifted interest towards Orage's Social Credit scheme.

Leighton, Putnam, Loomis and Whitcomb tried to persuade Gurdjieff to remain in the United States in view of the explosive political situation in Western Europe following the annexation of Austria and seizure of the Sudeten. Considering the war atmosphere in Germany, Gurdjieff's insistence on returning to France is puzzling. Margaret Anderson and Georgette Leblanc had taken up permanent residence in Paris, but The Rope had dispersed. Few French pupils awaited him. The so-called deposit on the Marne château was but a pretence.

When he boarded the *Normandie* on 19 May 1939 with Kathryn Hulme, Gurdjieff had given up hope for securing the work in America. From any perspective, Gurdjieff left America and his American relationships behind definitively. Then, before the summer of 1939 was over, the Wehrmacht invaded Poland, and France and England declared war on Germany. Mother World War II, following Grandmother Russian Revolution, showed her face to Gurdjieff.

13

1 September 1939–17 December 1948:
Survival

The Occupation of Paris

On the Monday morning German troops invaded Poland, Jane Heap was in England with her English group, and two days later, on 3 September, after France declared war on Germany, Margaret Anderson took refuge in the south of France until she found passage to America. Her friend Georgette Leblanc died of cancer in Cannes in October 1941. In the early days of the war, Gurdjieff was being aided in his small apartment by relatives who served as *factoti*. Before the war broke out it had been Nikolai de Stjernvall, Valia Anastasieff and Mikhail ("Michel") de Salzmann. Gurdjieff's indefatigable major domo George ("Gabo")—whose whole name no one seems to have known—was always on hand when needed.

During the period from September 1939 until the German Blitzkrieg attack through Belgium and the Netherlands into France on 10 May 1940, Americans heard little news of Gurdjieff. Fred Leighton wrote Toomer on 12 January 1940 to report: "Latest news from Mr. G. came only the other day (by Atlantic Clipper three weeks late). He wants all his old friends in America who wish to do so to sit down at once and write him a letter inviting him to America . . . This show of letters from different parts of this country will make it easier with regard to his necessary papers" (*Invention* 258). German troops marched into Paris on 14 June, and on 25 June terms of surrender were signed that divided France into occupied and unoccupied zones.

On 26 June Leighton wrote Toomer again, saying: "No one has heard from G or Miss Gordon since 20 days before Germans entered Paris. I would like to think of him as still sitting each morning at the Café de la Paix." He may well have been, though Miss Gordon was seized soon after as a citizen of a belligerent nation and interned for the duration.

Meanwhile in England, Ouspensky had been under government surveillance since 1937, and after Germany invaded Russia in the spring of 1941, he was threatened with house arrest because of his unknown political sympathies (*Circle* 439–40). He started to move his family one by one across the Atlantic. His wife's twenty-one year old grandson, Leonid ("Lonia"), sailed from Liverpool to New York aboard the *Samaria* on 21 August 1940, and Lonia's eleven year old half-sister Tatiana ("Tania") sailed from Glasgow aboard the *Empress of Australia* on 14 September 1940 along with ten other children. Four months later, on 15 January 1941, Sophia Gregorievna sailed on the *Warwick Castle* and arrived on the 24th in St. Johns, New Brunswick, and Ouspensky himself followed from Liverpool on 11 February 1941 aboard the *Georgic*. Helene ("Lenochka"), Sophia's daughter, remained in England another two years until 24 April 1943 when she sailed on the *Mauretania* from Liverpool and arrived in the United States on 2 May. Many of Ouspensky's pupils who remained in England joined the groups of Maurice Nicoll, Kenneth Walker, or J. G. Bennett (*Circle* 440–41). Not many were attracted to Jane Heap's group.

After the commencement of hostilities, Gurdjieff's former English and American pupils drifted into various wartime activities. Before the end of 1939, Elizaveta de Stjernvall and her twenty year old son Nikolai went by boat to Stockholm and then by rail to Finland. After the Soviet Union invaded Finland on 30 November, Nikolai served as a translator for Finnish intelligence throughout the war, after which he and his mother made their way in 1948 to Geneva where they took up permanent residence. Fritz Peters was drafted into the American Army and served as a company clerk in the European theater of Operations after allied forces landed in France in 1944. Valia Anastasieff joined the French Resistance and was rewarded with French citizenship after the war. Elizabeth Gordon, who had remained imprudently in Paris, suffered hardships of confinement and died soon after the war ended. Ethel Merston, Gurdjieff's housekeeper at the Prieuré, had moved to India where she remained until her death.

Bernard Metz took a post with the British Consulate in Algiers and later in Casablanca. In 1940, after the French-German Armistice, he transferred to the American Consulate. When American Forces landed in late 1942, he worked with the American negotiator with French forces, Robert Daniel Murphy. At the close of the North African Campaign he was rewarded for his service in August 1943 with passage to the United States where he took the name Bernard Mayne (he quipped that he had just changed his name from one French city to another, Mayenne).

In the United States, Nick Putnam was associated, he claimed, with the Office of Strategic Services. Before the war was over, he remarried, though he was still attached in religious bonds with Lida Gurdjieff. Loomis worked with Intelligence agencies until 1945 when he was employed by the United Nations as interpreter and translator. After the death of her husband, Jessie Orage returned to the United States in 1935 with her two children and resided in Santa Fe, New Mexico. Stanley Nott spent the war years with his wife and two sons in various locations in the United States. He wrote to Toomer 20 April 1940 asking if he might stay at the Mill House (*Invention* 263), and after Toomer turned down his request, Nott, his wife and two sons found refuge with the Wrights in Spring Green, Wisconsin, in Putney, Vermont, and in Westport, Connecticut with the Taylors, before returning to England in 1944 about the same time that Jessie Orage returned to England.

Meanwhile, with the substantial financial aid of Janet Collin-Smith and real estate scouting by Schuyler Jackson and other members of the Orage group, Ouspensky, his family and followers were able to move to Franklin Farms in Mendham, New Jersey, near Morristown, some fifty miles from New York City (*Circle* 442). Ouspensky also leased an apartment in New York where he gave series of talks throughout the war that attracted many of Orage's former group members.

In February 1942, Leighton, Israel Solon and Donald Whitcomb sent a letter to American pupils asking for contributions for visas and travel expenses for Gurdjieff to go to Cuba or Mexico. They assumed that Gurdjieff could manage to get to Lisbon from where he could travel to the Caribbean region without difficulty. With his current papers and alien status in Occupied France, however, he would most likely be *persona non grata* in the United States. The request raised $299 of which $200 was sent to Gurdjieff. Leighton wrote Toomer on 25 February 1942 to report Gurdjieff's reply to the offer: "Gladly go Cuba. For permission leave, necessary many things. Hope regulate independently, except taxes eighteen thousand, rent twenty-five thousand, and of course journey." Leighton considered that even if Mexico would be cheaper, Gurdjieff would need $3110. Soon after, word was received from Elizabeth Gordon's sister in Canada that Gurdjieff would remain in Paris.

One reason to sit tight in Paris that few Americans would have known at the time were the complex problems Gurdjieff faced to leave the zone of Occupation. He would have to apply and pay for an exit visa from France, but because of his status as an alien, he was probably ineligible for an official exit visa. Even if he managed to escape France over the Pyrenees, he would have to apply and pay for a transit visa from Spanish authorities. That done, he would have to pay the cost of boat passage and compete for passage with Americans and other non-French nationals by the thousands who were fleeing South and West. After the armistice, there were over a thousand Americans in Lisbon from where one might fly by Pan Am Clipper to the United States or sail to South America. All things considered, it was easier for him to stay and await further events.

Local French authorities gave Gurdjieff another incentive for sitting tight in Paris. On Christmas Eve 1942, the French Department of Immigration, in German, issued Gurdjieff a bilingual French German "Certificat d'identité de l'Office des Emigrés Caucasiens en France." Gurdjieff's talents at persuasion were certainly behind this fortunate shift in identity, since Nansen Identity Certificates were not issued after 1938, and his French visa on his *Fremdenpass,* a document not likely to be viewed with favor for very long by any French administration, had expired. The timing of Gurdjieff's shift of national identity is particular. The second half of 1942 was an axial period in the fortunes of Germany.

At the beginning of 1942, Germany had reason to feel that she had absolute dominion over all parts of Europe. By the middle of the year, however, certain signs of problems became evident in occupied France. In June Gauleiter Sauckel arrived from Berlin to demand 350,000 workers from the occupied zone. French authorities under the direction of Pierre Laval put into practice a forced labor program to transport young Frenchmen to factories and camps in Germany, a program formally established in February 1943 as the STO (Service du travail obligatoire). Before the end of the war some 7,500,000 laborers toiled for the German military machine, of whom 785, 000 were French (the German authorities had demanded 1,575,000). To avoid deportation, a large number of Frenchmen fled the occupied zone or found refuge in the mountains of Eastern France in the Savoys and Franche Comté where they were organized in the resistance movement known as the Maquis. Among them was Gurdjieff's nephew Valia Anastasieff. In May 1943 they were organized well enough to convene a National Council of the French Resistance.

Events in the second half of 1942 foreshadowed the end of

German expansionist ideals. On 19 August 1942, Canadian commandoes staged a daring raid on Dieppe, and despite heavy losses, the action presaged for the resistant French an eventual liberation. On 14 September the German Wehrmacht entered Stalingrad, but the Russian counterattack on 19 November turned the tide of Operation Barbarossa and signaled the beginning of German retreat from the Soviet Union. On 23 October 1942 Field Marshal Montgomery struck a decisive blow on Rommel's Afrika Corps at El Alamein, and between 8 and 11 November American forces landed in Algiers and Tunisia. North Africa as well as the Soviet Union was inexorably slipping from Germany's grip.

After allied forces landed in Africa without significant French armed resistance, German forces swept into the previously unoccupied zone of France, but failed to seize the huge French fleet whose ships were scuttled by Admiral Laborde in the Mediterranean off Toulon on 27 November. In the late fall of 1942, the news of these German setbacks incited among the French a feeling that the occupation of their country was in its dying moments. For his part, Gurdjieff may have felt somewhat secure, if displeased, with German identity papers as long as it appeared that Germany would remain in control in Europe. By Christmas 1942, he either petitioned personally or knew someone with influence who could persuade local immigration officials to grant him papers identifying him as a Caucasian Immigrant.

During this period, something of a make-shift French group was being organized in Paris by Jeanne de Salzmann. Candidates for such a group were sparse. Able-bodied men were either prisoners of war, deported to concentration camps if Jews (although the deportation of Jews was done progressively), or deported to forced labor camps and factories in Germany. Those who remained in Paris to attend Gurdjieff group meetings were mostly women, the aged and the infirm.

Jeanne de Salzmann was seldom in Paris in the early days

of the Occupation. She preferred to stay close to her hometown, Geneva, in neutral Switzerland. She moved between Peyvoux in the Hautes Alpes near Grenoble and Passy, and between Megève and Chamonix on the Plateau d'Assay in the Haute Savoie near the Swiss and Italian borders. When she visited Paris from time to time, she led some former pupils to Gurdjieff's apartment, and seconded him in the direction of his movement classes at the nearby Salle Pleyel. Most of the French were artists and writers who, for one reason or another, were exempt from military service or forced labor in Germany. The sole survivor from the Prieuré days was Tchesslav Tchechovitch, who had been with Gurdjieff in Constantinople twenty years earlier.

Among the group of French pupils that included the Orientalist Phillipe Lavastine, Bernard Lemaître, Pauline Dampierre, Marthe de Gagneron, Solange Claustres, Henriette Lannes Tracol, and Luc Dietrich, the best known to the public was the writer René Daumal who had been introduced to Gurdjieff's ideas by Alexander de Salzmann almost a decade earlier. Stricken with tuberculosis, Daumal spent most of the wartime in the Alps with his wife, Vera Milanova, whom he had married in New York in July 1939. Another reason for staying away from Paris was Vera's status as a Jew. Though she was from Brooklyn, she had acquired French nationality by marriage, and was threatened with the same treatment by the Germans as French Jews. Daumal died from his illness before the end of the war, and his younger friend Luc Dietrich, the talented writer of *L'Apprentissage de la Ville*, was killed in hostilities shortly before the liberation of Paris. After the war Vera moved to England and married the landscape architect Russell Page. In 1948, the journalist Louis Pauwels joined and spent some fifteen months in a Gurdjieff group. The physician Michel Conge also joined the French group, directed a Paris group himself and founded a group in Israel.

Many of Gurdjieff's talks during the war were later transcribed and translated into English before being circulated in England and the United States (Patterson, *Ladies*). In his wartime talks, Gurdjieff revealed a softened style of teaching resembling his Petersburg and Moscow manner during World War I. Because his audience consisted of many who had not read any of his writings, he directed his attention to individual concerns of his pupils, offering the same sort of psychological counseling he had given The Rope group.

Gurdjieff's Oil Wells

There was then and continues to be speculation on how Gurdjieff managed not only to support himself and the small entourage about him as well as contribute to the survival of residents in his quarter to whom he gave generously. He helped poor street artists by buying their works. His collection of art works of dubious value crowded his salon until after the war when he gave most of them away. The novelist Mary Howard, writing under the pseudonym Josephine Saxton, in a work of pure fiction described a man during the occupation in Paris who could be only Gurdjieff:

"Le Vielle [sic] Marchand du Viand," the strange Armenian who had conjured up foods from nowhere, right under the noses of the Occupation Forces . . . sat in his "office" in the Rue des Colonels Renard with strings of sausages hanging over his head, jars of strange fruits and pickles, whole sides of smoked salmon, sweetmeats, hams, herbs, garlic, strings of onions, cream, eggs, oh, riches in the wilderness! And much of this he would give to the poor of the district, the poor and the old. And he would play tunes on an ancient accordion, tunes that wrung the heart and said things to a person that could not be spoken. And it was because of him that her mother had said she was content to die and was not in anguish. Some kind of love had passed into her stricken old life along with the food parcels. And when he died there had been thousands of people at his funeral, a long train of weeping people (*Group Feast* 34).

None of his French pupils had sufficient influence with the authorities to protect Gurdjieff against charges of hoarding. Gurdjieff's own explanation, reputedly told to Fritz Peters, was: "I make deal with Germans, with policemen, with all kinds idealistic people who make 'black market.' Result: I eat well and continue have tobacco, liquor, and what is necessary for me and for many others" (*Gurdjieff Remembered* 92–93). James Webb assumed that Parisian authorities were somehow mollified or persuaded to tolerate his behavior. "How [else] in that occupied city had he acquired the vodka and the delicacies which gave his feasts their memorable flavor?" (*Circle* 469). Moore thinks that Gurdjieff began hoarding between the beginning of the war and the capitulation of Paris in May 1940, adding that "Gurdjieff admitted to working the black market and collaborating with the Germans" (*Anatomy* 276).

In what way Gurdjieff might have "collaborated" has not been divulged. If he told Peters he made "deals" with the Germans, he was not admitting to the serious charge of collaboration. In his quarter of Paris, he was known to the locals as one ready to help anyone in distress, but no one in his neighborhood accused him of collaboration. Moore remarks that "Gurdjieff—despite his commercial transactions with German 'idealists'—was wholly indemnified by his grandfatherly humanity and his support of Jewish group members" (*Anatomy* 283). Of course, being on a list of those who had close ties to Germany and had once held a *Fremdenpass* might have protected him from the Gestapo. Perhaps the German authorities assumed he had anti-Bolshevik views, though it is unlikely that any of them had heard them expressed. It is easier to suppose that Gurdjieff maneuvered among the Germans in the same manner he had managed with Bolshevik and White Russian administrations a quarter of a century earlier.

He told those who asked that he had credit from local merchants on the expectation that his income from American oil wells would recompense them handsomely (Moore *Anatomy* 278; Patterson, *Ladies* 174; Hulme, *Undiscovered* 215). Gurdjieff had represented himself once as an oilman on a train between Petrograd and Moscow almost twenty years earlier (Ouspensky *Search* 325–26), and he had told his American audience in 1924: "I participated in oil wells and fisheries" (*Meetings* 270). Nonetheless, despite his assurances of financial solvency, under wartime conditions in Paris, it is highly unlikely that he could have been granted indefinite credit of the amounts involved, considering the scarcity of foodstuffs available to the public in licensed shops. First of all, foodstuffs were extremely rare, especially meat. Soon after the occupation began, Wednesdays, Thursdays and Fridays were declared "meatless." Almost all foods were strictly rationed, and butchers and bakers were under strict control. One need only view the film *La Traversée de Paris* starring Bouvil and Jean Gabin, to appreciate the lengths to which Parisians went to secure food. Parisians took to eating cats, despite posters declaring that eaters of cats abet the proliferation of rats. The black market was also wanting throughout most of the war and depended upon foodstuffs smuggled in from the countryside. It is likely that Gurdjieff was able to get his stock of food from the supplies of the occupiers with whom he made "deals."

That access he had as well as the money to make deals with the Germans. His oil-well story was a calculated cover-up. His money source was the pocketbook of a hotel owner and race-horse breeder, François Dupré, who transferred money to Gurdjieff before, throughout, and after the war on behalf of his Hungarian-born wife, Anna Stefanna ("Anci"), whom Gurdjieff had cured of a life-threatening illness (*Invention* 264–68). Sometime in early 1939, Anci suffered painful intestinal problems, diagnosed as caused by an inoperable tumor adjacent to the liver. Someone, perhaps Daumal, told her husband to have her consult Gurdjieff. When she did, Gurdjieff felt about her abdominal and thoracic regions and then held the palm of his right hand over the tumor. He told her to return if the pain persisted more than twenty-four hours. Within a day, the pain and signs of the tumor were gone.

From that instant, Anci became devoted to Gurdjieff. With the prompting of Jeanne de Salzmann, to whom Gurdjieff had entrusted Daumal and his wife, she offered her husband's money to support Gurdjieff. Though Dupré did not care to deal with Gurdjieff himself, he was willing to satisfy his wife's wishes. Dupré's acquiescence in his wife's support of Gurdjieff was threatened when, on New Year's Eve, 1942, with expectation of her husband's joy, Anci announced that she was pregnant. Dupré, after disclosing to her that he was impotent, left her. Daumal's friend Luc Dietrich, the biological father of her unborn child, had neither means nor desire to take Anci into his care.

Dupré ordered Anci to have an abortion outside of France. Because of his business associations with the German Occupation forces—his luxurious hotels, the Plaza Athenée and George V. billeted Wehrmacht officers—he could obtain transit papers for her. With Jeanne de Salzmann, Anci passed through German border controls into Switzerland with the Ausweiss her husband procured from German authorities. In Geneva a gynecologist friend of Salzmann performed the abortion. Back in Paris, she and Dupré reached an amicable agreement to the effect that both his money and business connections with the German Occupation authorities would serve Gurdjieff (*Invention* 265–67).

Retrieval

After the liberation of Paris on 25 August 1944, French authorities arrested and imprisoned Dupré for collaboration because he had worked for the Werhmacht. He was released only after paying an exorbitant fine. Gurdjieff was also seized and imprisoned after the Liberation for illegal possession of foreign currency, but he was released a day or so later on the grounds that he was a poor old man who did not understand his crime.

In the last days of the war, Roger Manchester, son of Orage's friend Sherman Manchester, was in France piloting B-26 bombers for the United States Army Air Corps. On a three-day pass he visited Paris to see Gurdjieff. Though Gurdjieff had not met him before, Manchester was received with "Oriental" hospitality and asked news of various members of the American groups. About the same time, Fritz Peters visited Gurdjieff on leave from his duties (*Gurdjieff Remembered*, 76–113). Kathryn Hulme, attached to the relief organization UNRRA in Cotentin, France, in 1945 and 1946, managed to get to Paris to see him. Nick Putnam and Philip Lasell arrived in Paris by air the summer of 1946, and both reported back to New York that Gurdjieff was in good spirits.

In 1947, the American Annie Lou Stavely, who had been in England with Jane Heap during the war, crossed the Channel with her and other pupils and met Gurdjieff for the first time. Donald and Lillian Whitcomb arrived in Paris by air on 23 June and stayed five weeks until the end of July. They brought money raised by the New York group, but Donald, obviously psychologically out of sorts, was intent on having Gurdjieff give him exercises. Gurdjieff named him "Camel" to mark the burden Donald, two months shy of forty-seven years of age at the time, carried on his emotional back. Whitcomb recounted in great detail his personal talks with Gurdjieff in an yet unpublished "Notes of his Visit to Gurdjieff in Paris," in which he recalls the many American and English who were at Gurdjieff's during that period. They included Louise March and her children, Nick Putnam and his close friend, "Bobby" de Pomeroy, Wim and Ilonka Nyland, Stanley Nott, and Cynthia Pearce.

While Wim reported back to the New York group later that Gurdjieff had authorized the starting of a New York group with materials he would furnish before going to New York himself, Donald was ordered by Gurdjieff to start a group in Providence, Rhode Island where Donald was an engineer with the Narragansett Power Company. Directing a group was well beyond Donald's capacities as all who knew him realized. Besides engaging in group exercises such as movements during his stay, Donald performed several personal tasks for Gurdjieff, such as getting bank checks validated.

Besides typical physical exercises consisting of concentrating successively on different parts of the body, Gurdjieff had Donald and Lillian recall their affective relations with their parents. "He asked about my relations with my mother. I told him about what he had told me at the Prieuré about mother, and how my attitude had changed. He wanted to know if this was due to him."(27-28). Curiously Gurdjieff told Donald to bolster his feelings about his living mother with the spirit of Gurdjieff's departed mother.

On one occasion, Gurdjieff predicted suffering for the Ouspensky (page 27), as if he felt Ouspensky's approaching death within three months. Gurdjieff might have heard from his English guests that Ouspensky returned to England in 1947 where he died on 2 October. From Mendham where she was bed-ridden with Parkinson's disease, Sophia Gregorievna (known by then familiarly as "Madame Ouspensky") advised her husband's former pupils to seek out Gurdjieff.

Englishmen Lord Pentland (John Sinclair) and J. G. Bennett, and Americans Edwin and Dorothy Wolfe, Margaret Anderson and Dorothy Caruso visited from New York in the summer of 1947. When Jean and Annette Herter visited that summer, they noted that Gurdjieff had an American visa already in his French passport. Throughout the winter and spring of 1948, Gurdjieff met with both French and English pupils in his apartment and with Jeanne de Salzmann directed movements at the Salle Pleyel nearby.

In August 1948, Gurdjieff, with Philip Lasell beside him in the front seat and Lise Tracol behind, had a near-fatal accident near Montargis when a truck crashed into the Citroën he was driving. As he lay on the roadside, waiting for help to arrive, he kept Lasell's morale up with stories, though Lasell suffered only minor injuries compared to Gurdjieff's. When Nick and Vicky Putnam, who had come all the way from Los Angeles, stopped at Rue des Colonels Renard the next day for lunch, they found him not only strong, but joking about his accident. Though his body had suffered grievously, he had not the least qualms about returning to the United States as planned.

Throughout that autumn Jeanne de Salzmann communicated Gurdjieff's travel plans to Madame Ouspensky who advised her group at Franklin Farms to prepare to meet Gurdjieff in New York. Gurdjieff told Putnam to round up the vestiges of Orage's New York group, and to find lodgings near Columbus Circle for the large entourage he would bring with him. When Gurdjieff told Americans that all his French debts had been liquidated, and his passage paid for, it was assumed that Ouspensky's former group had advanced the money, but Anci Dupré had provided her husband's money for the trip.

14

17 December 1948–29 October 1949:
Infinity with Finity Conjoined

Eighth and Final Visit to America

Gurdjieff, with a French passport in his hand that listed his nationality as "stateless," arrived in New York on 16 December 1948 aboard the *America* accompanied by Jeanne de Salzmann. Appropriately, his eighth visit reflects the eight notes of the musical octave whose patterns sustain the structure of Gurdjieff's universe. Before leaving Paris, Gurdjieff had credited the English for paying his running accounts in Paris (Bennett, *Making a New World* 249), and former Ouspensky pupils in New York for paying the millions of French francs of debt he had incurred during the war. It was said *sotto voce* in New York that Lord Pentland had shouldered most of the financial burden of the trip to America, though Anci Dupré told Eve Taylor that she had paid for his passage. In New York Gurdjieff announced that he had made a down payment on the Château des Voisins in Rambouillet, south of Versailles, where he intended to re-establish the Institute. If he had done so, where he had found either the cash or the credit is perhaps no mystery.

In December 1948, Gurdjieff was back in his element in New York. He was there, he announced, to do what he had done nine years earlier; that is, to review and re-organize the American groups while raising money for the publication of the first series and the acquisition of the Rambouillet property. He would also name financial representatives, secretaries and treasurers in the United States, as in England and France. He was also intent on reviving the movements, and for that purpose he had sent Alfred Etievant ahead of him to initiate classes in New York. Jessmin Howarth was at the time directing movements at Franklin Farms, as she had in England earlier for Ouspensky people, so there were already a number of Americans familiar with the dances.

By the time Gurdjieff arrived in mid-December, some sixty people of all ages, many already instructed in Mendham, were enrolled in movement classes at Carnegie Hall. During his stay, Gurdjieff selected a number of young women, whom he called affectionately "calves," for the front line of six in demonstrations. The orphaned niece of Henri Tracol, Lise, who remained in France, was to be one, and the others designated were Dushka Howarth, Tatiana Savitsky Forman, Eve Taylor Zwaska, Iovanna Lloyd-Wright, and Marian Sutta. The younger Martha ("Patty") Welch and Mary Sinclair would be behind them. Vivian Heally in London would join the group in France.

Two in the front row were Gurdjieff's daughters he was particularly interested in seeing in New York. When Jessmin Howarth brought her twenty-four year old daughter Dushka to him, he addressed her as "Sophie," the name he had chosen for her himself after his favorite sister. Since 1935, he had not laid eyes on Edith Taylor's twenty-year old daughter Eve (whom he had named after his mother). He proudly addressed both as "Miss Gurdjieff," though Eve, contrary to Dushka, did not seem to appreciate the implication of the name.

Many former Ouspensky followers from Mendham and former members of Orage groups flocked to the Wellington Hotel to see him, some with their families, including Louise Welch and her husband Bill, Wim Nyland and his wife Ilonka, Paul Anderson and his wife Naomi, Maurice Sutta and his wife Evelyne, Tom Forman, Clive Entwhistle, Basil Tilley, Lonia Savitsky, William Segal and his wife Cora, and Irmis Popoff. A scant few of Ouspensky pupils declined to join the crowds swarming into the Wellington to see Gurdjieff.

From Spring Green, Wisconsin, Frank and Olgivanna Lloyd Wright with daughter Iovanna came and moved into the Plaza on Central Park South for the duration of Gurdjieff's stay. On Gurdjieff's behalf, Fred Leighton invited Jean Toomer to New York, but Toomer demurred, saying he would keep in touch with developments. There is no record of the attendance of many prominent members of the former Orage group such as Daly King, Waldo Frank, Gorham and Delza Munson, Tom Matthews, and Mabel Dodge Luhan. Curiously, neither Fritz Peters nor Bernard Metz showed up there. Metz told me later that he was not notified of Gurdjieff's presence. It is likely that no one knew of Metz's new name and address.

Many were surprised and pleased by Gurdjieff's demeanor. He seemed to be on a peace mission to mend broken bridges to former pupils of Orage, Toomer and Ouspensky. He had made peace with Jessie Orage in Paris months earlier, and with Edith Taylor and Jessmin Howarth right away in New York. He had not lost the combative spark and fire of the Institute days but for the most part kept it dampened. No more than ever would he suffer fools, but now he dismissed them with humor rather than with histrionic rage. Someone told Irmis Popoff, who was seeing Gurdjieff for the first time: "You did not know him when he was young. He was a devil" (*His Work* 138).

Gurdjieff paid particular attention to the children. He had often said that cognitive relations with those attached to him "in the skin" were more meaningful than blood strain. More than one pupil had said that Gurdjieff was a "father" to him. Frank Lloyd Wright said in an interview that Gurdjieff admitted to "104 sons of his own and 27 daughters, for all of whose education he has made provision and to which he has given attention" (*Madison Capitol Times*, 9 September 1934). Gurdjieff told children in New York that he had ten of his own children, but the names of only seven circulated and the blood ties of some of these were doubted. In New York Gurdjieff told Popoff that he had fifty sons in monasteries (*His Work* 148).

Others he probably never heard of claimed him as their be-getter (*Invention* 272–73). Gurdjieff's own view was that he was "father" to the many he treated with paternal care besides his nephew, nieces and the children of associates who had played on the lawns of the Prieuré. It seems strange that current biographies of Gurdjieff pay little mention to the children who were with him in the Caucasus, Constantinople, Berlin, France and the United States. Gurdjieff counted eleven children between the ages of one and nine with him in Essentuki in 1918, six of whom were his sister Sophia's (*Meetings* 278), though Sophia is not known to have had six children. Most of the children who gathered about him with their parents in New York in 1948 and 1949 were already in their teens or early twenties. Margery Toomer ("Argie"), daughter of Jean Toomer, was not there, but she attended movement classes after Gurdjieff left.

On the whole, the children were in awe of Gurdjieff, and he treated them as "candidates for initiation." A child invited to lunch for the first time might be seated at the long table set up in the largest bedroom of his suite at the Wellington. Occasionally, on a first visit to his table, a child placed on Gurdjieff's right was given an adult portion of vodka for the toasts to idiots. In the order of idiots, a child was an "unformed idiot," or "aspirant for ordinary idiot." It was considered an honor for a young person to receive from Gurdjieff's hand a special morsel of food, such as a sheep's eye.

Gurdjieff enjoyed "testing" and assigning tasks to the children and young adults. He gave one of the "calves" a thousand dollars with the task of buying Christmas presents for the holiday guests (*Shadows* 170n). A boy was given five hundred dollars to exchange for silver dollars (*Invention* 275). In both cases the changing of hundred dollar bills in banks proved difficult. The silver dollars played a role in testing children when, a few days later, Gurdjieff put a pile of five dollar bills next to a pile of silver dollars and had children chose either one bill or one silver dollar. The boys invariably chose the bill, while girls favored the silver (*March* 82).

After talks in the afternoon, Gurdjieff would throw handfuls of hard candies known as "jaw-breakers" to the crowd, but particularly to the children sitting cross-legged at the front of the assembly. He said that bon-bons were rewards for attention. Annie Lou Stavely recalls that a Prieuré pupil explained to her: "Of course he gives candy only to waiters and people like that because he is sorry for them. If people can't be helped any other way he gives them candy (*Memories* 33)." Rina Hands remembers Gurdjieff in Paris giving children sweets as reward for work (*Diary* 65).

After supper, guests assembled in the salon to listen to readings. After his arrival in January, John Bennett joined Edwin Wolfe, Stanley Spiegelberg and Fred Leighton as a reader. Evenings ended with Gurdjieff playing his harmonium, and when he stopped playing, it was time to leave. On Saturday evenings, Gurdjieff took others with him to steam baths, usually at the Luxor baths in the basement of the Lenox hotel at 121 West 46th Street. Sometimes the evening meal was taken at a restaurant. His favorite was Frank's Steak House on 125th Street in Harlem. Because the restaurant did not have armagnac on hand for the toasts, Gurdjieff gladly toasted with applejack, a brandy distilled from cider.

The concentration of activities in which Gurdjieff engaged himself in a few weeks in New York was mind-boggling. Besides hosting two meals a day, giving series of talks, playing music, taking the baths, going to restaurants, and attending movement exercises at Carnegie Hall, Gurdjieff held regular "office" hours at Child's on 57th Street where he received old and new pupils. Gurdjieff was obviously tired by the end of January, after celebrating what might have been his eighty-third (or seventy-second) birthday on the 13th (*His Work* 153).

On that day, Gurdjieff had Pentland sent out a circular letter under Gurdjieff's Paris address to all his "adepts" announcing the forthcoming publication of *An Objectively Impartial Criticism of the Life of Man*, or *Beelzebub's Tales to his Grandson*. The letter, written by Gurdjieff in Russian and translated by Loomis, read: "By this publication I shall begin to actualise the plans I have prepared for the transmission of my ideas to the whole of contemporary and future humanity." Gurdjieff announced that the first edition would be printed in four languages, and the American edition would be sold for $400, the English for £100, and the French for 25,000 francs (this is not entirely true, since Harcourt Brace promised that once the subvention cost was covered, the book would go on sale to the public for $5.00). The letter closes with the names of "the representatives whom I have appointed in the three countries for the collection of subscriptions": René Zuber for France, J. G. Bennett for England, and Lord Pentland for America. Separately, Gurdjieff appointed Edith Taylor "keeper of the books," Wim Nyland "comptroller," Rita Romilly Benson "reader," Carol Robinson "pianist for movements," Donald Whitcomb "recorder and keeper of music," and Jessmin Howarth head of movement instruction. Paul Anderson would serve as his American secretary and Edwin Wolfe was to be his American minister of finance. It was made clear that Pentland would be the "figurehead" of all operations in the United States, but he would prove to be the motor as well. These appointments made, Gurdjieff cut short his projected stay by two weeks and boarded the *Queen Mary* on 11 February with those who chose to accompany him. One of these was Iovanna Wright whose father initially refused to allow her to go, before relenting after his wife Olgivanna persuaded him that she would be secure in the company of the other "calves."

After his departure, Pentland directed the preparations for his return in the fall as well as negotiations with Harcourt Brace who had demanded a $25,000 subscription. Louise March wrote that it was E. P. Dutton, in negotiation with Christopher Fremantle, who demanded a subvention that $400 per copy would cover (*March* 86). Pentland also negotiated with Harcourt Brace over the publication of Ouspensky's *In Search of the Miraculous*, scheduled for publication in October 1949, for which no subvention was asked.

Last Days

After Gurdjieff arrived home in February 1949 at Rue des Colonels Renard in Paris, he consulted right away with Jeanne de Salzmann to set a calendar for the continuation of the work. He expected many visitors from England to join the Americans who had crossed the Atlantic with him. Some of each contingent, including Dushka Howarth and Marian Sutta, moved into the Hotel Belfast on the Avenue Carnot, just a hundred meters up from the Rue des Colonels Renard. Those on a tighter budget checked into the Hotel Rena on the Rue d'Armaillé across from Gurdjieff's apartment. Anci Dupré offered her house on the Square de Bois du Boulogne as lodgings for Tania Savitsky Forman, Eve Taylor and Iovanna Wright, and provided for their daily sustenance. To all of this hurly-burly, her husband François seems to have been indifferent.

Kenneth Walker, who assumed that Gurdjieff was dedicating the spring and summer to training the young, expressed this view of Gurdjieff's "children" in Paris that spring:

One of the most striking features of these last reunions was the number of young people who crowded round his table, especially after his return from America. Those of his followers who were parents seemed to have realized that the moment had come for taking their children to Paris. They might understand very little but they wanted them to be able to recall in later years having, a long time ago, met a very remarkable man in France, a certain Mr. Gurdjieff. To ensure their being able to do this, children, ranging in age from three to fourteen, were now being brought to Paris and invited to his flat. There they sat at his table warmly welcomed and specially entertained by him . . . For him, very young people were of far greater importance than the rest of us, for they were representatives of a future generation of men and women, a generation which had not yet been ruined and which, by right teaching and upbringing, might possibly be saved. . . . Gurdjieff as grandfather, dispenser of gifts and enjoyer of fun.

Rina Hands also offers a description of Gurdjieff with children in the summers of 1948 and 1949 (*Diary* 54–55).

The routine in Paris was much the same as in New York. The lunches were generally reserved for honored guests, though the table could only serve a dozen or so. Others stood in the narrow hallway balancing plates and glasses in their hands. Tchesslav recalls that often there were some seventy to eighty persons for lunch, and often over sixty for supper, and that the kitchen staff—Alfred Etievant, Luba Gurdjieff, Lise Tracol, Gabo and Sophia Kapanadze—were so pressed that Gurdjieff himself would go there and wash dishes until the early hours of the morning (*Tu l'aimerais*, 223–25). The majority of visitors were English, and few, if any, French. If any food were left over, a rare occurrence, someone would carry it around the block to St. Ferdinand hospital.

Movement exercises were directed at least twice a week at the Salle Pleyel under Jeanne Salzmann's or Etievant's direction. By the end of March, all six front-row calves were there and Gurdjieff would wander in regularly to comment. The Salle Pleyel in Paris where the movements were practiced had a lobby whose floor exhibited an enneagram design, and the participants in the movements moved through the mathematical stations of the octave in performing them. Gurdjieff appeared overweight and coughed often, but his energy seemed unlimited.

His evening meetings rarely changed in routine. After a

meal ended usually between ten and eleven, guests and others assembled in the salon whose walls were hung with Oriental rugs. Someone would read from a typescript of *Tales* while the others sat cross-legged on the floor. Gurdjieff was not always present at the beginning of the readings but entered the salon some minutes later to take a seat on a couch. After a while he would stop the reading and incite a discussion, often based on something from the reading.

Whenever someone questioned why Gurdjieff described himself to visitors as a rug merchant, he replied: "Why dealer in rugs? Answer simple. I sell knowledge. All is in rugs around you, all. Read! All life is hidden in design." The rugs on his floors and walls were texts, stories to be read. Rug or carpet designs, like folk stories, transmit traditional cultural lore from one generation to another. Gurdjieff had always insisted that story, myth, art and dance reduplicate objective language (Ouspensky, *Search* 279), and that symbols veil truths (*Search* 284).

Throughout the spring and summer of 1949, Gurdjieff kept to his habit of taking automobile trips with pupils. In the spring he drove to Nevers, Dieppe, Vichy and Cannes. He made a trip in July to Geneva to see Elizaveta de Stjernvall and son Nikolai, as well as the landscape architect Russell Page, soon to marry Daumal's widow, Vera. On this trip, which continued to Chamonix and Vichy before returning to Paris, he traveled with the "calves," Margaret Anderson, Dorothy Caruso, Lady Pentland, Cynthia Pearce, Elizabeth Bennett and Peggy Flinch (*Shadows* 175–80). By the last week in August, Tania Forman, Marian Sutta, and Iovanna Wright had left for the United States, and later Dushka Howarth and Vivien Healy for England. Though he had originally thought of returning to the United States in September, Gurdjieff finally set the date of 20 October for his departure.

Despite his anxiety over Gurdjieff's failing health, Pentland wrote American pupils on 28 September that "Mr Gurdjieff intends to return to this country later in this year." Then he outlined the preparations for his arrival, including movement exercises and readings. He announced the forthcoming publication of Ouspensky's *In Search of the Miraculous* and urged recipients of the letter to buy one or more copies of the first printing of "Beelzebub." The report on subscriptions given Pentland by Edith Taylor was not encouraging (*Invention* 301). Anci Dupré furnished the necessary balance to Harcourt Brace for the English language version to be printed. Curiously, at this time, Gurdjieff acquired a railway station hotel-restaurant "Talbot de La Grande Paroisse" in the town of La Grande Paroisse, just east of Avon. He recorded some music there, and after his death, Kapanadze and his wife, Sophia managed the property for some years afterwards.

On the last week in October, Gurdjieff cancelled his travel plans. On 27 October, thanks to Dr. William Welch's intervention, he was admitted to the American Hospital of Paris. Gurdjieff was in great pain from an abdominal edema associated with the terminal stages of a cancer of the pancreas. He died early in the morning of 29 October, two months before his seventy-first birthday. Had he been eighty-three years of age, as he was wont to indicate to others, he would have died at the same age as he reported his father had thirty-one years earlier.

15

Postscript: Gurdjieff and Meta-history

A few months after Gurdjieff's mortal body lost its breath, his spirit found a new life in the body of his book. A few months after Gurdjieff's death, the first series of *All and Everything* went to press after Anci Dupré advanced the difference between what had been collected through subscriptions and what Harcourt Brace demanded. Within a few years, his life found other matrices in the books written about him by those who knew him "in the skin," as he would say. Shortly before he died, as I was about to return to New York, he told me that I owed him stories, and I have been spinning stories about him for the past several years but have not yet acquitted my debt.

It would be difficult to find among the volumes written about Gurdjieff's life and about pupils' personal relations with him what I could call a "disinterested" or "objective" view. The best known of his biographers, James Moore, had been a long-time member of the Gurdjieff Society of England when he wrote his Gurdjieff biography. James Webb, who preceded Moore as a biographer of Gurdjieff, was associated with pupils of Ouspensky. The score or more personal accounts by Fritz Peters, J. G. Bennett, Stanley Nott, Margaret Anderson, Georgette Leblanc, A. L. Stavely, Rina Hands, Dorothy Caruso, Jean Toomer, Louis Pauwels, René Zuber, among others, were all by Gurdjieff pupils. More recent accounts of Gurdjieff's life tend to draw upon these, often unwittingly repeating non-truths.

There is little history that is not, in fact, meta-history; that is, objective facts shaped into subjective designs. The historian interprets facts by his style, organization of materials and, often unwittingly, by his personal view of his subject. I myself cannot claim disinterest in Gurdjieff's life. Since my birth I have been closely associated with the families of Orage, Toomer and Gurdjieff himself. I spent much of my first four years with Orage and his family, and when I was a child in Fontainebleau and Paris, Gurdjieff's niece Luba was my nurse. I was informally adopted by Jean Toomer after my mother brought me and my sister to the United States. In New York City in 1948 and in Paris after the war I "worked" with Gurdjieff.

After his death I kept in close contact with Luba and her sister Lida, with Orage's son, Dick, and daughter, Ann, and more closely with Jean Toomer and his daughter Margery ("Argie," "Margot"). All of this is to say that my writing on Gurdjieff, Orage, and Toomer had been influenced heavily by my personal experience with them, despite my attempt to assume a neutral, or objective, stance toward my subject. Though I have written about people in Gurdjieff's milieu, I knew only a dozen or so very well: Stanley Nott's family (Rosemary Lillard Nott was my godmother), Nick Putnam, Philip Lasell, Fred Leighton and Wim Nyland's family. I was several times in the company of Jeanne de Salzmann but had not been with her since the early nineteen fifties. I knew neither J. G. Bennett nor Lord Pentland beyond a handshake introduction and listening to their reading and dialogues. I met P. D. Ouspensky but once in New York. I went often to Franklin Farms in the early fifties, but I never saw Madame Ouspensky, though I knew Lonia and remained close to Tania since I met her in 1948. I have known some of Gurdjieff's children very well: Nikolai de Stjernvall in Geneva, Dushka Howarth in New York and my half-sister Eve always and everywhere. The only pupil of Gurdjieff with whom I felt uncomfortable was Fritz Peters because of his big-brotherly bullying of me in the late thirties and early forties

These "facts" comprise an admission of my filtered observation or slanted perspective, if you will, on the life of Gurdjieff. That perspective has influenced my reading and my appreciation of the biographical work of others. Though I consider James Moore a friend, we have exchanged salvos of criticism at each other for the past dozen years. I have been critical of his entertaining style, his wit of *invention*, a tendency to inject humor where it seems inappropriate and to shape a story in a manner that demeans pupils, Orage and Toomer in particular. Despite my observation of my own stance toward Gurdjieff, my concern is with known and likely "facts." In my writings I have struggled to expose what I feel is not quite the truth in the process of elaborating what is, for the moment, what appears to be the truth.

James Webb, who neither knew Gurdjieff "in the skin" nor was a member of any group studying his ideas, published the first scholarly biographical account of Gurdjieff's entire life, *The Harmonious Circle* in 1980, that included biographical sketches of major pupils P. D. Ouspensky, A. R. Orage, and N. J. Toomer. Webb constructed his account of Gurdjieff's life from various sources, including the three series of *All and Everything*. He cautiously read much of the fictional *Beelzebub's Tales to his Grandson* as autobiographical, and speculated on its verifiable history (*Circle* 27, 81). For Gurdjieff's early life, Webb placed Gurdjieff within the complex political and cultural histories of Russia and Asia at the end of the nineteenth century and early years of the twentieth.

Impressive as Webb's research is, particularly his interviews with people associated directly with Gurdjieff, the reader is blocked from verifying his findings. Disdaining footnotes and endnotes, he left his readers without means of consulting his putative sources. Disarming is his caveat that "in only a very few cases have I introduced the names of living persons whose role in events has hitherto been unknown . . . The reader will have to accept my word that (to take some examples), 'a pupil of Ouspensky,' 'a follower of Orage,' or 'an inmate of the Prieuré' actually exists, and my judgment of each as a reliable source of information"

(*Circle* 12). This is asking more of readers than they can reasonably concede, particularly when his reliability is put into question in several instances where one can trace sources. It is disarming to find on the same page as this disarming statement that, in acknowledging the kind reception of Elizaveta de Stjernvall, he misspells her name as Stoerneval. It is unnecessary to enumerate the other manifest errors in his account, but one can only regret that others after him take some of his errors for fact. Of recent critics I know and respect, I admire Roger Lipsey and his *Gurdjieff's Reconsidered*, though I have taken exception to his expressed view that Gurdjieff's unsatisfactory command of English was responsible for a faulty text of the 1950 *Beelzebub's Tales*.

Willy-nilly, every historian "interprets" the facts he lays out. The literary structure which encloses them is not strictly "history"—if that term suggests a compilation of facts placed in a chronological order—but "meta-history"—a narrative of fact shaped by the style and personal view of the writer. There are as many histories of any single event and biographies of any one person as there are writers describing them. In Moore's case, his work is marked by a lively wit and wry humor that entertains, often by a personal coloring of a minor or even hypothetical event. Nonetheless, the entertainment quality of his writing is undoubtedly responsible for drawing attention of readers to Gurdjieff and his work.

I cannot measure accurately my own "slant" on Gurdjieff. I have been told that my writing suggests that I disliked, even "hated" him. If so, I am unaware of the informing emotion. Were I to state my own general assessment of Gurdjieff's career, I would say that he possessed and exercised an exceptional genius for influencing other people to work for their own "perfection of being." If there was a flaw in his method, it was an implicit conception of self as a model for emulation, whereas the man, in my opinion, could not be emulated. Perhaps he judged the intellectual, moral and physical possibilities of others too highly. Major pupils such as Ouspensky, Orage and Toomer thought that he both held and held out a key to the secret of life. I would say from the distance of over a half century that the life of the man was inseparable from the life of his work that contains that key. I suspect that should someone grasp it, he or she would be unable to turn it in the lock of universal truth. For me, the key opens up both the man and his works. For those who realize the man in the book, Gurdjieff, like Boethius's Lady Philosophy, spans the space between the above and below, the infinity and finity, and the all and everything. Gurdjieff the man embodies his work. What one knows of the man can be revedaled in his work.

Nothing illustrates this point better than his own reply to the question posed by a listener to a talk. "What will become of your work when you die?" "I not die," Gurdjieff thundered back. What he meant, of course is, that he remains alive in his writing and teaching after his body is no longer visible.

Excursus 1

Gurdjieff and Women

Perhaps nothing is a more contentious issue for readers of Gurdjieff's work and hearers of stories of his life than his attitude and behavior toward women. That man is superior to women is apodictic in his writings. In general, men are innately positive, or "affirming," while women are by nature negative or "denying," while the sexual force that brings them together is neutral or "reconciling" (*Tales* 278). This triad reflects in a manner the Christian Trinity of the Holy Family of Joseph, Mary and Jesus.

Well-known to readers is Beelzebub's citing Mullah Nassr Eddin's repeated assertion that "the cause of every misunderstanding must be sought only in woman" The context is Beelzebub's explanation that man did not evolve from apes, but apes from "women" (*Tales* 274), but Nassr Eddin's axiom is general and not restricted to a historical anomaly. In effect, Beelzebub's story reflects transitional Christian lore that has Eve the "author of all our woe." Just as the Christian Platonist exegetes attributed the Fall to the separation of Adam's reason from Eve's passion, Gurdjieff characterized men with better developed intellects (A), and women with better developed emotions (B), "but what is essential for real understanding," he concluded, "is the fusion of A and B. This produces a force we shall call C" (*Views* 87), a force that reproduces the natural moral conditions of humankind's prelapsarian state.

One would like to think that Gurdjieff means that marriage is an honest exercise of love that can engender real understanding, but such a conclusion is not apparent in Gurdjieff's teaching or in what is known of his own relations with women. Gurdjieff's fictional speakers often place women in one of two classes—wife and prostitute or woman-mother and woman-female

265

(*Tales* 987)—and it is the confusion of these roles, or the misuse of them, that causes loss of one's proper nature. In his talks with the women of the Rope, he made this point by comparing the women of Occidental and Oriental households. A woman's natural role in the Orient is as man's "handkerchief," an aid to her husband. When once Solano made herself up at the table, Gurdjieff roared, "I am Oriental and man. Never can I see woman making prostitute thing without my insides turning over . . .This idiot fashion put paint on face exist only in New York and in territory around Place Opera" (*Invention* 245–46).

Regardless of Gurdjieff's pronounced views of women and sexual activities that condemned onanism, homosexuality and prostitution—exercise of sex for pleasure alone— Gurdjieff's own sexual relations with women confused pupils and observers alike. It might have been that he had one attitude toward his grandmother, mother, sisters and wife, and quite another toward his women pupils. To his blood relatives and wife his attitude was protective and reverential. To some of his women pupils he appeared immoral, exhibiting what Samuel Johnson characterized as the morals of a Turkish pasha, and yet they respected him none the less.

Gurdjieff's reverence toward his mother and his wife conceived them as beings in rapport with nature. None of his writings makes this clearer than his Christmas Eve 1927 reflection upon the two of them while sitting on a bench between the Prieuré and the Paradou: ". . . they frequently used to come and sit down by me on this bench, on each side of me, two near beings, the only ones close to my inner world." He then recalls his mother always approached the bench from the Paradou in the company of a cat, two peacocks and a dog, while his wife approached from the Prieuré: "I remembered how it often happened that they would sit by my side . . . My mother knew not a word of the language which my wife spoke and my wife in turn understood no word of the language which my mother spoke" (*Life Is Real* 38–39). All seven, three human and four animal beings, communicated perfectly with one another in a silent transcendental language. This extraordinary scene of a mutual consciousness of the highest order places Gurdjieff and the women he loved best in a mythic and spiritual context. To others in his family and his nieces in particular his behavior was consistently protective.

With other women, the picture is starkly secular and mundane. Gurdjieff wielded uncanny sexual power over women. The apocryphal story Rom Landau tells of Gurdjieff in 1933 producing an orgasmic sensation in a woman sitting away from him in a restaurant (*God is My Adventure* 244) is repeated by Webb and Moore, though Gurdjieff was not in the United States anytime that year, and the woman mentioned, Zona Gale, was happily ensconced in Wisconsin with her husband William Breese. That he slept with various women and sired children is well known and documented. Jessmin Howarth in 1924 and Edith Taylor in 1928 bore him daughters. Both were unmarried. It is remarkable that he sired sons upon both Elizaveta de Stjernvall and Jeanne de Salzmann whose husbands were working with him at the time. His affair with Lily Galumnian, who was married, produced a son in 1927. There is oral testimony that he made sexual advances to Olga de Hartmann and Jessie Orage in 1930. It is notable that when Jessie complained to Orage about Gurdjieff's advances, her husband replied that, ordinarily, he would take offense at such a man's comportment with his wife, but he didn't consider Gurdjieff a man (*Gurdjieff and Orage* 162).

Gurdjieff typically insulted women, not just by identifying them as squirming or harmful idiots, but also by identifying them as animals, Jessie was a "dog" and Peggy Matthews was a "sow" (*Gurdjieff and Orage* 176). He called Orage and Toomer "sheep" only when they exhibited a loss of leadership power. He insulted Waldo Frank for marrying badly. Notwithstanding the anti-feminist charges that could be brought against him, women flocked to him with enthusiasm that seems unreasonable. Reviewing the inter relations he had with the women of the Rope, one wonders why he tolerated their presence and why they frequented him so regularly and ardently when his relations with them, according to reports, were superficial. His words to them do not seem to have had the moral or spiritual depth that words carried in conversations with Ouspensky, Orage and Toomer, for example. He favored women as performers of sacred dances and movements because of their capacities to create and display meaning in motion. Women in physical movement were often fluid icons.

In his autobiographical memoir, Nikolai de Stjernvall recalls that Gurdjieff's "nocturnal pleasures" exercised his "sexual potency" (*My Dear Father Gurdjieff* 37). In 1945, a woman who identified herself as Princess Nina Toubaïz-Malinowski sent him a poem in Russian that highlighted his appetite for food and sex, which I render here in English:

At present I am aware of naught but this
Life without money is far from bliss
As far as I care, all may go to hell.
I need only to eat in order to feel well.

Making love is not necessarily good
Unless the spirit is well supplied with food
And one feels like passing gas,
Having happily stuffed a mouth like an ass.

So, go preach the health of masturbation
Or pay the price of senseless fornication.
You may pay the sluts with pearls
Since you know well what to do with girls

Georgiivanich in loving you have no fears
As you teach your moves to girls of any years.
Of your soul you give nary a single thought or more
Whether you mount a princess or a whore.

Teaching a class in Love's rude school
Exposes you to the risk of playing the fool

Jessmin Howarth wondered to my mother in 1949 why women thought it was necessary to sleep with a master in order to obtain his ideas. In Oriental, Hellenic and Hebrew traditional lore, a woman does indeed draw from a man something of his power with his seed. The mythic dimension of Gurdjieff's sexual relationships with women can be appreciated vividly in W. B. Yeats' poem "Leda and the Swan" which closes:

Did she put on his knowledge with his power
Before the indifferent beak could let her drop?

What conjoining of knowledge and power was carried in the blood strains engendered by Gurdjieff's seed is impossible to calculate, but neither Jessmin nor Edith were the poorer for their experience, and their daughters were exceptional women.

Excursus 2

Gurdjieff's Age

According to all known extant official records I have cited earlier, Georgii Ivanovich Gurdjieff was born on 28 December 1877 (new style) and died on 29 October 1949, two months shy of his seventy-second birthday. According to all records of his conversations with others, including his nieces, he was born on 1 January 1866 (old style), 13 January 1866 (new style). One niece, Luba, daughter of Dmitri Ivanovich (b. 1880 or 1883), understands that he was 82 years old in the last year of his life. There is no extant testimony of his mother, father, brother and sisters concerning his date of birth. Though the great majority of records indicate 1877 as the year of his birth, there is no "official" proof of it. The national Soviet of the Transcaucasus at Tiflis on 20 May 1928 noted Gurdjieff's age as forty, which supports a birth date of 28 December 1877. No birth certificate in either municipal, state or church records has been found, but they, as well as all his passports, have 28 December 1877 as his date of birth. The Alexandropol 1907 census lists Ivan Ivanovich Gurdjiff, his wife Eva, sons Georgii (b. 1880), Dmitri (b. 1883), and daughter Sophia (no birth year).

At the age of twenty-three, in 1871, when he was twenty-four years of age, Gurdjieff's father, Ivan, married eighteen-year old Evdokia Eleptherovna (b. 1852), the daughter of a Greek merchant Elepther Eleptherov, Elepheriadis in its Greek form. Ivan was born in 1847 according to Church and census records. Therefore, it is unlikely that he would have sired a son, Georgii, four years before his marriage. Gurdjieff told others that he was the third-born of his mother, but the first to survive more than a few days.

His own known "natural" children were born after World War I when he was in his forties. Had he been born in 1866, he would have been a father for the first time in his fifties, and in November 1928, when his youngest known child was born, he would have been almost sixty-three years of age. Since Gurdjieff's statements about his age contradict official records and papers, the question is: Why did he "invent" a birth date and age?

Nonetheless, nowhere in his autobiographical writings does he state that he was born in 1866, though his reports of his adventures suggest that he could not have been born in 1877. According to tales he told in conversations and interviews, as well as his autobiographical reports in *Meetings*, *Herald* and *Life Is Real*, Gurdjieff traveled extensively in Asia, from Persia to Mongolia, at times and places he mentioned in his autobiographical conversations and writings. Now, some hundred years later, the official records concerning travels in India, Sikkim, Afghanistan, Tibet and Mongolia, as well as written records of travels by European travelers, reveal the names of scores of "Westerners" who have traversed these areas and were known to local inhabitants as well as bureaucratic records. What is extraordinary is that the name "Gurdjieff" has not been found mentioned among those official and personal recollections. During the period of the "great game," when Russian and British interests clashed in Tibet and India, names and materials were carefully monitored, particularly in ports of India, and though most of those with Tibet and Mongolia as destinations have their names remembered in both written and oral records, the name Gurdjieff is absent.

Besides Pyotr Kozlov's brief mention of Gurdjieff in 1901 on the Chitral, his name is absent from the extensive records of European explorers in Central Asia. Nikolai Przhevalsky (1839–1888), Francis Younghusband (1863–1942), Sven Anders Hedin (1885–1952), Auriel Stein (1862–1943), Paul Peliot (1878–1945), Albert von Le Coq (1860–1930), Otani Kozui (1876–1948), Gustav Mannerheim (1878–1951) and Nikolai Roerich (1874–1947) often mention the names of others who traveled the same paths; but, Gurdjieff's name does not appear a single time in any of their writings.

The names of many Russians who were in Tibet about the turn of the century are well known (see "The Great Game" (*Circle* 48–73, and *Anatomy* 341). The names of mountains, rivers, lakes and tribes that explorers recorded assiduously are not found in Gurdjieff's writing. No one seems to have doubted that Gurdjieff, at the turn of the century, did indeed wander through Central Asia, as he has Beelzebub do in The First Series of *All and Everything*, but since the name "Gurdjieff" is absent from records of the period, one is led to conclude that he traveled under other names. Attempts to identify him with Dordjieff or Narzunoff are dismissed by Moore (*Anatomy* 241), and I have refuted Moore's assertion that Gurdjieff assumed the name "Prince Ozay." The Gurdjieff who arrived in Moscow in 1912 is a man of mystery who strikes many as one who constructed his own history and knowledge out of which he constructed his real worlds.

So, we are left with two crucial questions: First, why did Gurdjieff claim to be eleven years older than the age recorded on official records; and, second, who was the Gurdjieff that was present in Central Asia at the turn of the twentieth century? Somehow, these two questions are connected, but how is a mystery. To begin with, one can put, side by side, dates of events Gurdjieff refers to in his autobiographical reflections with the age he would be in relation to the official date of his birth, 28 December 1877. To begin with, in *The Herald of Coming Good*, 16, Gurdjieff says that in 1892, after a period of research into the essence of things, he retired into isolation. He would have been fourteen years of age for almost all of 1892. A year later, according to a talk he had Olga de Hartmann make in Essentuki in 1918, twenty-five years earlier, that is, 1893, he was in Egypt where he, a young Greek guide, met a Russian Prince and an archeologist. After comparing past histories, the three decided to go different ways in search of knowledge of "something absolute" in the world. All three had years of searching behind them (*Our Life* 1992 70-73.).

In Paris in 1922, Gurdjieff told his students another version of the story, saying that one can consider 1895 the year that the Institute originated when three Russians met by the pyramids: Prince L., an archeologist, and Gurdjieff, the youngest of the three. In the Institute prospectus, printed in 1923, Gurdjieff says that in Alexandropol in 1895 he joined a society called "Seekers of Truth" that set out eastward on an eighteen-year quest (p. 5). These dates indicate that Gurdjieff was between fifteen and seventeen years of age when he started his travels into central Asia. Olga de Hartmann mentioned India, Tibet and Ceylon as places visited before the searchers re-assembled in Kabul. In all, Gurdjieff's searching spanned twenty-one years between 1892 and 1913; that is, between his ages of fourteen and thirty-five.

In interviews and talks, Gurdjieff mentioned other activities in which he must have been engaged during those years. He told an interviewer in Boston that he had been a student in the University of Athens Medical School. In 1909, according to 1927 Soviet trial records, Gurdjieff directed a Masonic temple in Saint Petersburg that had Nikolai Roerich and his wife Helena among its members. It was about this time that he married Julia Ostrovska, who had served relatives of the Tsar. In his early thirties, he would have been at an appropriate age for marriage. Julia did not bear him children.

Looking back at Gurdjieff's birth date to mark the ages at which he did certain acts, one finds it difficult to believe that, before he reached the age of twenty, he had already travelled extensively, done extensive research into esoteric matters, studied medicine at university level, and acquired skills of a hypnotist. It is no wonder that the question of his age continues to be a matter of confusion. Dr. Welch, who attended him at the end, did not doubt that he was treating a man of eighty-three years. Photographs and films of him in his last years show what appears to be a very old man.

There are at least three possible explanations for this apparent discrepancy between Gurdjieff's official age, his own reported age and the ages suggested in his writings and conversations when he underwent adventures in the East. One is that, having done these things at such a young age, he added eleven years to his age in speaking of them in order to lend credibility to them. A second possibility is that he simply altered the dates of the times when these things occurred. A third possibility is that these occurrences did not take place in either the times or the places mentioned, and that Gurdjieff fabricated a personal history.

There is negative evidence supporting the third possibility. No one who took the baths with Gurdjieff in Russia, Fontainebleau or New York reported seeing scars of bullet wounds. In his description of the places he moved through between 1892 and 1913, Gurdjieff is very sparing in the kind of details other explorers mentioned, particularly names of mountains, rivers, towns, villages, and hamlets. He says very little of the flora and fauna on landscapes. That his name does not appear in Asian records of the day can be explained by the supposition that he traveled in disguise and, though others have tried in vain to discover the name or names he took to traverse areas, it is clear that Gurdjieff had an uncanny capacity to appear as different persons in different locations. The major obstacle to understanding what "facts" lay behind Gurdjieff's "stories" is the blurred line between fact and fiction in his writings. It is remarkable that in his writings—Institute prospectus, *The Herald of Coming Good*, *Meetings*, *Life Is Real*, *Glimpses of Truth*, and the front and back matter of *Beelzebub's Tales to His Grandson*—Gurdjieff tells stories which contain "facts" that do not contradict the narrative of other stories. Gurdjieff had a prodigious memory, and he seems to have in mind at all times what he has said at other times about his self.

One may, finally, after a careful scan of his words in all contexts, come to the conclusion that Gurdjieff "invented" his past; that is, his life before records appeared by others. Gurdjieff read a good deal in many languages. He traveled throughout the Caucasus, Persia, Turkey and other countries nearby. It is open to some doubt that he spent time in Tibet and India where the political tensions in those countries prompted careful record-keeping on strangers.

Given that Gurdjieff's reading and travels gave him access to sufficient information to "invent" an alter ego, it is difficult to dismiss the visible discrepancy between ages on his papers, the age he declared himself to be, and the apparent age assumed by those who spent time with him. For example, when Ouspensky met Gurdjieff in the spring of 1915, he saw "a man no longer young . . . who astonished me first of all because he seemed to be disguised and completely out of keeping with the place and its atmosphere (*Search* 7) Since Ouspensky was born on 4 March, 1878, and Gurdjieff on 28 December 1877, they were both thirty-seven years of age at that time. It is curious, therefore, that Ouspensky saw a man "no longer young" who was almost the same age as himself.

If one considers that Gurdjieff was, supposedly, eleven years older than Ouspensky, it is curious that throughout Gurdjieff's travels in the company of others who must have noticed his passport information, no one seems to have questioned the discrepancy of dates of birth. On the other hand, never did Gurdjieff, as far as it is known, deny the accuracy of the date of birth on his papers. In effect, though Gurdjieff, who looked several years older than he was reported to be officially, did not bother contradicting the reports. One is tempted to consider a fourth possibility that would put the problems to rest should it be verified. That possibility is that he was, indeed born in 1866, and carried falsified papers with the 1877 as date of birth, and that he did look his

275

age; that is, just short of eighty-three years of age or, if one accepts the day of birth he celebrated, when he died a couple of months short of his eighty-fourth birthday.

There is one other possibility. Imagine that the man who carried the name "Gurdjieff" when he died, was not the Georgii Ivanovich born in 1877, but was an older man who assumed the identity of that person. It is not difficult to invent a fiction to fit that hypothesis. Let's say that sometime in the 1890s, Ivan and Evdokia's son died, for some reason they permitted someone eleven years older than their departed son to assume his identity. It is not implausible that an identity shift could have taken place somewhere far from his home, for the person with Georgii's identity would not have been accepted at home by his mother and father. There are no obvious telling physical features that Gurdjieff shares with his parents, brother and sisters. Dmitri was considerably lighter of skin and rounder of face. In *All and Everything* Gurdjieff concludes "The Arousing of Thought," by reporting that: "in childhood was called 'Tatakh'; in early youth 'Darky'; later the 'Black Greek; in middle age the 'Tiger of Turkestan' . . . the nephew of Prince Mukransky." He identified himself also as the nephew of Giorgii Merkurov (*Meetings* 71), but to which parent Giorgii Mercourov was related is not mentioned. The sculptor who directed Ouspensky to Gurdjieff, and who was one of Gurdjieff's first followers in Moscow, might have been Sergei Dmitrivich Merkurov (1881–1952), and he was most likely the Merkurov that Olga de Hartmann says lived next door to Gurdjieff's parents in Alexandropol. The Mercourovs are reported to be Greco-Russian. I have no information neither on Prince Moukhransky's origins.

Could it be then, if one assumes that the man called Gurdjieff who appropriated the identity of the son of Ivan, was a "false" Gurdjieff related to these Russians? The complex relationship of the Gurdjieffs with the Merkurovs is difficult to detail. A certain

Valerian Merkurov, his wife Nina, and their son Anatole lived at the Prieuré in the 1920s. He was probably a cousin of Sergei's and, while Sergei remained in the Soviet Union, Valerian emigrated to France, where he joined Gurdjieff at the Institute. They probably left the Prieuré before Gurdjieff went to the United States in January 1924, and the name Merkurov does not appear on French department census lists.

So, we can return now to the hypothesis that Georgii died soon after birth. About that time, 1878, Sergei left Armenia for the north of Russia. He and his wife may have left an eleven-year-old son behind to board with their neighbors and friends, the Gurdjieffs, or the boy may have been part of the family already. It was not unusual for families to board children who were attending school or working in the area. It is possible that some time later, they adopted the children informally, and the child asked to carry the name of their lost son. When the son Dmitri and the daughters Anna and Sophia were born, they would not have had to know that Georgii was not a blood brother.

The "false" Georgii Ivanovich, whatever his real genetic origins were, possessed a viable identity and, struck by a wanderlust and unquenchable thirst for knowledge, he set out to explore the reality of the world as a Greek. In 1892, the year he reported that he left home to search for universal knowledge, he would have been twenty-four years old.

Selected Bibliography

Anastasieff, Valentin Feodorovich. "Preface" to *Life Is Real Only Then when "I Am"* (unpublished).

Anderson, Margaret. *The Fiery Fountain*. London: Rider & Co., 1953.

————. *The Unknowable Gurdjieff*. London: Routledge & Kegan Paul, 1962.

Bell, Mary C. "Some Memories of the Prieuré." *Gurdjieff International Review* 1, no. 4, 1998.

Bennett. J[ohn] G[odolphin]. *Gurdjieff: Making a New World*. London: Turnstone Books, 1973.

————. *Gurdjieff: A Very Great Enigma*. Kingston-upon-Thames: Coombe Springs Press, 1969.

————. "An Introduction to Gurdjieff's Third Series 'Life is Real only then, when I AM.'" Combe Springs Press, no date.

Blom, Gert-Jan. *Gurdjieff/de Hartmann: Oriental Suite*. The Complete Orchestral Music 1923– 1924. Netherlands: Basta Audio Visuals, 2006.

Butkovsky, Anna Hewitt. *With Gurdjieff in St. Petersburg and Paris*. London: Routledge & Kegan Paul, 1978.

Dukes, Sir Paul. *The Unending Quest*: Autobiographical Sketches. London: Cassell, 1950.

Everitt, Luba Gurdjieff. *Luba Gurdjieff: A Memoir with Recipes*. Berkeley, CA: Ten Speed Press, 1993.

Friedland, Roger, and Harold Zellman. *The Fellowship*, New York: HarperCollins, 2006.

Gill, Brendan. *Many Masks*. New York: Da Capo, 1998.

Gordeziani, Rismag Venianovich. *The Greeks in Georgia*. Tbilisi, 1990.

Gregova, Tatiana Ivanovna. Tibetskaya Meditsina v Rossii: istoriya v Sud'bakh y Litsakh. (*Tibetan Medicine in Russia*). St. Petersburg: Anton, 1998.

Gurdjieff, G[eorgii] I[vanovich]. *Beelzebub's Tales to His Grandson*. New York: Harcourt Brace and Co., 1950.

———. "Glimpses of Truth" (1915). *Views From the Real World*. London: Penguin Compass, 1973.

———. "G. Gurdjieff's Institute For the Harmonious Development of Man." Privately printed, 1924.

———. *The Herald of Coming Good*. Paris: Private Printing, 1933.

———. *Life Is Real Only Then, When "I Am."* London: Penguin Arkana, 1991.

———. *Meetings With Remarkable Men*. London: Arkana, 1985.

———. *Views From the Real World*. London: Penguin Compass, 1973.

Hands, Rina. *Diary of Madame Egout Pour Sweet*: With Mr. Gurdjieff in Paris 1948–1949. Aurora, OR: Two Rivers Press, 1991.

Hartmann, Thomas de. *Our Life with Mr. Gurdjieff*. Baltimore: Penguin Books, 1972.

———. *Our Life with Monsieur Gurdjieff*. Revised and enlarged from notes of Olga de Hartmann, San Francisco: London: Arkana, 1992.

Howarth, Dushka and Jessmin. *It's up to Ourselves*: A Mother, a Daughter, G. I. Gurdjieff. New York: Gurdjieff Heritage Society, 1998.

Hulme, Kathryn. *Undiscovered Country*: A Spiritual Adventure. Boston: Little Brown, 1966.

Kerman, Cynthia Earl and Richard Eldridge. *The Lives of Jean Toomer*. Baton Rouge: Louisiana State University Press, 1987.

Kharitidi, Olga. *Entering the Circle*: Ancient Secrets of Siberian Wisdom Discovered by a Russian Psychiatrist. San Francisco: Harper, 1996.

Khomeriki, Manana. "About the the Origins of Gurdjieff and His Activities in Georgia." G. I. Gurdjieff from South Caucasus to Western World. Edd. Constance A. Jones and Leven Khetaguri. *Shota Rustavelli* Theatre and Film University, 2008, 28–36.

King, C. Daly. *The Oragean Version*. New York: privately printed, 1951.

Kun, Miklós. *Stalin: An Unknown Portrait*. Budapest: Central European University, 2003.

Landau, Ron. *God Is My Adventure*. London: Ivor Nicolson and Watson, 1935.

Lipsey, Roger. *Gurdjieff Reconsidered*. Boulder, Colorado: Shambhala Press, 2019.

McAlmon, Robert and Kay Boyle. *Being Geniuses Together* 1920–1930. Garden City, NY: Doubleday, 1968.

March, Louise Goepfert. *The Gurdjieff Years 1929–1949*: Recollections of Louise [Goepfert]

March. Ed. Beth McCorkle. Walworth, NY: The Work Study Association, Inc, 1990.

Montefiore, Simon Sebag. *Young Stalin*. New York: Alfred A. Knopf, 2007.

Moore, James. *Gurdjieff: The Anatomy of a Myth*. Boston: Element, 1991.

Morris, Lawrence S. "Notebooks of L.S.M.: Orage lectures. New York 10 January 1927–28 May 1928" (unpublished).

Négrier, Patrick. *Le Travail selon Gurdjieff*: L'ennéagramme–La science des Idiots. Groslay, Val d'Oise, France: Editions Ivoire-Claire, 2008.

Nott, C[harles] S[tanley]. *Journey Through this World*. London: Routledge & Kegan Paul, 1969.

———. *Further Teachings of Gurdjieff*. York Beach, ME: Samuel Weiser, 1984.

———. *Teachings of Gurdjieff*: Journal of a Pupil. London: Routledge & Kegan Paul, 1961.

Ouspensky, P[yotr] D[emianovich]. *In Search of the Miraculous*: Fragments of an Unknown Teaching. New York: Harcourt, Brace and World, 1949

———. *Remembering Pyotr Demianovich Ouspensky*. Ed. Merrily E.

Taylor. New Haven: Yale University Library, 1978.

———. "Memorial Collection." Sterling Library, Yale University.

Paléologue, Maurice. *An Ambassador's Memoirs*. New York:George H. Doran, 1925.

Parton, Anthony. *Mikhail Larionov and the Russian Avant Garde*. Princeton University Press, 1993.

Patterson, William Patrick. *Ladies of the Rope*. Fairfax CA: Arete Communications, 1999.

———. *Struggle of the Magicians*. Fairfax, CA: Arete Publications, 1996.

Pauwels, Louis. *Gurdjieff*. Douglas, Isle of Man: Times Press, 1964. First published in France with the title *Monsieur Gurdjieff* (Paris: Seuil, 1954).

Petsche, Johanna M. *The Gurdjieff/de Hartmann Piano Music and its Esoteric Significance*. Leiden: Brill, 2015.

Peters, Fritz. *Boyhood with Gurdjieff*. London: Victor Gollanz, 1964.

———. *Gurdjieff Remembered*. London: Victor Gollanz, 1969.

Philpotts, Dorothy. *Discovering Gurdjieff*. Author House: Central Milton Keynes, 2008.

Popoff, Irmis B[arret]. *Gurdjieff: His work on myself with others . . . for the work*. New York: Samuel Weiser Inc., 1978.

Robinson, Carol. "Letters to Jane Heap." Heap Papers in custody of Barbara Walker Todd Smyth.

Saxton, Josephine. *Group Feast*. New York: Doubleday Science Fiction, 1971.

Seabrook, William. *"Our Modern Caliostros." Witchcraft: Its Power in the World Today*. New York: Harcourt, Brace, 1940.

Spinage, C. A. *Cattle Plague: A History*. New York: Kluwer, 2003.

Stavely, A. L. *Memories of Gurdjieff*. Aurora, Oregon: Two Rivers Press, 1978.

Stjernvall, Nikolai. *My Dear Father Gurdjieff*. Dublin: Bardic Press, 2013.

Storr, Anthony. *Feet of Clay*: Saints, Sinners and Madmen. New York: The Free Press, 1996.

Taylor, Paul Beekman. *Gurdjieff in the Public Eye*. Utrecht: Eureka Editions, 2010.

———. *Gurdjieff's Invention of America*. Utrecht: Eureka Editions, 2007.

———. "Gurdjieff and Prince Ozay." *Gurdjieff: A Reading Guide*. Third Edition, ed. Walter Driscoll, 2004, and *Gurdjieff International Review*.

———. *Gurdjieff's Worlds of Words*. Utrecht: Eureka Editions, 2014.

———. *Orage and Gurdjieff: Brothers in Elysium*. York Beach, ME: Weiser Books, 2001.

———. *Real Worlds of G. I. Gurdjieff*. Utrecht: Eureka Editions, 2012.

———. *Shadows of Heaven*: Gurdjieff and Toomer. York Beach, ME: Weiser Books, 1998.

Tchechovitch, Tchesslav. *Tu l'aimerais*: souvenirs sur Georgii Ivanovitch, Gurdjieff. Paris: L'Originel, 2003.

Webb, James. *The Harmonious Circle*. New York: G. P. Putnam's Sons, 1980.

Welch, Louise. *Orage with Gurdjieff in America*. London: Routledge & Kegan Paul, 1982.

Welch, William J. *What Happened In Between*. New York: George Brazillier 1972

Wilson, Colin. *The War Against Sleep*: The Philosophy of Gurdjieff. Wellingborough, Northants: Aquarius Press, 1980.

Young, James Carruthers. "Experiment at Fontainebleau." London: The New Adelphi, 26–40. 1927.

Zarcone, Thierry. *La Turquie moderne et l'islam*. Paris: Flammarion, 2004.

INDEX

It is hardly necessary to refer to every mention of persons in Gurdjieff's inner circle: Hartmann, Salzmann, Stjernvall, Tchechovich, Olga Wright, Galumnian, Orage, and Ouspensky.

E-book and printed by Amazon

March 2020

© **Eureka Editions**
ISBN 978 94 92590 046

Herenstraat 4-A
3512 KC Utrecht
The Netherlands

www.eurekaeditions.com
info@eurekaeditions.com

Printed in Great Britain
by Amazon

64565610R00189